For the love of food

For the love of food
Denis Cotter

First published in 2011 by Collins
an imprint of HarperCollins*Publishers*
77–85 Fulham Palace Road
London W6 8JB

www.harpercollins.co.uk

13 12 11 15 14
9 8 7 6 5 4 3 2 1

Text © Denis Cotter 2011

Photography © William Lingwood 2011
Food styling: Fergal Connolly
Styling: Roísín Nield
Design: MARiA.MARiA

A catalogue record for this book is available from the British Library.

ISBN: 978-0-00-731275-7

Printed and bound in China by South China Printing.

for Maureen, for the love

Contents

Introduction

'There is no love sincerer than the love of food'
George Bernard Shaw, 'The Revolutionist's Handbook,' *Man and Superman*

This is a book of recipes and this bit at the start is the introduction, where I tell you about the themes and concepts that bind the collection of recipes together. The thing is, though, there is no concept. The book took more time than should have been necessary to put together because I spent so long at the beginning writing bits and pieces of essays that would form the core themes of a serious food book. A few recipes would be added later to flesh out the concepts.

Then one morning, I typed out a recipe for what we'd eaten for dinner the previous evening. The next morning I did the same thing and for the next few months I set myself small targets of a few recipes a day of dishes that were simply nice things to eat. Some were records of meals eaten, others ideas for later occasions. For a while I thought I would get back to big themes, but the day came when I realised that perhaps a book of nice things to eat would be of more use than an addition to the growing list of serious food tomes. Not that there's anything wrong with serious food books. The so-called first world is still a long way from putting right our relationship with food. But how many books do you need to tell you to shop local, eat more greens and stop supporting big, nasty corporations? Browsing a bookshop one day, I drifted to the food section, as I tend to do, and spent some time poring over a couple. One was a perfect, eloquent summation of the state of our eating habits and the way back to reality. The other seemed like just another repetitive bandwagon jumper. The first made me feel that enough had been said and the second galvanised my sense that I wanted to do something more useful than add weight to the bookshelves.

I went home and wrote another recipe, something nice to cook for dinner that could be shared and might bring pleasure to the cook and the people sharing the food. Then I made dinner. Nothing fancy or elaborate, but it took a while, mostly because I like to

potter in the kitchen. It wasn't a dish that called for reverence or any acknowledgement more than an occasional 'mmm...' We ate it watching a movie, the food just one part of a lovely evening.

Perhaps there is a theme here after all, and if there is, it is something to do with love and food. The love of the act of cooking itself, something we are discouraged from feeling when the media is full of ideas on how to make dinner in five, 10 or 20 minutes. And the love expressed through food prepared for those that you love. Food is survival fuel first and foremost, but it is surely one of humanity's highest marks of evolution that we have turned the preparation and shared eating of it into a generous act of love. When you cook for someone, you are saying – here, eat this, I hope you will love it. When you share food, you are sharing the pleasure of taste and of hunger satisfied.

So here, enjoy this book of simple pleasures. Share it with those you love.

Breakfast

Breakfast

What's your breakfast routine? A slice of cold toast rejected by
the kids, eaten standing at the kitchen counter, hair dripping,
wondering where your socks might be and trying to make school
lunch sandwiches? Or a bowl of yoghurt, optional sliced banana
depending on time, while checking email and applying lipstick at
the same time? Mine's the latter, minus the lipstick. Porridge, at a
stretch. We have less time for breakfast than we do for dinner, and
most of us go out the door in the morning with some degree of guilt
about how chaotically we approach the officially branded 'most
important meal of the day'.

Don't worry, I'm not here, having a Martha Stewart moment, to
add to your guilt with tales of pumpkin pancakes and portobello
florentine. Though – come on now – you could get up a tiny bit
earlier and make some porridge or boil an egg. No? Okay, never
mind. It's also true that guilt and stress will get you sooner and
worse than the lack of a good breakfast anyway.

These recipes are for those mornings when you've got all the time
in the world and you've decided to spend it eating with lovers,
friends, family or the whole lot in one go. Food to cook and share at
a leisurely pace. It's probably the weekend, let's imagine the sun is
shining, the newspapers are full of interesting stories and the radio
is playing all your favourite songs. Someone even brought a bottle
of bubbly, meaning the meal can stretch slowly far into the day.
Brunch might be the proper term for it, the original fusion cooking,
breakfast and lunch in one go. A meal without rules about courses,
quantity, combinations, structure; or whether you eat the sweet or
savoury things first.

That last one's an interesting divider of people – whether, given one
hard choice to make at the breakfast diner, they order sweet or
savoury brunch. I'm a hollandaise dope. No matter how much I try to
order the most interesting thing on the menu, my mouth opens and I
name the dish with the most hollandaise. Yet, when I subconsciously
twist my own arm, it always surprises me how pleasurable it is to eat
sweet treats for the first meal of the day.

At home, it's unlikely you'll be presenting a menu, nor would I recommend it. If doing separate courses seems like a good idea, make the first one cold, from stuff that can be grazed on while you get on with the main act. Put delicious things on the table – fruit, yoghurt, granola, crackers, jams, chutneys and cheese.

For anything more than a cosy couple, breakfast/brunch is something of a juggling act, whether you're cooking for four or a hundred. This is especially true when it comes to eggs, when the result can flip from perfect to gone too far in a few seconds, and there is so much that needs to come together at the same time. Make sure everything but the eggs, including people, is ready before the final stage of cooking begins.

Eggs are on something of a comeback from the graveyard of medical condemnation. Apparently, we don't actually die from eating more than a couple of eggs a week. Phew! I never could figure out, with a fondness for the occasional five-egg omelette, how to stay within view of the old limits, never mind operating below them. This readjustment of the official ruling on eggs came just in time for me. I was getting to the age when some doctor was sure to start telling me to swap the hollandaise for a Hollywood egg white omelette. Double phew! Mind you, some eggs might as well be all white for all the flavour they've got. Eggs, almost more than anything else, get their flavour and richness from how they are produced. This is no preacher book, but I will say this – keep chickens or get to know your source, and don't poach an egg that's only fit for making cake.

Vanilla & coconut risotto with spiced mango and pistachio

You can think of this as risotto for breakfast, which sounds strange, or rice pudding for breakfast – less weird and only a little naughty. Or you can think of it as rice porridge for breakfast, for what is risotto anyway but rice porridge? This procedure follows the classic risotto method of absorbing liquid into rice in stages, though I would be inclined to let the rice cook a bit more than for a savoury risotto.

The recipe calls for sweet wine. This doesn't mean you have to crack open your precious expensive dessert wines. A slightly sweet Riesling or Muscat is what's needed, though you might get away with that Liebfraumilch you've got hidden away for visiting aunties.

- First make the spiced syrup for the mango: put the sugar, star anise, cloves and ginger in a small saucepan with 5 tablespoons of water and bring to the boil, then remove from the heat and leave to cool and infuse. Pass the syrup through a fine sieve.

- Peel the mango and slice the flesh from the stone. Put half of it in a food processor, add 2 tablespoons of the spice syrup and blend to a purée. Add a little water, if necessary, to get a pouring consistency. Check for flavour and sweetness, and add a little more syrup to taste if it needs it.

- Slice the remaining mango into matchsticks and put them in a bowl with a tablespoon of the mango sauce.

- To make the risotto: put the milk, coconut milk and sugar in a saucepan and bring to the boil, then reduce the heat to a simmer. Split the vanilla pod lengthways and scrape the pulp into the milk.

- Heat the butter in a wide, heavy pan over medium heat, add the rice and toast it, stirring, for 5 minutes. Add the white wine and simmer until it has been absorbed. Add a ladle or 2 of the hot milk mixture. Stirring often, let this simmer until it has been absorbed, then add more of it. Continue in this way for about 20 minutes, until the rice is tender and you have a nice porridgey texture. Stir in the citrus zest.

- Serve the risotto in shallow bowls. Pour over a little mango sauce and place some of the sliced mango on top. Scatter over the pistachios, grate over a little nutmeg and serve.

for 4

for the spiced mango
100g/3½oz caster sugar
1 star anise,
    coarsely ground
4 cloves
1 tsp finely grated
    fresh ginger
1 large ripe mango

*for the vanilla
and coconut risotto*
400ml/14fl oz milk
1 x 400ml/14fl oz tin
    of coconut milk
2 tbsp caster sugar
1 vanilla pod
15g/½oz butter
200g/7oz Carnaroli
    or Arborio rice
4 tbsp sweet white wine
finely grated zest
    of 1 orange
finely grated zest of 1 lime

to serve
2 tbsp shelled pistachio
    nuts, coarsely chopped
nutmeg, for grating

Lucy's breakfast sausages with spiced tomato chutney

makes about 30 sausages

for the sausages
400g/14oz cooked
    chestnuts
250g/9oz firm tofu, mashed
1 onion, grated
2½ tsp finely chopped
    fresh sage
1 tsp finely chopped fresh
    rosemary or thyme leaves
125g/4½oz strong hard
    cheese, such as Cheddar,
    grated
1 tbsp soy sauce
juice of ½ lemon
½ tsp chilli powder
1 egg, beaten
200–250g/7–9oz fine
    breadcrumbs
butter and/or olive oil,
    for cooking

for the spiced tomato chutney
2 onions, finely chopped
3 garlic cloves, crushed
2 red peppers, deseeded
    and finely chopped
1 fresh red chilli,
    finely chopped
1 kg/2lb 2oz ripe
    tomatoes, chopped
450ml/16fl oz malt
    or white wine vinegar
350g/12oz soft brown sugar
100g/3½oz raisins
2 tsp black mustard seeds
2 tsp black onion seeds
2 tsp smoked paprika
1 cinnamon stick

If you've ever stayed at the guesthouse that is part of Gort Na Nain Farm on the south coast of County Cork, where much of the produce used in Café Paradiso comes from, you have surely had Lucy Stewart's homemade chestnut sausages for breakfast. If you're anything like me, you will have asked what's in them to make them taste so good. For those of you too shy to ask, and for the rest of you who have yet to go there, I asked on your behalf. Lucy, in her generosity, said yes.

She makes occasional batches and freezes them, and the quantities below are about as small as it is worth doing. The sausages behave better in the pan if cooked straight from the freezer, so it is best from every aspect to make and freeze rather than getting up at the crack of dawn to start from scratch.

Use pre-cooked vacuum-packed chestnuts, firm tofu and a hard, strongly flavoured Cheddar or similar. The chutney will keep for as long as you have it, if properly sealed in sterilised jars, so it can be made well in advance. However, it can also be used on the day it is made, once it has cooled. Opened jars should be kept in the fridge.

- Well ahead, make the tomato chutney: put all the ingredients in a large saucepan and stir, bringing slowly to the boil. Simmer gently for an hour or so, stirring occasionally. When the mixture is thick and jam-like, remove the cinnamon stick. Spoon the chutney into hot sterilised jars and screw the lid on tight.

- To make the sausages: put the chestnuts in a food processor and pulse to get a fine crumb texture. Put this in a bowl and add the rest of the ingredients, except the breadcrumbs and butter and/or oil. Add enough breadcrumbs to get a firm consistency that can be shaped.

- Form into sausage shapes and store in the freezer. The best way to do this is to place a few in plastic freezer bags with baking parchment separating the sausages to prevent sticking.

- To cook the sausages, heat a little butter and/or olive oil in a frying pan over medium heat. Put in a few sausages and fry for 5–7 minutes, turning occasionally to brown all over.

- Serve them with a good generous dollop of the tomato chutney.

Scrambled eggs with avocado, rosemary & chilli and grilled sourdough

Scrambled eggs are more forgiving than poached, and the technique allows some scope for varying the timing of the dish by simply adjusting the heat. There still comes a point when the eggs are done, after which you're going to start getting cranky unless everything else is ready, so do whatever you can to make the last few minutes' cooking time as stress-free as possible. Bread toasted? Butter soft? Table set and people sitting? That's the hardest part of breakfast, organising fuzzy-brained humans.

The rosemary and chilli in the eggs are a lovely combination of fragrance and heat. It is an exception to how I usually cook with rosemary in that the herb is finely chopped and left in the dish rather than being used as an infusion. Fresh coriander, a natural companion for chilli and avocado, and evocative of Mexican breakfast eggs, is an effective alternative to rosemary if you want to swing that way instead.

for 2

5 eggs
2 tbsp milk
15g/½oz butter, melted
1 sprig of fresh rosemary, leaves only, finely chopped
1 fresh green chilli, finely chopped
1 avocado
olive oil, for tossing and brushing
1 tsp lemon juice
2 thick slices of sourdough bread
salt

- In a shallow stainless steel bowl, beat the eggs lightly with the milk and a pinch of salt. Stir in the butter, rosemary and chilli.

- Set the bowl over a pan of simmering water, making sure the bottom of the bowl is clear of the water, and cook the eggs slowly, stirring occasionally with a spatula or wooden spoon, until the eggs are scrambled to your liking.

- While the eggs are cooking, cut the avocado in half, remove the stone and skin, and slice the avocado flesh thickly. Toss the avocado gently in olive oil and season with salt and the lemon juice.

- Heat a griddle pan over medium heat. Brush the bread with olive oil and place it on the griddle, turning once, until browned on both sides.

- Serve the eggs with the avocado slices on top and the grilled sourdough on the side.

Portobello & roast tomato florentine

The ultimate solution to the issue of eggs and bread – the problem of there usually being too much of the latter at breakfast – is to replace the bread with something else. In this case, roasted portobello mushrooms take the place of English muffins in a variation on the classic eggs florentine.

The method I've given here for hollandaise sauce is the simplest food processor technique. Don't feel guilty about not standing for ages over a bowl, whisking furiously and frettingly in the traditional way. Cooking isn't actually intended to be stressful; it just feels that way sometimes.

Speaking of stress, the best way to get the timing right here is to make sure the tomatoes, mushrooms and hollandaise are ready before you start poaching eggs. Turn the oven off and leave the vegetables in there to keep warm. Use baby spinach – it cooks in seconds and won't hold up your service.

for 2

1 large beef tomato
1 tsp balsamic vinegar
2 large portobello
  mushrooms
2 sprigs of fresh thyme,
  leaves only
45g/1¾oz butter
1 tsp white wine vinegar
4 eggs
2 tbsp olive oil
2 handfuls of baby
  spinach leaves
salt and pepper

for the hollandaise sauce
3 egg yolks
1 tbsp lemon juice
1 tsp Dijon mustard,
  or similar
pinch of cayenne pepper
225g/8oz butter

- First make the hollandaise sauce: put the egg yolks, lemon juice, mustard and cayenne in a food processor and blend for 15 seconds. Melt the butter in a saucepan over medium heat. Start the food processor again, and slowly pour the hot butter into the egg mixture while it is running. When the sauce has thickened, transfer it to a heatproof bowl and season with salt and pepper. Keep this warm by sitting it over a pan of water at a low simmer, or by simply putting it in a warm place.

- Preheat the oven to 200°C/400°F/gas mark 6.

- Slice the top and bottom off the tomato and cut the rest in half to get 2 thick slices. Place these on an oven tray lined with baking parchment and sprinkle with salt. Roast in the oven for 15 minutes, until beginning to colour. Drizzle with the balsamic vinegar and return to the oven for 1 minute.

- Put the mushrooms on an oven tray, gill sides up. Sprinkle with the thyme leaves and dot with 15g/½ oz of the butter. Season with salt and roast in the oven with the tomato for 8–10 minutes, until tender and juicy.

Continued on following page ...

Continued from previous page...

- Fill a shallow saucepan with water to a depth of 5–7.5cm/2–3in, bring to the boil, then add the wine vinegar and turn the heat down to keep the water at a gentle simmer.

- Crack 1 egg into a small cup or ramekin and gently lower it into the water. Repeat with the other eggs. Poach the eggs for 2–3 minutes, until done to your liking. Lift them out, one at a time, with a slotted spoon.

- While the eggs are cooking, heat the olive oil in a frying pan over medium heat. Add the spinach and cook, stirring, for 1 minute, until wilted. Season with salt and pepper.

- To serve, place a mushroom on each plate, and top with a slice of tomato. Spoon over a little hollandaise sauce and cover with spinach and 2 poached eggs. Drizzle some more hollandaise around the plate.

Snow cakes

Check the ingredients list for these miraculous little cakes... snow and corn. That's about as primitive as it gets. May you never find yourself in a situation where you have to eat snow out of necessity rather than for the fun of baking it.

The night before I first made these, my girlfriend Maureen had decided it was time for me to read *From Stone Orchard*, a memoir by the great Stratford storyteller, Timothy Findley, or Tiff, as she knew him (Canadian Stratford, that is, the one in the Ontario Snow Belt). Flicking through the book, and reading snippets aloud, she came across a recipe for 'snow bread' – a recipe for those mornings when the water pipes are frozen and the car has a foot of snow riveted to it. Or, in another scenario, for one of those days when, for the sheer fun of it, you feel like taking two quick steps into the back garden – pyjamas optional – to gather a bowl of freshly fallen snow.

The morning in question, I awoke with a Christmas feeling, giddily excited to find out if the promised snowfall had transpired. Good ol' Mr Weatherman... the snow was falling very gently in feathery flakes, but had already reached more than a foot deep. I scooped a bowlful from a picnic table that was optimistically waiting for summer a few feet from the door.

The freshly fallen bit is essential – that beautiful, fluffy stuff that seems like it fell from heaven and is as full of air as a bowl of lightly whipped egg white (which, incidentally, you can add to the mix to give the cakes a lighter texture). The rest is simple. Fold the mixture together gently and bake it hot and fast. The cakes will rise in the oven, then fall when they come out. Which is fine – this isn't haute cuisine, it's breakfast fun. Spread with butter and maple syrup, you could easily eat half a dozen, and they're strangely compulsive.

makes 12 small cakes

butter, for greasing, plus extra to serve
1 cup of fine yellow cornmeal
pinch of salt
4–5 cups of fresh fluffy snow
maple syrup, to serve

- Preheat the oven to 200°C/400°F/gas mark 6. Grease a muffin tray.

- Put the cornmeal in a bowl with the salt. Go outside and collect the cupfuls of clean snow. Gently fold this into the cornmeal and spoon the mixture into the muffin tray indents.

- Bake in the preheated oven for 15 minutes.

- Remove the tray from the oven and leave for 5 minutes before lifting the snow cakes out on to a plate. Serve with butter and maple syrup.

Brioche french toast with pears & walnuts in gingered maple brandy sauce

for 2

for the lime mascarpone
100g/3½oz mascarpone
100ml /3½fl oz double
  cream, whipped to
  soft peaks
finely grated zest of 1 lime

for the French toast
2 eggs
100ml/3½fl oz milk
1 tsp ground cinnamon
1 vanilla pod, interior
  pulp only
4 slices of brioche
about 15g/½oz butter

for the pears and walnuts in
gingered maple brandy sauce
50g/2oz butter
2 medium pears, cored
  and thickly sliced
  lengthways
1 piece of stem ginger in
  syrup, thinly sliced
3 tbsp maple syrup
1 tbsp brandy
1 tbsp chopped walnuts

French toast and bread and butter pudding have this much in common – you can perceive them as good ways to use up leftover bread where the quality of the bread will make a huge difference. Brioche works really well for both, because of its rich flavour and almost cakey crumb texture.

If you make brioche, wonderful – next time you do, make an extra loaf to set aside for French toast. It will keep for a few days and it also freezes well. Otherwise, track down a source of good brioche and be thankful you live close to one. If neither is an option for you, use a good country loaf, something with a dense texture.

- First prepare the lime mascarpone: beat the mascarpone to soften it and fold in the whipped cream and lime zest.

- Make the French toast: whisk the eggs, milk, cinnamon and vanilla together in a large bowl. Soak the brioche slices for 1 minute in this egg mixture.

- Preheat the oven to 180°C/350°F/gas mark 4.

- Melt the butter in a frying pan over medium heat. Remove the brioche slices from the egg mixture and place 2 of them in the pan. Cook on one side until golden, then turn and repeat with the other side. Repeat with the remaining slices, adding a little more butter if necessary, and arrange on an oven tray.

- Place the tray in the oven and bake for 10 minutes.

- Make the pears and walnuts in gingered maple brandy sauce: in another frying pan, heat 15g/½oz of the butter over medium heat and sauté the pear slices in it for 5–7 minutes, turning them to colour all sides. Add the ginger, maple syrup and brandy, and continue cooking for a further minute.

- Remove from the heat and add the walnuts and the remaining butter to give the sauce a pouring consistency.

- Serve 2 slices of toast per portion, topped with the pears, walnuts and sauce poured over. Add a dollop of the mascarpone and serve.

Buttermilk pancakes
with honey & berries

for 4–6

260g/9½oz plain flour
2 tsp baking powder
¼ tsp bicarbonate of soda
2½ tbsp caster sugar
½ tsp salt
450ml/16fl oz buttermilk
4 tbsp sunflower oil
2 eggs, separated
clarified butter, for cooking

to serve
fresh fruit (see right)
honey
lightly whipped double
   cream

This is the simplest prototype of an endlessly useful recipe – a stack of pancakes, some berries, a well-flavoured honey and a little whipped cream. As the year unfolds, you can use just about any fresh fruit, from berries to summer peaches and exotic mangoes. When you're in the mood, and especially in the colder months, think about caramelised or stewed apples, pears, rhubarb or a compote of blueberries. Try adding some coarsely chopped almonds, hazelnuts or pistachios. Substitute maple syrup for the honey, or citrus-scented mascarpone or a jug of warm custard for the cream. You write your own script on this one.

By the same token, I'm not going to tell you how to make a pretty picture on the plate. Certainly, if it's a cosy romantic breakfast, do take the trouble to make it look pretty. But if you're feeding a small gang, the best and most fun way to set this up is to put a piled platter of pancakes in the centre of the table, surrounded by the optional extras – fruit, cream, honey or syrup – and let people make their own combinations one pancake at a time for as long as it takes to get to the end.

• Sift the flour, baking powder, bicarbonate of soda, sugar and salt together into a large bowl. In another bowl, stir together the buttermilk, oil and egg yolks. Stir this liquid into the dry ingredients, without mixing too much.

• Whisk the egg whites to stiff peaks, and fold them into the batter.

• Heat a non-stick frying pan over medium heat. Brush it with clarified butter and add separate tablespoonfuls of the batter to the pan. Fry the pancakes until lightly coloured, then flip them over to cook the other side until they become light and fluffy. The pancakes can be served immediately or kept warm in an oven at low heat.

• Serve 2 or 3 pancakes per portion, with fruit, honey and lightly whipped cream.

Spiced polenta almond cake with blood orange & pink grapefruit salad

It's definitely the weekend when you're eating cake for breakfast, but this is a lovely way to get your daily dose of citrus fruit. Served with a generous dollop of yoghurt, it's got all the ingredients of a good breakfast, just in a way that looks like dessert. Nice.

The cake is one of those very simple mix-and-pour recipes, and it gets most of its flavour from the sweetly spiced syrup poured on top after it cools down. The syrup soaks into the cake but the top remains sticky, so if you're saving any leftovers, wrap them up in the tin, making sure that the cling film doesn't touch the cake.

- Preheat the oven to 180°C/350°F/gas mark 4 and line a 30x20cm/12x8in rectangular cake tin with baking parchment.

- First prepare the blood orange and pink grapefruit salad: peel the blood oranges with a knife, removing the white pith. Slice the oranges into thick rounds and put them in a bowl. Peel the grapefruit in the same way, then cut out the individual segments, leaving all of the pith behind. Add these to the bowl with the grapes, sugar and cinnamon. Leave for 30 minutes (10 minutes will do if you are serving this on its own) before serving.

- While that infuses, make the spiced polenta almond cake: mix together the polenta, sugar, almonds and baking powder. Stir in the oil and eggs, and pour the mixture into the tin. Bake for 20–25 minutes, until the cake has set. Remove from the oven and leave to cool in the tin.

- While the cake is baking, make the spiced orange syrup: put the orange juice and zest in a saucepan with the sugar, cinnamon stick, cloves and star anise. Bring this to the boil and simmer for a few minutes, until slightly syrupy. Remove from the heat and leave to infuse for 10–20 minutes.

- When the cake has cooled, warm the syrup again and pour it over the cake. Leave to cool again briefly, then cut the cake into squares.

- Serve the fruit draped over the squares of cake, with a dollop of yoghurt on the side.

for 4

for the blood orange and pink grapefruit salad
4 blood oranges
1 large pink grapefruit
1 small bunch of seedless black grapes, each grape halved
2 tbsp caster sugar
large pinch of ground cinnamon

for the spiced polenta almond cake
70g/2¾oz medium polenta
300g/11oz caster sugar
225g/8oz ground almonds
2 tsp baking powder
200ml/7fl oz sunflower oil
5 eggs, beaten

for the spiced orange syrup
finely grated zest of 1 orange and 100ml/3½fl oz freshly squeezed orange juice
100g/3½oz caster sugar
1 cinnamon stick
5 cloves
2 star anise

to serve
200ml/7fl oz natural yoghurt

Macroom oatmeal
with whiskey sultanas,
honey & cream

for 4

150g/5oz Macroom
  oatmeal
½ tsp salt

for the whiskey sultanas
100ml/3½fl oz Irish
  whiskey, plus extra
  to serve
150g/5oz caster sugar
200g/7oz sultanas

to serve
4 tbsp honey
pouring cream

You can think of this as a simple twist on porridge – use your usual oats, cook them as you like to and then add the whiskey sultanas. Any good pinhead oatmeal will work here, but if you can get access to Macroom oatmeal, it really is a unique product that will make the best porridge you've ever had. The oats are slow-roasted to bring out their nutty flavour before being stoneground, which cuts the grain into something like coarse polenta. The wonderful thing about this operation is that it isn't some expensive resurrection of traditionalism as marketing tool. No, the Creedon family, who run the mill, do it this way because they have done so for generations, and there's never been a reason to change. The other great thing about Macroom oatmeal is simply that it comes from Macroom, my home town.

Macroom oatmeal takes a little longer to cook than your average rolled oats, but it's not like you have to stand over it, fussing. In fact, the classic method is to make the porridge the night before and leave it to sit in the pot on the stove. Start with a bit more water, and in the morning you might have to add a splash more to loosen it up.

The whiskey sultanas are best made at least a few hours ahead. The recipe is for more than you will need, but they keep very well in the fridge for a couple of weeks at least.

- At least 2 hours ahead, make the whiskey sultanas: put the whiskey, sugar and 5 tablespoons of water in a saucepan. Simmer until reduced to a slightly thickened syrup. Allow to cool, then pour it over the sultanas in a bowl. Leave for at least 2 hours.

- Bring 600ml/1 pint of water to the boil in a large saucepan. Whisk in the oatmeal and salt and bring back to the boil. Lower the heat to the lowest setting, cover the pan and simmer for 20 minutes, uncovering occasionally to stir.

- After 20 minutes, check the consistency and adjust, if necessary, by boiling off some water while stirring, or adding more water if the porridge is too thick. Stir in 4 tablespoons of the sultanas.

- Brush warmed shallow bowls with a little whiskey. Spoon in the porridge and drizzle the honey over. Serve with cream on the side, to be poured around and over the porridge.

Shallot & thyme eggy bread with rocket and spiced pepper compote

for 2

1 tbsp olive oil
4 small shallots, finely chopped
3 eggs
4 tbsp milk
4 sprigs of fresh thyme, leaves only
40g/1½oz hard cheese, such as Cheddar, finely grated
4 thick slices of bread
15g/½oz butter
2 handfuls of rocket leaves
salt and pepper

for the spiced pepper compote
1 tbsp olive oil
1 red onion, finely chopped
2 garlic cloves, finely chopped
1 fresh red chilli, deseeded and thinly sliced
1 red pepper, roasted and peeled
1 tbsp chopped tinned tomatoes
1 tbsp balsamic vinegar
1 tbsp soft brown sugar

Eggy bread is peasant-speak for French toast, or a blunt definition of a dish by people not in the mood to give the French credit for anything. That's everyone on the planet at one time or another, I think. The Irish were ambivalent about the French for centuries, given the Gallic tendency to be at war with the English and occasionally even throwing a few boatloads of soldiers behind some of our pitchfork uprisings. Their selfish motivation was always blatant, mind you, so gratitude never came into it. The infamous handball incident in Paris 2009 ended all that, and the Irish stepped formally over to enemy status. Now we'd hardly credit them for inventing Paris.

Anyway, shaking off the endlessly recurring image of hand on ball – twice – what we're trying to do here is to not only serve eggy bread in a savoury way, but to bring savoury flavours to the bread itself by adding onion, cheese and herbs to the batter. It struck me while I was doing this that another approach would be to use a flavoured bread from the start. The fashion for putting all sorts of ingredients into bread dough might be waning a little, but you can still find some lovely oniony herbed loaves. I've said in the instructions to cut off the crusts. It depends on the loaf, obviously, and I was using country-style bread with a very thick crust. Make your own call on it.

The spiced pepper compote is something you can knock up fairly quickly, especially if you have a roasted, peeled pepper in the fridge. The quantities are tiny, and it is also the kind of thing that will keep for a few days in the fridge, so it's best to make a bigger batch, preferably the day before – or use your favourite jar of chutney.

- First make the spiced pepper compote: heat the olive oil in a small saucepan over medium heat. Add the onion and fry for 2 minutes, stirring. Add the garlic and chilli, and continue to cook for 1 minute more. Dice the pepper, discarding its seeds and membrane, and add it to the pan with the tomato, vinegar and sugar. Bring to the boil and simmer for 10–15 minutes, until you get a jammy consistency. Remove from the heat.

- Make the eggy bread: heat the olive oil in a small saucepan over a medium heat. Add the shallots and sauté them, stirring, for 3–4 minutes, until soft.

- Whisk the eggs and milk together in a large bowl. Add the shallots, thyme leaves and cheese. Season with salt and pepper.

- Cut the crusts off the bread and soak the slices in the egg mixture for a minute.

- Melt the butter in a frying pan over medium heat. Remove the bread slices from the egg mixture and place them in the pan. Cook on one side until golden, then turn and repeat with the other side.

- To serve, place a slice of fried bread on each plate. Put some rocket on top and set another slice of bread leaning on that. Spoon some of the spiced compote on each plate.

Spiced pumpkin maple pancakes with orange cream & walnuts

for 4

for the spice mix
½ tbsp baking powder
½ tsp ground ginger
½ tsp ground cinnamon
¼ tsp freshly grated
    nutmeg
pinch of ground cloves

*for the spiced pumpkin
maple pancakes*
200g/7oz diced pumpkin
    or squash
180g/6¼oz plain flour
1 tbsp caster sugar
¼ tsp baking powder
large pinch of salt
200ml/7fl oz buttermilk
1 large egg, lightly beaten
2 tbsp melted butter, plus
    extra for brushing
1 tbsp maple syrup

for the spiced maple sauce
100ml/3½fl oz maple
    syrup
¼ tsp ground ginger
¼ tsp ground cinnamon
⅛ tsp freshly grated
    nutmeg
small pinch of ground
    cloves

for the orange cream
200ml/7fl oz double cream
finely grated zest of
    1 orange

to serve
60g/2½oz walnuts,
    chopped

If you like pumpkin and maple together – and why would you not? – then this is the breakfast, brunch, afternoon tea or dessert for you. Pumpkin, maple and spices in a pancake doused with pumpkin, maple and spices! No further comment required except to say that, if you can't get buttermilk, you will get a similar result by substituting half milk and half yoghurt.

- First make the spice mix by mixing together all ingredients.

- Prepare the spiced pumpkin maple pancakes: bring a saucepan of water to the boil, add the pumpkin and simmer for 10–15 minutes, until tender. Drain the pumpkin and purée, adding a little water for a smooth paste. If it seems in any way stringy, pass through a sieve.

- In a large bowl, combine the flour, sugar, baking powder, half the spice mix and the salt.

- In another bowl, stir together the buttermilk, egg and melted butter. Add the maple syrup and 100g/3½oz of the pumpkin purée. Add to the flour mixture and stir briefly to create a thick batter.

- Preheat the oven to 150°C/300°F/gas mark 2.

- Heat a frying pan over medium heat and brush lightly with melted butter. Pour 1 tablespoon of the batter into the hot pan for each pancake, making as many at a time as possible without overcrowding the pan. Cook for 3 minutes, then turn the pancakes and continue cooking for 1 or 2 minutes more. Repeat with the remaining batter, keeping the cooked pancakes warm in the oven.

- While the pancakes are frying, make the spiced maple sauce: pour the maple syrup into a small saucepan over low heat. Add 2 tablespoons of the remaining pumpkin purée and the remaining spice mix. Warm gently, whisking to get a syrupy pouring texture. Add a little water if the sauce seems too thick.

- Make the orange cream: whip the cream to soft peaks and fold in the orange zest.

- Serve the pancakes with a generous amount of spiced maple sauce poured over them and some orange cream on top. Scatter each portion with some chopped walnuts.

Grilled asparagus with poached eggs & avocado cherry tomato salsa

for 2

6–8 asparagus spears
olive oil, for brushing
4 eggs
1 tsp white wine vinegar
2 slices of bread
salt

*for the avocado
cherry tomato salsa*
12 cherry tomatoes, halved
1 fresh green chilli,
    deseeded and thinly
    sliced
2 tbsp olive oil
1 avocado, peeled,
    stoned and diced
1 tbsp lemon juice

The quantities below are for two people, mostly because poaching eggs for more than two at a time can be a bit of a stressful juggling act. Do-able, certainly, but you wouldn't volunteer for it. How then, I hear you ask, is it done in restaurants that serve tens or even hundreds of people? One or two, maybe three, portions at a time, over and over and over. Sometimes, the eggs are poached ahead of time and stored in chilled water to keep them at that perfect just-done state. Nothing wrong with that; it's a practical solution to a tricky problem. If you're thinking of poaching for more than six at home, you should consider one or other of those options.

Use a fairly shallow pan with no more than 5–7.5cm/2–3in of water in it. The vinegar will help the eggs to hold together, as will keeping the water at a very gentle simmer. Sometimes you will hear that swirling the water into a whirlpool at the centre is a good idea, and it does help with the first egg, but I've never figured out where to put the second one.

Like most breakfast dishes involving eggs, the stress is in the timing of getting everything ready at the same moment. Keep in mind that the one element that won't hold, wait or sit around is the eggs themselves. Have everything else in some partial state of readiness and do a quick mental and visual scan just before you slide the eggs into the water.

Finally, I've included just two slices of bread in the ingredients. I always find it disappointing when there is more bread than egg in my breakfast, believing that you really only need just enough to soak up stray egg yolk.

- First make the avocado cherry tomato salsa: put the cherry tomatoes and chilli in a small saucepan with the olive oil and a pinch of salt. Warm gently over medium heat for a few minutes, until the tomatoes are beginning to soften. Remove from the heat, but keep warm.

- Heat a griddle pan over high heat. Just before you poach the eggs, brush the asparagus spears with a little olive oil and place them on the hot pan. Sprinkle with salt and grill for 3–4 minutes, turning once or twice.

- Fill a shallow saucepan with water to a depth of 5–7.5cm/2–3in, bring to the boil, then add the wine vinegar and turn the heat down to keep the water at a gentle simmer. Crack an egg into a small cup or ramekin and gently lower it into the water. Repeat with the other eggs. Poach the eggs for 2–3 minutes, until done to your liking. Lift them out, one at a time, with a slotted spoon.

- Toast the bread while the eggs are cooking. Stir the avocado and lemon juice into the salsa.

- Serve the eggs on the toast, with the salsa spooned over and around them, and the asparagus draped across the top.

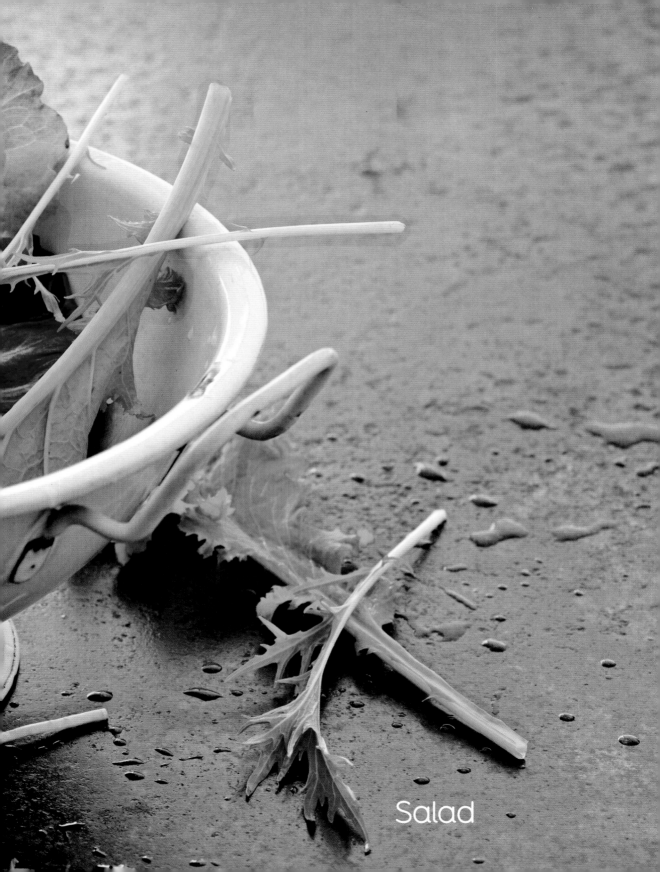

Salad

Salad

By the simplest definition, salad is a bunch of leaves tossed together with a touch of oil and vinegar, an accompaniment to the main business of dinner or lunch. During the preparation of food, if someone volunteers to make salad, or is asked to do so, this simple throwing together of greens and dressing is usually what is meant. The volunteer, or the commandeered, is likely to have a favourite dressing: a little mustard or honey, maybe a touch of herbs, garlic or spices; they might start with a few spoons of yoghurt or sesame paste and go from there.

The French eat their salad after dinner, the Italians before, or is it the other way around? Where I was brought up, salad was strange foreign food, and almost the only time we indulged in it was as a substitute for a cooked evening tea on the warmest of sunny summer days. Then, it was an arrangement of a dish rather than a composed one. Soft lettuce leaves laid on a plate were covered with sliced tomato and cucumber, spring onion, hard-boiled egg (also sliced, on a specific gadget dedicated to that job alone) and – every child's nightmare – pickled beetroot, also sliced. Fun times, so much that we couldn't wait for the rain to come back so we could revert to hot food.

Funny, but the idea of composing a plate by arranging some like-minded ingredients around or on top of a pile of fresh green leaves is still at the heart of much of what trades under the banner of 'salad', in this book and everywhere else too. Sometimes the ingredients are warm, sometimes cold. Still salad. Sometimes there is no leafy green of any kind, but still it is a salad, even if the dish is warm. Sometimes, as in at least one dish here, the salad consists of some braised vegetables served hot from the pan and dressed with a sharp, tangy sauce. Salad too. So that's cleared that up then – it's a salad if the person making it says it is. That's my kind of definition, loose and arbitrary, with total control in the cook's hands.

Once you've decided to call it a salad, you're free to serve it as a starter, a side dish or a meal in its own right. I've taken a fondness to adding fruit to salads, though it might be a stretch to say you can serve those recipes as dessert.

With one or two exceptions, the recipes here don't have elaborate dressings. This is mostly because the flavours in the salads come from the combination of ingredients, and the dressing is there, like any sauce, not to dominate the dish but to add a little background zing to it.

In the notes attached to each recipe are suggestions on how it might best be used, and any variations I think might work with it. For example, the above-alluded-to hot dish of kai-lan in a peanut dressing can be a starter, a side dish or part of a feast. A noodle salad might do the same, while it can also make a fine lunch, or go on a picnic with you. You may have to adjust the quantities for some of these changes of use, but you'll figure that out after making a dish once.

Also, while some of the dishes are quite specific in their ingredients, especially the more composed salads with a fine-ish balance between fruit and vegetables, many of the others can be read as either prototypes or the sum of their parts. If the only thing that appeals in a salad is the dressing, take it and compose your own salad. Replace vegetables, noodles or grains with others, change the proportions within a salad or leave out something you know you don't like. Don't leave out something you're merely not sure you like – this might be the time you fall for it!

Salad of watercress, quince, glazed pecans & fresh sheep's cheese with citrus-hazelnut dressing

This elegant starter has lovely contrasting sweet, acidic and nutty flavours mixed through the peppery punch of watercress leaves. There is a bit of preparation in the pecans and quince, but you can do those well ahead and the rest is simple assembly.

Quince isn't a lot of fun to eat raw, but it comes into its own when poached for a while with a little vanilla. If you can't get quince, roasted chunks of pear would be a good substitute.

In Ireland, I use Knockalara sheep's cheese whenever I need something light and creamy with a little touch of acidity. A mild rindless goat's cheese would also be good, as would feta.

- First make the glazed pecans: preheat the oven to 130°C/250°F/gas mark ½.

- Melt the sugar and maple syrup in a small saucepan and stir in the pecans. Spread on an oven tray lined with baking parchment. Place the tray in the oven for 20 minutes, then remove and leave the pecans to cool and become crisp.

- Make the vanilla-poached quince: bring the sugar and 250ml/9floz water to the boil in a saucepan and add the vanilla pod. Peel the quince and slice it into thin wedges. Place these in the syrup and simmer until the quince is soft. Remove from the heat and leave to cool.

- Make the citrus-hazelnut dressing by combining all the ingredients.

- In a salad bowl, mix together the watercress, cheese, pecans and quince. Pour on some of the dressing, toss gently and share out between 4 plates.

for 4

200g/7oz watercress
100g/3½oz fresh sheep's or goat's cheese, crumbled

for the glazed pecans
30g/1¼oz caster sugar
1 tsp maple syrup
60g/2½oz pecans

for the vanilla-poached quince
150g/5oz caster sugar
1 vanilla pod, split
1 large quince

for the citrus-hazelnut dressing
finely grated zest of 1 orange, juice of ½
juice of 1 lemon
2 tsp toasted hazelnut oil
150ml/5fl oz olive oil

Spiced sweet potato pancakes with avocado, pumpkin seed, pomegranate & feta salad and herbed yoghurt

Is it a pancake with toppings or a salad on a pancake? Is it a pancake at all or simply a fritter? Not that fritters are inferior, mind, but the naming of things can become a pedantic tribunal when something is going on a restaurant menu for the first time. Which is why I make up names for dishes if a debate looks like going on for too long, even in the case of things for which names already exist. Lack of professional training, I explain, if caught out.

Flipping a coin, this one's a salad on a very versatile pancake. The basic batter will accommodate carrot, potato, parsnip or even beetroot. After that, it's simply a matter of choosing a salad combination that works with the pancake. Watercress and goat's cheese with beetroot pancake? Artichokes, rocket and pecorino on a potato version of the pancake?...You can do the rest.

- First make the herbed yoghurt: in a small bowl, mix together all the ingredients.

- Make the pancakes: in a bowl, combine all the ingredients well with 125ml/4½fl oz water. Heat a thin layer of vegetable oil in a large frying pan over medium heat. Put in 4 separate generous tablespoonfuls of the pancake mixture to make 4 cakes about 7.5cm/3in in diameter and 5mm/¼in thick. Cook for 5 minutes, until crisp and browned, then flip them over and cook the other side until lightly coloured.

- While the pancakes are cooking, prepare the salad: peel the avocados, remove the stones and slice the flesh thickly. Toss the avocado slices with the pomegranate and pumpkin seeds, feta and salad leaves.

- Drizzle some yoghurt on 4 plates and place a pancake on each. Arrange some salad on top, squeeze the lemon juice over and serve.

for 4

for the herbed yoghurt
200ml/7fl oz natural yoghurt
1 tbsp finely chopped fresh mint
1 tbsp finely chopped fresh coriander
1 tbsp finely chopped fresh dill

for the spiced sweet potato pancakes
100g/3½oz sweet potato, peeled and grated
1 small red onion, finely diced
2 fresh green chillies, finely chopped
2 tsp cumin seeds
1 tsp black mustard seeds
1 tsp fennel seeds, ground
2 tsp coriander seeds, ground
1 tsp baking powder
75g/3oz gram (chickpea) flour
40g/1½oz semolina
vegetable oil, for frying
salt

for the salad
2 avocados
seeds of ½ pomegranate
1 tbsp pumpkin seeds, lightly toasted
100g/3½oz feta cheese, crumbled
100g/3½oz small salad leaves
juice of ½ lemon

Spiced haloumi on a warm Puy lentil, spinach & beetroot salad

for 4

2 medium beetroots, washed, cooked and peeled
1 tbsp balsamic vinegar
olive oil, for tossing and cooking
200ml/7fl oz vegetable stock
100ml/3½fl oz red wine
100g/3½oz Puy lentils
2 sprigs of fresh thyme
4 garlic cloves, sliced
2 spring onions, thinly sliced
2 dried bird's eye chillies, ground
2½ tsp cumin seeds, ground
finely grated zest of 1 lime and juice of 2
200g/7oz haloumi cheese, cut into 8 slices
100g/3½oz baby spinach leaves
salt and pepper

While the beetroot is caramelising in the oven with a splash of balsamic vinegar, the Puy lentils are simmering in a stock of red wine and thyme. When they come together, it makes for a deeply satisfying combination that can form the basis of any number of dishes. Will it be a stew or the foil for some ravioli? Or will we put a few spoonfuls under some rich aubergine and cheese parcels? Or will we turn up the vinegar, add some olive oil and call it a salsa? No, today, it's going to be a warm salad with a very comfortable partner for both beetroot and lentils – fresh baby spinach leaves.

Sitting atop the earthy and familiar combination, bringing a touch of fiery heat to the show, are a few slices of salty fried haloumi that have been seared with chillies, lime and cumin. This combination of comfort food and challenging spices is one of my favourite ways to liven up a dish or a meal. You can easily turn down the drama by reducing the amount of chilli.

- Preheat the oven to 180°C/350°F/gas mark 4.

- Slice the beetroot into thin wedges, toss with the balsamic vinegar and a little olive oil and roast in the preheated oven for 20–30 minutes, until beginning to caramelise.

- While the beetroot is roasting, bring the vegetable stock and red wine to the boil in a large pan. Add the lentils, thyme and garlic, and simmer for 15–20 minutes, uncovered, until the lentils are just tender but still firm. If there is any liquid left in the pan, turn up the heat and boil until the liquid is all but gone. Stir in the roast beetroot and spring onions, and remove from the heat. Season with salt and pepper.

- Mix together the chillies, cumin and lime zest. Halve the haloumi slices diagonally.

- Heat a little olive oil in a frying pan over medium heat and fry the haloumi until browned on both sides. Sprinkle the spice mix and the juice of 1 of the limes over the cheese and toss to coat it evenly.

- Place some baby spinach on each plate and scatter some of the lentil mix over it. Arrange the haloumi slices on top and finish with the remaining lime juice.

Roast aubergine, avocado & chicory salad with honey, chilli & cardamom and a tahini-yoghurt dressing

In this composed starter, the aubergines are dressed twice: once with a spiced marinade that is absorbed as the aubergines cool, and then on the plate with the creamy tahini and yoghurt sauce. The combination creates a layered flavour impact, evocative of the Eastern Mediterranean – or South Cork, or wherever comes to mind when you eat cardamom, chilli, honey, sesame and yoghurt.

I've specified chicory because it's a crisp salad leaf with a touch of bitterness to offset the honey-sweetened aubergines. Radicchio would also be good. If you're not keen on bitter greens at all, then a Cos or Little Gem lettuce is probably the best bet.

If you don't have a hothouse full of aubergines, from which to pick the most appropriate size and variety, try to find small ones that can be sliced lengthways without overhanging the plate! Most importantly, make sure they are firm and fresh and don't have a lot of bitter seeds.

- Preheat the oven to 200°C/400°F/gas mark 6.

- Prepare the aubergine: slice the aubergines lengthways about 1cm/½in thick. Brush these on both sides with olive oil and roast them on a baking tray in the oven for about 8–10 minutes, until lightly coloured, turning once if necessary.

- Transfer to a shallow dish or plate and brush with the honey. Mix together the cardamom seeds, chillies, salt and the 2 tablespoons of olive oil. Spoon or brush this marinade over the aubergines and leave to stand for 10 minutes.

- Meanwhile, make the tahini yoghurt dressing: whisk some water into the tahini to get a thick pouring consistency. Add the garlic, lemon juice and yoghurt, and whisk to combine. If too thick, dilute with a little more water.

- Peel the avocados, remove the stones and slice the flesh thickly.

- Lay 3 slices of roast aubergine on each plate and arrange some avocado in the centre. Drizzle over a little tahini yoghurt dressing. Dress the chicory and red pepper with some of the dressing and place it on top of the avocado. Drizzle some more dressing over the salad and around the plate, and scatter sesame seeds on top.

for 4

3 small aubergines
2 tbsp olive oil, plus extra for brushing
2 tbsp honey, warmed
12 green cardamom pods, seeds only, crushed but not ground
4 dried bird's eye chillies, ground
pinch of salt
2 avocados
1 head of chicory, halved and thinly sliced
1 red pepper, deseeded and sliced into thin matchsticks
1 tbsp sesame seeds, lightly toasted

for the tahini-yoghurt dressing
1 tbsp tahini
1 garlic clove, crushed
juice of ½ lemon
4 tbsp natural yoghurt

Braised kai-lan & shiitake with crisped vermicelli and a peanut, ginger & chilli dressing

for 4

vegetable oil, for stir-frying
100g/3½oz shiitake
   mushrooms, halved or
   thickly sliced
16 kai-lan (Chinese kale)
   stems
1 fresh red chilli, deseeded
   and sliced
1 tbsp soy sauce
2 spring onions, thinly
   sliced at an angle

for the crisped vermicelli
vegetable oil, for
   deep-frying
1 handful of thin rice
   vermicelli

*for the peanut, ginger and
chilli dressing*
2 tbsp peanuts, lightly
   toasted in a dry pan
150ml/5fl oz lemon juice
3 tbsp soft brown sugar
2 tbsp grated fresh ginger

Kai-lan or Chinese kale, to give it only two of its many names, is a thick-stemmed sprouting green, something like fat sprouting broccoli with juicy tender stems. Here, its strong flavour is combined with shiitake mushrooms, then dressed with a sweet hot and acidic peanut sauce. It doesn't need to be a big portion to have quite an impact.

The dressing, like many in the Asian style, is based on sugar and citrus juice, with no oil, making it at once both light and flavour-packed. It will keep for a couple of days, no more, so don't make any more than you can use.

I see this as a warm salad, because I like to serve it alone as a first course. You could also serve it in a communal way as part of a multi-dish meal with loosely Chinese tendencies.

- First prepare the crisped vermicelli: pour enough oil for deep-frying into a medium saucepan and heat to a moderate temperature. To test, drop in a strand of vermicelli – it should turn golden in about 10 seconds. Break up the vermicelli in your hand, then drop it into the oil. It will swell quickly. When it has turned golden, remove it with a slotted spoon and drain it on kitchen paper. Leave to cool.

- Make the peanut, ginger and chilli dressing: put the peanuts in a food processor and chop coarsely. Remove half the peanuts, add the rest of the ingredients and pulse briefly. The dressing should not be fully emulsified. Stir back in the reserved peanuts.

- In a wide pan, heat a little oil and stir-fry the shiitake over medium heat for 2 minutes. Add the kai-lan, chilli and soy sauce, cover and cook over medium heat for 3–4 minutes more. Remove the lid, add the spring onions and turn up the heat to boil off most of the liquid.

- Lift out the kai-lan and lay the stems side by side on serving plates. Spoon some mushrooms, spring onions and a little pan juice over each portion, and pour on a generous coating of the dressing. Scatter some crisped vermicelli on top and serve warm.

Strawberry, hazelnut & sheep's cheese salad with honey & raspberry dressing

Because I don't often get around to eating dessert, this has been my favourite way to eat strawberries over the past summer. Mind you, if you take out a few words from the middle of the title above, this could easily be read as a dessert. Strawberries, hazelnuts, honey and raspberries… make no mistake, it has its share of sweet notes, though the sheep's cheese and raspberry vinegar help to balance those. The most important element in making this a savoury dish, however, is the salad leaves. Make sure that these include a decent amount of fragrantly peppery leaves such as watercress, rocket and mustard. Then, lo and behold, what we really have here is a peppery salad balanced with the sweet notes of summer berries.

- First make the dressing by blending all of the ingredients to get a slightly thickened consistency.

- Mix all of the salad ingredients gently with enough of the dressing to lightly coat the leaves.

- Divide the salad between 4 plates, season with coarsely ground black pepper and drizzle a little more of the dressing over.

for 4

250g/9oz mixed small salad leaves
12 strawberries, hulled and quartered lengthways
2 tbsp hazelnuts, lightly toasted in a dry pan and halved
125g/4½oz fresh sheep's cheese, crumbled.
pepper

for the honey and raspberry dressing
2 tbsp raspberry vinegar
1 tbsp honey
10 raspberries
200ml/7fl oz sunflower oil

Warm chickpea, aubergine & broccoli salad with bulghur, sunflower seeds and a lemon yoghurt dressing

Bulghur is a tricky beast because it is so easy to get it wrong and end up with a stodgy mess. Because of this you will find lots of different instructions on how to cook it. I'm not claiming this to be the best way, only the one that works for me. And I didn't invent it, so don't give me a hard time if it doesn't work for you – switch to another method instead. Bulghur isn't cracked wheat. It is whole wheat kernels that have been boiled, dried and then crushed. It might be crushed finely, coarsely or in the middle, which is why I have specified a medium grind here. The best advice is to fix on a source of the grind you like, learn how you like to cook it and stick to that. Now, as you can see from the tiny weight of it in the ingredients list, this salad isn't so much about the bulghur at all. Think of it as a vegetable salad with a vibrant herb and creamy yoghurt dressing with a little grain stirred in for texture. Serve it at room temperature for lunch with some warm flat bread, or as part of a mezze plate for a party. If I had to choose one thing to go with it, it would have to be fried haloumi. You can sometimes buy sunflower seeds that have been toasted in tamari or soy sauce. They are very easy to make at home and, as well as adding a salty crunch to salads, they are a great snack. Make a big batch.

- Preheat the oven to 200°C/400°F/gas mark 6.

- Toss the aubergine slices lightly in olive oil, spread them out on oven trays lined with baking parchment and roast for 10–12 minutes, until well coloured on both sides, turning once if necessary.

- Toast the sunflower seeds in a dry heavy frying pan over low heat for 8–10 minutes, until lightly coloured. Stir in the soy sauce and remove the pan from the heat. Transfer the seeds to a bowl and leave to cool.

- Prepare the bulghur: put it in a small, dry frying pan over a medium heat to toast it for 5 minutes, stirring frequently. Add 125ml/4½fl oz hot water and stir once, then cover the pan, remove it from the heat and leave for 15 minutes. Fluff up the bulghur with a fork and put it in a large mixing bowl.

Continued on following page…

for 4

2 medium aubergines, halved lengthways and cut into slices 1cm/½in thick
olive oil, for tossing
25g/1oz sunflower seeds
2 tsp soy sauce
400g/14oz broccoli
salt and pepper

for the bulghur
50g/2oz bulghur (medium grind)
4 tbsp olive oil
200g/7oz soaked and cooked dried chickpeas
2 tsp cumin seeds
1 fresh red chilli, halved and thinly sliced
3 garlic cloves, sliced
3 tomatoes, deseeded and diced
3 spring onions, sliced thinly at an angle
3 tbsp chopped fresh parsley
3 tbsp chopped fresh coriander

for the lemon yoghurt dressing
200ml/7fl oz natural yoghurt
juice of 1 lemon

Continued from previous page...

- In a wide pan, heat the olive oil over medium heat and fry the chickpeas for 5 minutes, stirring often. Add the cumin seeds, chilli and garlic, and fry for 2 minutes more. Stir in the tomatoes, spring onions and herbs, then pour the contents of the pan over the bulghur.

- Break the broccoli into florets, and halve any really big ones. Bring a saucepan of water to the boil, drop in the broccoli and simmer for 3–4 minutes, until just tender but still crunchy. Drain and cool in cold water. Drain again, then add the broccoli to the bulghur. Add the aubergines and stir gently.

- Make the dressing by combining the lemon juice and yoghurt, thinning to a pouring consistency with water if necessary.

- Stir half of the dressing into the salad and season to taste with salt and pepper. Serve on a wide, flat dish or in individual bowls, with the seeds and the remaining dressing on the side, to be added at the table.

Crisped artichoke fritters with tarragon aioli and a broad bean, roasted onion & new potato salad

The artichokes and aioli make a fine starter in their own right, with just a few lightly dressed leaves on the side. For that matter, the broad bean, onion and potato salad is certainly substantial enough, depending on portion size, to be a starter or light lunch. Putting the two together makes a wonderfully complex dish. For a first course, make sure the salad portion is the smaller part; to make a meal of it, increase the salad quantities. The artichoke fritters can be prepared and crumbed earlier in the day, then kept in the fridge until frying time.

- First prepare the artichokes: squeeze the juice of the lemon into a bowl of cold water and throw in the lemon too. Prepare the artichokes by pulling away the outer leaves and peeling the stem back to the edible core. Slice off the top of the remaining leaves, and cut the artichokes in half lengthways. If there is any hairy choke, scrape it out with a knife and discard. Put the prepared artichokes in the water to keep them from discolouring.

- Bring a saucepan of water to the boil, drop in the artichoke halves and simmer for 7–10 minutes, until the they are tender. Drain and cool them in cold water. Pat them dry with kitchen paper.

- Beat the egg and milk together. Coat the artichokes in the flour, then coat them in the egg and milk mixture and finally coat them in the breadcrumbs. Repeat a second time if necessary to get a thick coating of crumbs.

- To make the tarragon aioli: put the garlic, tarragon, egg, extra egg yolk and mustard in a food processor. Blend for a minute, then slowly add the oil until you get a thick pouring consistency. Taste and adjust by adding some or all of the white wine vinegar. Season with salt and pepper.

- Prepare the vegetables for the broad bean, roasted onion and new potato salad: preheat the oven to 200°C/400°F/gas mark 6. Toss the red onions in a little olive oil on an oven tray. Season them with salt and place in the oven to roast for 10–12 minutes, until the onions are browned. Remove from the oven and stir in the balsamic vinegar.

for 4

for the artichoke fritters
1 lemon
6 small globe artichokes
1 egg
100ml/3½fl oz milk
100g/3½oz plain flour
200g/7oz breadcrumbs

for the tarragon aioli
1 garlic clove, chopped
3 tbsp chopped fresh
 tarragon
1 egg, plus 1 extra egg yolk
1 tsp smooth mustard
250ml/9fl oz olive oil
1 tbsp white wine vinegar
salt and pepper

for the broad bean, roasted onion and new potato salad
2 red onions, halved and
 thinly sliced
olive oil, for tossing
1 tbsp balsamic vinegar
300g/11oz podded fresh
 broad beans
200g/7oz waxy new
 potatoes, thinly sliced
125g/4½oz rocket leaves
125g/4½oz baby spinach
 leaves
juice of ½ lemon
100ml/3½fl oz olive oil
salt and pepper

Continued on following page...

Continued from previous page...

- While the onions are in the oven, cook the broad beans in boiling water for 7–10 minutes, until tender. Drain and cool briefly, but not completely, under cold running water.

- At the same time, do the same with the new potato slices, then add them to the broad beans and season with salt and pepper.

- Make the artichoke fritters: heat olive oil to a depth of 1cm/½in in a frying pan over medium heat. Add the artichoke halves and fry them for 7–8 minutes, turning occasionally, until browned and crisp all over. Drain on kitchen paper and keep warm in the oven while you assemble the salad.

- Add the rocket and spinach to the broad beans and potatoes. Add the lemon juice and olive oil, and toss gently to mix.

- Place the salad on 4 plates and drizzle some aioli around each portion. Place 3 of the artichoke fritters on each plate and serve.

Couscous salad with fresh apricots, broccoli, feta and a minted tomato dressing

for 4

300g/11oz couscous
275ml/10fl oz warm
 vegetable stock or water
400g/14oz broccoli
1 tbsp olive oil
1 red onion, halved and
 thinly sliced
3 garlic cloves, sliced
2 tsp cumin seeds
1 tbsp each coarsely
 chopped fresh parsley
 and coriander
juice of 1 lemon and
 ½ orange
4 fresh apricots, stoned,
 quartered and sliced
200g/7oz feta cheese,
 crumbled

*for the minted tomato
dressing*
100g/3½oz sun-dried
 tomatoes, chopped
40g/1½oz fresh mint
2 tsp smoked paprika
large pinch of cayenne
 pepper
200ml/7fl oz olive oil

The dressing for this substantial combination of fruit, greens, cheese and couscous is more like a pesto than a delicate salad dressing. For that reason, I add just a little of it to the salad, then spread more of it on the plate, underneath the salad in a pretty design. It looks good, if I may say so, and gives the eater the pleasure of deciding from one forkful to the next just how much dressing to have each time. Same goes for the feta, which in another approach might be stirred into the salad. So the dish is to some extent deconstructed.

Feel free to take any different approach that appeals. And that goes for the ingredients too. Change the greens to beans, use dried apricots instead of fresh or try oranges or cherries instead. Start with millet instead of couscous. Write your own recipe!

- Put the couscous in a bowl and stir in the stock or water. Leave for 15 minutes, then fluff up the couscous with a fork or your hands.

- Cut the top of the broccoli into short florets, and cut the larger of these again in half or into quarters. Peel the remaining stem and chop it into thin batons about 4cm/1½in long.

- In a wide pan or wok, heat the olive oil over medium heat. Stir-fry the red onion and broccoli with the garlic and cumin seeds for 2–3 minutes. Add to the couscous.

- Make the minted tomato dressing: put the sun-dried tomatoes and mint in a food processor with the paprika and cayenne, and blend to a paste. Add the olive oil and blend again to achieve a pouring consistency.

- Add the remaining fresh herbs to the couscous with the citrus juices and the apricots. Stir in 2 tablespoons of the dressing.

- To serve the salad, drizzle some dressing on to plates and spoon some salad on top. Scatter the feta over each portion.

Salad of rosé-poached rhubarb, baby carrots, rocket and fresh goat's cheese with hazelnut citrus praline

We put this on the Café Paradiso menu one week when the poached rhubarb dessert was selling slowly and we needed to shift the rhubarb before the next batch arrived. I wanted to try the rhubarb in a savoury setting. It is, as people keep pointing out, a vegetable, and one that works well with carrots and hazelnuts.

If you don't want to go to the trouble of making the praline, simply roast some hazelnuts instead, chop them up and sprinkle them over the salad.

- First make the hazelnut citrus praline: peel the lemon and orange rind in wide strips, and put them in a small saucepan with the sugar and 1 tablespoon of water. Simmer over very low heat until the sugar has melted and turned a light golden colour. Stir in the hazelnuts and immediately spread the mixture on a large sheet of baking parchment. Leave to cool.

- Break the praline into pieces and pulse these in a food processor to get a fine, crisp crumb.

- Preheat the oven to 180°C/350°F/gas mark 4.

- Put the rhubarb pieces in an ovenproof dish. In a large saucepan, bring to the boil the sugar, ginger, wine and 300ml/11fl oz water. Pour this over the rhubarb and place the dish in the oven for 15–20 minutes, until the rhubarb is just tender but still firm. Transfer the rhubarb pieces to a container to cool.

- While they cool, make the dressing: whisk the olive oil with the juice of the lemon and a tablespoon of the juice from the orange used for the praline.

- Bring another saucepan of water to the boil, drop in the carrots and simmer for a minute. Transfer the carrots to a bowl of cold water, then drain them again and dry them on kitchen paper.

- Toss the carrots, rocket and goat's cheese together with a little of the dressing.

- Divide the salad between 4 plates and place some of the rhubarb in and around each portion. Drizzle a little more dressing over, and sprinkle some praline on top.

for 4

3 rhubarb stalks, cut into 2cm/¾in pieces
100g/3½oz caster sugar
4cm/1½in piece of fresh ginger, peeled and thinly sliced
100ml/3½fl oz rosé wine
100ml/3½fl oz olive oil
150g/5oz tiny carrots, peeled
200g/7oz rocket leaves
150g/5oz fresh goat's cheese, crumbled

for the hazelnut citrus praline
1 lemon
1 orange
100g/3½oz caster sugar
50g/2oz hazelnuts

Fingerling potato, watercress & walnut salad

for 4

1kg/2lb 2oz fingerling
  potatoes, washed and
  unpeeled
4 spring onions, finely
  chopped
125g/4½oz watercress,
  coarsely chopped
50g walnuts, coarsely
  chopped
salt and pepper

for the dressing
4 tbsp mayonnaise
2 tbsp yoghurt
2 tbsp olive oil

The densely firm texture and rich nutty flavour of fingerling
potatoes – those small, finger-shaped varieties like La Ratte or Pink
Fir Apple – make great salad material. What's more, they don't
need to be peeled, which wipes out a chore and retains a lot more
character in the dish. Watercress adds a peppery and acidic bite,
toned down by a good dollop each of mayonnaise and yoghurt.

The quantities will serve 4 generously but, as this is such a
great party food, you might want to double the recipe or more. It
will keep well for a few days in the fridge.

- Boil the potatoes until just tender. Drain and cool under cold
  running water. Slice the ends off each potato and discard, then
  chop the rest into slices 1cm/½in thick and put in a large bowl.

- Add the spring onion, watercress and walnuts, and season well
  with salt and pepper.

- Make the dressing: mix together the mayonnaise, yoghurt and
  olive oil, and stir enough of this dressing into the potatoes to coat
  them generously.

Sugar snaps with garlic, cherry tomatoes, shallots & basil

for 6–8

500g/1lb 2oz sugar snap
  peas, strings removed
2 tbsp olive oil
4 small shallots, very finely
  diced
3 garlic cloves, finely
  chopped
1 small bunch of fresh
  basil, coarsely chopped
100g/3½oz cherry
  tomatoes, halved
salt and pepper

This is as simple as food gets, yet it simply won't do what you want unless you've got great ingredients. I knocked it together for a midsummer outdoor affair centred around the barbecue. A local grower gave me a couple of kilos of sugar snaps when I called to the farm to get salad leaves. Nice, I thought, now I've got a big pile of snaps to string. I did the sensible thing. Bribed children to do it for me and forgot to pay them.

Well, it's not taking anything away from the rest of the food to say that all the guests raved about the sugar snaps. It's a nice recipe, full of happy summer flavours, but I absolutely know that what people were really getting so excited about was the intrinsic flavour of the snaps themselves. So don't use this recipe as a way to sweeten up some tired old supermarket produce. Get it out to honour a bag of pods that deserves it.

- Bring a large saucepan of water to the boil and drop in the sugar snaps for 30 seconds. Drain in a colander and cool under cold running water briefly – just enough to stop the cooking and bring the snaps back to room temperature. Put the snaps in a serving dish.

- In a small frying pan, heat the olive oil over a medium heat. Add the shallots and garlic, and cook for 30 seconds, stirring. Then add the basil and cook for 30 seconds more.

- Add to the sugar snaps and mix well. Stir in the cherry tomatoes, and season with salt and pepper.

Salad of roasted courgette, green beans & puy lentils with coriander, mint & yoghurt dressing

A gently flavoured summer salad with a light herby dressing, this is a very versatile little number. By adjusting the quantities, you might eat it as a starter or one course of many, or it can be a lunch in itself with a hunk of bread on the side. You might decide to increase the lentil quota, or add some new potatoes to the mix.

As it stands, the courgettes are the main item and they need to be good. Try to find – down your own garden, maybe – smallish courgettes that are firm all the way through and have little or no seeds. If, god forbid, you are determined to make it despite having only large truncheons of courgettes, cut them at a slight angle into slices about 2cm/¾in thick.

- Bring a saucepan of water to the boil, add the lentils and simmer for 20 minutes, until tender but still with a little bite. Drain through a sieve.

- While the lentils cook, heat the olive oil in a wide pan over medium heat, add the red onion and fry for 1 minute. Add the garlic and cumin seeds, and cook for a few seconds before adding the drained lentils and half of the herbs. Fry for 1 minute more, then transfer the lentils to a large bowl, and season with salt and pepper.

- Preheat the oven to 200°C/400°F/gas mark 6.

- Put the halved courgettes in a bowl and add enough olive oil to coat them lightly. Season with salt and lay the courgettes on an oven tray. Roast in the oven for 8–10 minutes, until beginning to colour but still firm. Add to the lentils.

- While these roast, bring another saucepan of water to the boil, drop in the green beans and simmer for 2 minutes. Drain the beans, cool them under cold running water and add to the lentils with the remaining herbs.

- Make the yoghurt dressing: whisk the olive oil into the yoghurt, add the lemon juice and gently stir half of this dressing into the salad.

- Serve the salad piled up in the centre of each plate, with more of the dressing drizzled over and around each portion.

for 4

100g/3½oz Puy lentils
2 tbsp olive oil, plus extra for coating
1 small red onion, halved and thinly sliced
2 garlic cloves, sliced
1 tsp cumin seeds
4 tbsp chopped fresh coriander
2 tbsp chopped fresh mint
400g/14oz small courgettes, halved lengthways
200g/7oz green beans
salt and pepper

for the yoghurt dressing
100ml/3½fl oz olive oil
200ml/7fl oz natural yoghurt
juice of 1 lemon

Minted bean salad
with cumin crispbread

for 4

400g/14oz fine green
   beans
200g/7oz soaked and
   cooked dried haricot or
   cannellini beans
4 tbsp olive oil
2 small shallots, thinly
   sliced
2 garlic cloves, thinly sliced
1 bunch of fresh mint,
   coarsely chopped
2 tbsp sherry vinegar
salt and pepper

for the cumin crispbread
1 tbsp cumin seeds,
   ground
3 tbsp olive oil
2 slices of day-old bread

A warm or room temperature side dish combination of fine
summer beans and more substantial dried white ones, this is
a fresh and vibrant accompaniment to rich food, whether sitting
beside a tart at the dinner table or outside as part of a barbecue
or picnic feast. One thing's for sure though – the simplicity of the
salad requires very fresh, crisp beans, so it's no place to be trying
to use up old or wrinkly ones. If you have them to hand, mix some
sugar snaps and/or mangetout with the green beans.

• First make the cumin crispbread: preheat the oven to 150°C/
  300°F/gas mark 2. Stir the cumin seeds into the olive oil. Cut the
  crusts off the bread and discard. Brush the bread lightly with the
  spiced olive oil and place it on an oven tray lined with baking
  parchment. Bake for 10–15 minutes, until the bread is crisp.
  Leave to cool, then break the bread into bite-size irregular pieces.

• Bring a saucepan of water to the boil, drop in the green beans and
  cook for 1 minute. Drain and cool briefly under cold running
  water so that the beans are at warm room temperature. Put them
  in a serving bowl with the cooked white beans.

• In a wide pan, heat the olive oil over medium heat. Add the
  shallots and garlic, and sauté for 1 minute. Add the mint and cook
  for 30 seconds more. Add this to the beans and stir in the vinegar.
  Season with salt and pepper.

• Just before serving, stir in the crispbread. Serve the salad at
  room temperature.

Toasted millet, sugar snap & avocado salad with ginger, honey & pumpkin seed dressing

for 4

1 tbsp olive oil
300g/11oz millet
4 spring onions, finely
  chopped
150g/5oz sugar snap peas,
  strings removed and
  halved
2 avocados
1 handful of micro salad
  leaves or watercress
salt and pepper

for the ginger, honey and
pumpkin seed dressing
150g/5oz pumpkin seeds,
  toasted
juice of 1 lemon
2 tbsp grated fresh ginger
1 tbsp honey
125ml/4½fl oz olive oil

The method below describes how to make this into four good-looking, individually plated portions that make lovely starters or a light lunch. However, perhaps the nicest way to eat this salad is to treat it as mini mezze. Put the base mix of toasted millet mixed with spring onion and sugar snaps in a bowl on the table, surrounded by separate dishes containing generous amounts of salad leaves, sliced avocado, pumpkin seeds and a jar of dressing. Some halved radishes would be good too, as would alfalfa and sprouted beans or lentils (not the long commercial beansprouts, which are too watery and unwieldy). Then everyone can construct their own mini salads, as often as they like, and in any way they like.

That's how I first encountered it, over a leisurely dinner between card games. Every time someone tried to get the game going again, someone else mixed up just a smidgeon more salad. And on it went until there was no more dressing to be finger-licked out of the jar. Cards and sticky fingers don't mix.

My girlfriend Maureen's sister, Pati, made the salad with bulghur wheat but said it was usually done with millet, out West in British Columbia, where the dish is loosely called 'the diggidy dank'! The evening started me on a millet kick. That said, I think millet, couscous and bulghur dishes can be largely interchanged, so don't postpone the pleasure of this one if you can't get hold of millet.

- First prepare the ginger, honey and pumpkin seed dressing: set aside 2 tablespoons of the pumpkin seeds and chop them coarsely. Put the rest in a food processor and grind to a fine powder. Add 150ml/5fl oz water and blend to a paste. Add the lemon juice, ginger, honey and olive oil, and blend briefly to get a pouring consistency. Season with salt and pepper.

- Heat the olive oil in a heavy saucepan over low heat. Add the millet and toast it for 7–8 minutes, stirring often. Add 600ml/ 1 pint of boiling water and a pinch of salt. Lower the heat, cover the pan and simmer the millet for 15 minutes, until all the water has been absorbed.

- Stir the spring onion and sugar snaps into the millet. Spoon this into shallow bowls and drizzle some dressing over.

- Peel the avocado, remove the stone and cut the flesh into thick dice. Toss with the salad leaves and a little of the dressing.

- Spoon some of this salad on each portion of the millet, and drizzle some more dressing over and around the salad. Scatter the reserved chopped pumpkin seeds on top and serve.

Roasted beetroot & squash salad with smoked almonds, capers, spinach and a goat's cheese dressing

The first inspiration for this salad came from staring at a bunch of beets sitting beside a squash in a basket, thinking how nice it would be to put those together on a plate. Especially if they were sitting on some fresh greens... oh, the colours! OK then, so it's a vain little plate, carefully composed and proud of its flamboyant hues, but it packs a flavour punch too, with the sweetness of the main acts against the tang of capers and goat's cheese, and a touch of smoke in the almonds. Would that all pretty things were so feisty.

- Preheat the oven to 200°C/400°F/gas mark 6.

- Bring a saucepan of water to the boil, drop in the beetroots and simmer for 20–30 minutes, until tender. Drain, then peel under cold running water. Place the beets in an oven dish and toss with a little olive oil and salt. Roast in the oven for 15–20 minutes, until starting to caramelise. Remove from the oven and stir in the vinegar.

- While the beets are cooking, toss the squash or pumpkin with a little olive oil and salt in another oven dish. Roast for 15–20 minutes, until tender. Stir in the chillies and cumin, and return the squash to the oven for 2–3 minutes more.

- Make the goat's cheese dressing by whisking together all of the ingredients, adding a little water, if necessary, to get a thin pouring consistency.

- Start the plating by drizzling some dressing on each plate. Toss the spinach with a little of the dressing and put a little in the centres of 4 plates. Carefully put some squash on top of each portion, without covering the spinach completely, then tuck some beets into the edges of the salad. Drizzle a little more dressing over the top of the squash, and scatter some capers and smoked almonds over the whole plate.

for 4

20 small beetroots, washed
olive oil, for tossing
1 tbsp balsamic vinegar
500g/1lb 2 oz squash or pumpkin, peeled, deseeded and cut into 2cm/¾in dice
2 fresh red chillies, deseeded and thinly sliced
2 tsp ground cumin
250g/9oz baby spinach leaves
1 tbsp tiny capers, rinsed
2 tbsp smoked almonds, thinly sliced
salt

for the goat's cheese dressing

100g/3½oz fresh goat's cheese, crumbled
1 garlic clove, crushed
2 tbsp olive oil
2 tbsp natural yoghurt

Rice vermicelli & cabbage salad with almond-coconut dressing and coriander-radish salsa

I have to say I'm still undecided about whether this should be made with very thin or very fat noodles. It's fun to eat with everything from these ultra-thin rice vermicelli through the spectrum to fat udon wheat noodles, about twice the thickness of standard spaghetti. It's certainly easier to mix if you use the fatter noodles. Try to shorten the vermicelli by breaking them before cooking, though not so much that there is no fork-twirling involved in the eating of the dish.

It's a simple dish with not too many elements or flavours, and I think it's best that way. I use Savoy cabbage, and the lack of crowding allows its crisp texture and sweet flavour to shine. The salsa on top gives the dish a contrasting liveliness that might be lost if the radish and coriander were simply stirred into the mix.

There may be more of the sweet, nutty dressing than you need for four portions of this salad, but it keeps well in the fridge for a few days, and doubles up nicely as a dip for vegetables or flat breads.

- First make the almond-coconut dressing: put the almond butter in a bowl and whisk in the coconut milk and the same amount of water to get a freely pouring consistency. Stir in the soy sauce and vinegar.

- Heat the vegetable oil in a wide pan over medium heat. Add the shallots, chillies, garlic and ginger, and sauté for 1 minute. Add the cabbage and continue to cook for 3–4 minutes more, stirring often, until the cabbage is tender but still quite crisp. Tip this into a mixing bowl and stir in enough of the almond-coconut dressing to coat the noodles generously.

- At the same time, bring a large saucepan of water to the boil, drop in the rice vermicelli, turn the heat off and leave for 5–10 minutes (or according to the packet instructions) until the noodles are tender. Drain and cool the vermicelli under cold running water, then stir into the cabbage and mix well.

- To make the coriander-radish salsa: mix the radishes, spring onions and coriander together in a bowl, then add the lime juice.

- Serve the salad in deep bowls with some of the salsa sprinkled over each portion.

for 4

1 tbsp vegetable oil
2 small shallots, finely chopped
2 fresh green chillies, finely chopped
2 garlic cloves, finely chopped
2 tbsp grated fresh ginger
400g/14oz cabbage, cut into thin slices about 4cm/1½in long
200g/7oz thin rice vermicelli

for the almond-coconut dressing
100g/3½oz almond butter
100ml/3½fl oz coconut milk
4 tbsp soy sauce
2 tbsp white wine or rice vinegar

for the coriander-radish salsa
8 radishes, finely diced
2 spring onions, finely chopped
1 handful of fresh coriander, chopped
juice of 1 lime

Maple chilli-roasted beetroot with glazed pecans wild rice, bitter greens & orange yoghurt

for 4

100g/3½oz wild rice
2 tbsp olive oil
1 small red onion, halved
and very thinly sliced
200g/7oz cime di rapa,
broccoli raab or kai-lan
(Chinese kale)
salt and pepper

for the maple-coated pecans
2 tbsp soft brown sugar
2 tbsp maple syrup
50g/2oz pecan nuts

for the maple and chilli roasted beetroot
400g/14oz beetroots,
washed, cooked and
peeled
2 tbsp maple syrup
juice of 1 orange
2 tsp balsamic vinegar
2 dried bird's eye chillies,
chopped
1 tbsp olive oil

for the orange yoghurt
rind of 2 oranges, in
long strips
200ml/7fl oz natural
yoghurt
1 tbsp finely chopped
fresh chives

Beetroot loves sweet and acidic flavours that both echo its own and contrast with them, and it gets all its wishes here in a combination of spices, maple, citrus, bitter greens and acidic yoghurt.

In the recipe for Wild Rice, Haloumi and Ginger-braised Leeks with Sweet Pepper, Chilli and Caper Sauce on page 225, the wild rice is cooked as you might pasta – in a saucepan of water at a rolling boil. You can also cook it by the absorption method at a ratio of two volume measures of liquid to one of rice over low heat, as here. However, it's tricky cooking such a small amount of rice, so I would suggest you do a much bigger batch and find a use for the leftovers tomorrow.

I have suggested adding just six tablespoons of rice to the beets, making this much more a vegetable than a grain dish, and the proportions and quantities would suggest using it as a starter or light meal. You can easily turn it into something much more substantial by adding more rice to the beets, effectively creating a pilaf, and cooking more greens to drape across the top.

- Preheat the oven to 130°C/250°F/gas mark ½.

- Put the wild rice in a saucepan with 200ml/7fl oz cold water and a pinch of salt. Bring it to the boil, cover and simmer over low heat for 40 minutes. The water should have evaporated and the rice be cooked through but still firm and chewy.

- While the rice is cooking, prepare the maple-coated pecans: in a small saucepan, gently heat the sugar with the maple syrup. Stir in the pecans to coat them, then spread them on an oven tray lined with baking parchment. Put the tray in the oven for 20–30 minutes, then leave in a cool place until crisp.

- Make the maple and chilli roasted beetroot: increase the oven temperature to 180°C/350°F/gas mark 4. Slice the beetroot into thin circles, about 3mm/⅛in, and put them in an oven dish. In a saucepan, gently heat the maple syrup with the orange juice, balsamic vinegar, chillies and olive oil. Pour this over the beets and stir to mix. Cover loosely with baking parchment and roast in the oven for 20–25 minutes.

- Meanwhile, prepare the orange yoghurt: bring 2 tablespoons of water to the boil in a small saucepan, drop in the orange rind and simmer for 1 minute. Strain out the rind and allow the water to cool before stirring it and the chives into the yoghurt.

- In a wide pan, heat the 2 tablespoons of olive oil over high heat. Add the red onion and the greens, and cook, stirring, for 5–7 minutes, until tender. Season with salt and pepper.

- Stir 6 tablespoons of wild rice into the beets. Drizzle some yoghurt in a wide arc on each plate and place a neat pile of beets in the centre. Drape some greens over each portion. Chop or slice the pecans and sprinkle some over the greens. Pour a little more yoghurt over the top.

Roast cauliflower salad with green beans and a peppered walnut & caper dressing

for 4

1 medium cauliflower
3 tbsp olive oil
1 tbsp coriander seeds, cracked
200g/7oz green beans
juice of ½ lemon

for the peppered walnut and caper dressing
2 tbsp walnuts, finely chopped
1 tbsp small capers, rinsed
1 tsp freeze-dried green peppercorns, cracked
½ red pepper, deseeded and finely diced
2 tbsp chopped fresh coriander
juice of ½ lemon

Roasting brings out the strong brassica flavour that cauliflower has when raw but loses so easily when boiled. The other cooking method, very similar to roasting, that gives a similar result is braising the florets with just a touch of olive oil in a covered heavy iron pan. With either technique, check often to make sure the cauliflower isn't sticking, and that you get it out at the point where it is roasted but still firm and crisp.

Cauliflower also tends to be either forgotten or limited to a tiny few traditional roles like curry and that cheesy pasta thing that half the world loves while the other half can't figure out the fuss. In this salad, not a dairy product in sight, the cauliflower stands up to a very strong dressing with flying colours.

Serve in a communal bowl as a side dish, or give cauliflower its day in the sun by making this a course on its own.

- Preheat the oven to 200°C/400°F/gas mark 6.

- Break the cauliflower into florets, then cut these in half and put them in an oven dish with 2 tablespoons of the olive oil and the cracked coriander seeds. Roast for 10 minutes, until the cauliflower is tender and beginning to colour.

- Bring a saucepan of water to the boil and cook the green beans for 2–3 minutes, until tender but still firm. Drain and partly cool under cold water, then put them in a large, shallow serving bowl and dress with the remaining olive oil and the lemon juice. Stir in the cauliflower.

- Meanwhile, make the peppered walnut and caper dressing: combine the walnuts, capers, green peppercorns, red pepper and fresh coriander. Scatter this over the salad and squeeze the lemon juice on top. Alternatively, put the vegetables in individual bowls before scattering the walnut dressing over each portion.

Salad of leeks, hazelnuts, fennel & watercress with a blackcurrant balsamic dressing

Fruity salads seem to have become something of a minor obsession of mine. Desserts and salad leaves aren't near the top of my food preferences, so maybe I'm trying to combine both? Whatever, it works, in both senses – I eat more leaves and the salads have a lovely yin-yang balance, especially when strongly flavoured leaves like watercress are in the mix. In this case, however, the usual roles are reversed. Blackcurrants are notoriously sour and usually need a lot of sugar to make jams, tarts, fools and the like. So, here, the fruit is actually providing some of the acidity to balance the natural sweetness in the leeks and fennel. Blackcurrants freeze well, so don't feel guilty about using frozen ones if you don't have a bush in the garden.

- Heat the olive oil in a wide, shallow pan over medium heat. Add the leeks and sauté for 1 minute. Add the wine and some salt and pepper, cover the pan and simmer over low heat for 7–8 minutes, until the leeks are just tender. Remove the pan from the heat and leave the leeks to cool down a little.

- Discarding any imperfect outer leaves of the bulb, halve the fennel, trim off the tops of the leaves and cut out the core. Slice the remaining leaves as thinly as possible and toss with the watercress and citrus juices.

- Meanwhile, make the blackcurrant balsamic dressing: heat a little olive oil in a small saucepan over medium heat, add the shallots and blackcurrants, and cook for 2 minutes, until the blackcurrants are beginning to soften. Remove from the heat, add the balsamic vinegar and maple syrup and transfer to a small bowl.

- Place some watercress on each plate and scatter some of the still-warm leeks over and around them. Drizzle some of the dressing over the salad and spoon a little around the plate too. Scatter the hazelnuts over the top.

for 4

1 tbsp olive oil
2 leeks, well washed and cut at an angle into 1cm/½in slices
100ml/3½fl oz dry white wine
1 medium fennel bulb
250g/9oz watercress
1 tbsp lemon juice
1 tbsp orange juice
2 tbsp hazelnuts, lightly toasted in a dry pan and coarsely chopped
salt and pepper

for the blackcurrant balsamic dressing
olive oil, for cooking
2 small shallots, finely chopped
2 tbsp blackcurrants
1 tbsp balsamic vinegar
1 tsp maple syrup

Warm salad of roast pumpkin, Brussels sprout tops & borlotti beans with a maple-sesame dressing

for 4

400g/14oz peeled and
  deseeded pumpkin, cut
  into 2cm/¾in dice
olive oil, for tossing and
  cooking
200g/7oz small shallots,
  peeled
1 head of Brussels sprout
  tops
200g/7oz podded fresh
  or frozen borlotti beans,
  or drained tinned beans
1 fresh red chilli, deseeded
  and thinly sliced
4 spring onions, thinly
  sliced at an angle

*for the maple-sesame
dressing*
3 tbsp maple syrup
3 tbsp light tahini
juice of 1 lemon
1 tbsp grated fresh ginger
1 garlic clove, crushed
1 tsp toasted sesame oil
1 small bunch of fresh
  coriander, chopped
salt

A winter salad that is a meal in itself, this is essentially a combination of pumpkin and greens with a sweet and nutty dressing. Brussels sprout tops are the cabbage-like leaves that grow from the tops of the plants towards the end of their life in late winter. If you've got some in the garden, don't let them go to waste. If not, use the dark green leaves of a cabbage or some cavolo nero (black kale) instead. If you don't have your own borlotti beans stashed away in the freezer, you can often find really good tinned ones. Chickpeas are good in this too, as are butter beans.

- Preheat the oven to 200°C/400°F/gas mark 6.

- Toss the pumpkin in a little olive oil on an oven tray and roast in the oven for 20–30 minutes, until beginning to brown. Do the same with the shallots on a separate tray, until soft and coloured.

- While these are in the oven, chop the sprout tops into thin slices, 4–5cm/1½–2in long. Blanch them in boiling water for 2 minutes, then cool in cold water, drain again and pat dry with kitchen paper.

- Make the maple-sesame dressing: blend all of the ingredients except the salt in a food processor. Add a few tablespoons of warm water to get a pouring consistency and then season with salt.

- If using fresh or frozen borlotti beans, cook them in just enough boiling water to cover for 7–10 minutes, until just tender. If using tinned beans, warm them through. Transfer the beans to a bowl.

- Stir 2 tablespoons of the dressing into the beans while they are still warm.

- In a wide pan, heat a tablespoon of olive oil over medium heat. Add the sprout tops and chilli, and fry for 1 minute.

- Transfer to a serving dish and add the pumpkin, shallots and 2 tablespoons of the dressing. Divide between 4 plates and scatter the beans and spring onions on top. Drizzle a little more dressing over.

Risotto

Risotto

Something that I consistently come across when teaching or doing demos is a mental block against certain ingredients or techniques. Well, maybe I don't so much come across it as go looking for it, because I know it's out there. It can be expressed as simply as 'that's too much trouble' or as extremely as 'I couldn't ever do that'. Aubergine can be a good place to open the conversation. In my mind, it is one of the most useful vegetables, but for others it is a no-go area. 'It takes too much oil' – it doesn't have to but it starts out with none so it might as well. 'It has a horrible texture' – only when hopelessly undercooked by chefs who never eat the thing but cook it for unwelcome 'vegetarians'. And the five-star not-doing-that block – 'don't you have to salt it and rinse it or something?' No, you don't. That's part of the lazy, handed-down stuff that keeps getting perpetuated by people who write by reproducing old text without checking for themselves.

After the aubergine conversation, you can divide a class into those who know they can make risotto and those who think it's a mystery beyond them. It bothers me that people get put off the simple pleasures of cooking because of misinformation or foggy mystique. Fair enough if you have to put your hand up and say you're not much use at making puff pastry. My hand is up too.

But risotto is essentially a very simple rice dish that rewards a little attention to detail. It might be worth looking at that detail and some of the myths that make people back away, thinking they could never go to all that bother, or expect to get it right if they did.

The basic version is made from rice, stock, wine plus one, two or three featured ingredients, some butter and possibly some cheese to finish.

Working backwards, the butter and cheese are easy, you've got those. There is a purist element that frowns on the cheese; you can join them or ignore them as you please. I like cheese, but I leave it out if it really is going to clash with the other ingredients.

The featured ingredients might be as simple as the ubiquitous mushrooms, or it might be one or two ingredients that go well together in any setting. Peas and mint, parsnip and thyme, beetroot and broad beans. I do agree that a risotto can only take a few complementary ingredients and after that it becomes too much like a rice pilaf. Nothing wrong with a fragrantly spiced rice pilaf, but it isn't risotto.

The distinguishing feature of risotto is the cooking method, the toasting of the grains followed by the repetitive dousing with, firstly, wine and then stock.

To get the wine out of the way quickly, use any dry white. Unless you're making red risotto – beetroot for example – in which case use red wine.

Whether you need an amazingly complex stock for risotto or not depends on whether you want to taste anything else in the dish. I like my risotto to taste of the added vegetables. I think this goes against the received wisdom a little, but I don't want my risotto to taste of the stock, especially not one made from dead chickens. I do like the rice to be humming a gently complex tune in the background, but not screaming blue murder up front. In Café Paradiso we make a simple multi-purpose vegetable stock every morning, but at home I use a good stock powder or liquid concentrate. This is a crucial point in the mental block scenario – 'I can't make risotto because I don't have the time or ingredients to make a good stock'. Buy a good stock powder and stop fretting about the propriety of it.

'But you have to stir it all the time and it will be overcooked in the time it takes me to get the plates out'. This depends on the temperature at which you cook the rice and stock. Again, there is a certain amount of disagreement about this – whether to keep the rice at a very low heat or have it hopping along at a rate that makes the occasional grain pop excitedly up in your face. I generally lean towards the ping-ping lively end of the scale, but it honestly depends to some extent on my mood, and in a very Zen state I'll happily let the rice muddle bubble slowly along and do less stirring.

Letting your mood dictate how you cook is always a useful piece of advice. If you're on the slow train, you can walk away and do other things for up to five minutes at a time. Do come back before the grains are getting stuck to the pan, toss in another ladle of stock and go check your emails again. Or you can stand there fussing over a volcano, if you prefer that kind of drama. The result will be more or less the same, though you'll need more stock for the high tempo routine.

However, when it comes close to the endgame, pay attention to the pot. Test separate grains from different areas and get a sense of how close they are to done. Have everything ready – people sitting, cheese grated, plates warm, side dishes on the point of done too. When the rice is to your liking, make a quick decision about whether it is wet enough or too wet for your taste. The last ladle of stock is the most important. Adjust the texture by adding a splash of stock as you remove the pan from the heat, or by turning the heat up high for the last few seconds, to boil off some liquid.

There is no right consistency, that's just part of the mystique. How do you like your potatoes? That's personal, right? Well, risotto is too. I like some risotto wet and soupy, and others I like drier but with broths, oils, salsa or side dishes to add extra flavour and liquid on the plate.

That leaves the rice, I think. I have consistently written the words 'Carnaroli or Arborio rice' in the recipes that follow. Arborio is the most commonly available. Carnaroli is a slightly bigger grain and seems to hold its shape better in the cooking process. It gives a restaurant kitchen a slight advantage in avoiding making a mess of the risotto, and it will do the same for you. Both taste of nothing. There are others, less widely available, but they are of the same type. Risotto rice is probably the least flavourful rice in the world, and I would pity anyone trying to survive on it in a marginal way without a decent supply of good cheese and butter. Try a taste test sometime, risotto rice against any generic long grain. Boil both, add nothing and taste. Now see why there is a mystique around it, and why it is always cooked with stock, butter and cheese?

Like many cooking techniques that intimidate people, it is a matter of ownership. Instead of believing it to be the territory of experts, decide how you want yours to be and take a little time to learn how to make it to your taste.

The recipes here are typical of how I like risotto. They use the classic technique that allows the rice to become creamy with gradually added stock, but the dominant flavours are all about the highlighted ingredients. Watercress risotto tastes of watercress, parsnip risotto of parsnip and so on. Often, I add other flavours and textures outside the rice itself. These, as you can see from the recipes, might be strongly flavoured broths, side dishes, oils, butters, nuts or crisp crumbs. As with puréed soup, I become bored eating simple risotto, with the exception of the very rare pleasure of risotto with white truffles. Classic risotto is best as a small course in an elaborate meal. To make it a main course, as it so often is now, it needs more drama, and you can only fit so much inside the risotto. Instead of overkilling the risotto, add elements to embellish it.

In many of the recipes I have listed a hard cheese to be added to the end of the cooking and/or grated over the top of the finished dish. There are classic Italian varieties that are well known and very suitable. I prefer to use local cheeses wherever I happen to be. In Ireland, my favourites are Cratloe Hills mature sheep's cheese, Oisin mature goat's cheese or Gabriel, a cow's milk cheese. In Canada, I use Toscana, a wonderful hard sheep's cheese from Ontario. I would encourage everyone, and especially vegetarians, to find a local cheese rather than use fake 'Parmesan' varieties.

Leek & cauliflower risotto with chilli walnut crumbs & fried capers

for 4

2 slices of day-old bread
2 tbsp walnuts, chopped
4 dried bird's eye chillies, crushed
2 tbsp chopped fresh parsley
4 tbsp olive oil
2 tbsp small capers, rinsed
vegetable oil, for deep-frying
1 medium cauliflower
1.2 litres/2 pints vegetable stock
2 leeks, well washed and thinly sliced
4 garlic cloves, sliced
300g/11oz Carnaroli or Arborio rice
100ml/3½fl oz dry white wine
60g/2½oz butter
75g/3oz hard cheese, finely grated
salt and pepper

The spiced, crisp and nutty crumbs and the deep-fried capers add dramatic flavour and texture to this otherwise quietly comforting risotto. The rice is cooked in the classic way and, with no added external broth or oil, should be served in the classic wet – just short of soupy – way.

- Put the bread in a food processor with the walnuts, chillies and parsley, and pulse to get a coarse crumb. Heat 2 tablespoons of the oil in a frying pan over medium heat, add the crumbs and fry for 5 minutes, stirring, until browned and crisp. Drain on kitchen paper.

- Deep-fry the capers in vegetable oil in a small saucepan, until crisp. Drain on kitchen paper.

- Cut the cauliflower into quarters and trim off the tops of the florets, breaking them into small pieces. Chop the stalks into small dice.

- Bring the stock to the boil in a saucepan and hold it at a low simmer.

- Heat the remaining 2 tablespoons of olive oil in a wide, heavy pan over medium heat and sauté the leeks, cauliflower stalk and garlic for 5 minutes, stirring often. Add the rice and toast it, stirring, for 5 minutes more. Add the white wine and simmer until it has been absorbed. Add a ladleful or two of the hot stock. Stirring often, let this simmer until all the liquid has been absorbed, then add more stock. Continue in this way for about 20 minutes, until the rice is just tender and the liquid is almost all absorbed.

- While the risotto is cooking, heat 15g/½oz of the butter in another wide pan over medium heat. Add the cauliflower florets and sauté them for 8–10 minutes, stirring often, until tender.

- Stir the cauliflower florets into the rice with the remaining butter, half of the cheese and some salt and pepper.

- Serve the risotto in warmed shallow bowls. Scatter the capers around the edges and sprinkle the fried crumbs over the top. Finish with the remaining grated cheese.

Risotto of cavolo nero
with saffron-chilli leeks

Cavolo nero – also known as black kale – is about as dark a green as you can get in the natural world. When cooked, it lightens up a little. In this recipe, the cooked kale is finely chopped, then fried and stirred into the cooked risotto. The result is a beautifully green dish that looks like it is speckled with herbs but has the intense flavour of the kale.

For an alternative to the leeks, try some roast cherry tomatoes and chillies in olive oil for a sweet and hot pepper stew, or some buttery braised root vegetables.

- Bring the stock to the boil, add the cavolo nero and cook for 2 minutes, then remove it from the stock, squeeze it dry and chop it very finely, as you would a herb. Keep the stock at a low simmer.

- Heat 2 tablespoons of the olive oil in a wide, heavy pan over medium heat and sauté the shallots and garlic for 5 minutes. Lower the heat, add the rice and toast it for 7–8 minutes, stirring often. Add the white wine and simmer, stirring, until it has been absorbed. Add a ladleful or two of the hot stock. Stirring often, let this simmer until it is absorbed, then add more stock. Continue cooking the risotto in this way for about 20 minutes, until the rice is just tender and the liquid is almost all absorbed.

- Heat the remaining olive oil in a frying pan over medium heat. Add the cavolo nero and sauté for 5 minutes, stirring. Add this to the risotto with half of the butter and half of the cheese. Season well.

- While the risotto is cooking, prepare the saffron-chilli leeks: slice the white part of the leeks into thin rounds and the useable green parts into similarly thin strips. Heat the remaining butter in a wide, heavy pan over low heat. Add the leeks, saffron threads, chillies and orange rind. Add a ladleful of the vegetable stock and bring to the boil. Reduce the heat, cover with baking parchment and simmer for 15 minutes, until the liquid is almost gone. Remove the orange rind. If the dish is too dry, add a little more stock and butter. Season with salt.

- Serve the risotto in warmed shallow bowls. Spoon some leeks around each portion, pouring the pan juices over them. Sprinkle over the remaining cheese and serve.

for 4

1.3 litres/2¼ pints vegetable stock
400g/14oz cavolo nero (black kale), stalks discarded
4 tbsp olive oil
4–6 small shallots, finely chopped
3 garlic cloves, sliced
300g/11oz Carnaroli or Arborio rice
125ml/4fl oz dry white wine
125g/4oz butter
75g/3oz hard cheese, finely grated
salt and pepper

for the saffron-chilli leeks
2 leeks, well washed
¼ tsp saffron threads
6 dried bird's eye chillies, crushed
rind of 1 orange, in wide strips

Beetroot risotto with lemon-fennel oil, goat's cheese and broad beans

There are a lot of recipes for beetroot risotto out there in the virtual world of cooking, so I was in two minds about including this one here. Two things changed my mind. Firstly, from the comments on many of the online recipes and from the photos attached to others, it seemed a lot of people were getting a dirty brownish pink hue to theirs. I know that particular colour; sometimes you get it if beetroot is overcooked or if it is diluted too much in a dish, as it can be in risotto. Secondly, the feedback from the Café Paradiso version was so good, it would be plain wrong not to share it.

The essence of a good beetroot risotto is getting the intensity of beetroot flavour and colour right. The deep colour in this version is achieved by adding some puréed roast beets to the stock, so that every ladleful is adding to the colour rather than taking from it. If you have a juicer, you could simply add some beet juice to the stock, although you would then be missing out on the intensified roasting flavours.

Speaking of roasting, as well as the boiling method overleaf, it is also possible to cook beets by wrapping them individually in foil and roasting them in the oven until tender. When cool, they will then peel easily. You can also cut the tops and bottoms off the beets, stand them in an oven tray and pour in 2.5cm/1in of water. Cover the dish with foil and roast for an hour or so, then peel the beetroot.

I know... you're only half concentrating because you're back on the first line wondering if I raid the Internet for recipes. The answer is no, not for recipes, but yes for general flavour combination testing.

Here's a thing I do – you can try it yourself in the safety of your home with the parental controls turned on. Say you're at the 'blank page' early stage of a recipe and you're wondering whether a bunch of ingredients go together or not. Maybe you're determined to make a recipe with cabbage, but you're a bit fixated with rhubarb today.

At this stage you haven't even decided whether you're making a soup, breakfast or a dessert. So you type the words into the Internet to see if anyone else is putting them together, and if it looks like it works. The answer to the first part is almost always yes... someone has tried it.

Continued on following page...

for 4

500g/1lb 2oz beetroots,
  washed
2 tbsp olive oil, plus extra
  for tossing
1.3 litres/2¼ pints
  vegetable stock
4–6 small shallots, finely
  chopped
3 garlic cloves, sliced
300g/11oz Carnaroli or
  Arborio rice
125ml/4½fl oz red wine
60g/2½oz butter
200g/7oz podded fresh
  broad beans
115g/4oz fresh goat's
  cheese, crumbled
salt and pepper

for the lemon-fennel oil
200ml/7fl oz olive oil
finely grated zest and juice
  of 1 lemon
3 tbsp finely chopped
  fennel leaves

Continued from previous page...

Not so often does it look or sound appetising. Now try 'beetroot, chocolate, ginger'. You might expect to get a wacky dessert, and maybe you will, but you'll also get risotto. I did consider nicking that one, but I decided it was more important to get the beetroot part right first. After that, you can add any crazy ingredients you like to the dish.

• First make the lemon-fennel oil: combine all of the ingredients in a jug or jar. Shake well or blend and set aside.

• Put the beets in a saucepan of water, bring it to the boil and simmer for 20–40 minutes, until they are tender. Check by sticking a small knife into one of the larger ones. Don't check too often, as you don't want to bleed the colour from the beets. When they are done, drain off the water and cover the beets with cold water. With the tap still running, pull the skin off the beets with your hands – it should slip off easily.

• Preheat the oven to 180°C/350°F/gas mark 4.

• Chop the beetroot into 1cm/½in dice and toss them with a little olive oil and salt in an oven dish. Roast for 15 minutes.

• Keeping the oven on, remove half of the beets and put them in a food processor. Blend to a purée, adding about 400ml/14fl oz of the vegetable stock to get a smooth liquid. Pass this through a sieve and add it to the rest of the stock. Bring to the boil and hold it at a low simmer.

• Return the rest of the beets to the oven for 10–15 minutes more, until beginning to caramelise.

• Heat the 2 tablespoons of olive oil in a wide, heavy pan over medium heat, and sauté the shallots and garlic for 5 minutes. Lower the heat, add the rice and toast it for 7–8 minutes, stirring often.

- Add the red wine and simmer, stirring, until it has been absorbed. Add a ladleful or two of the hot beetroot broth. Stirring often, let this simmer until it is absorbed, then add more broth. Continue in this way until the rice is just tender and almost dry. It will take about 20 minutes. Now add the roasted beets and the butter. Season well with salt and pepper.

- While the risotto is cooking, bring a small saucepan of water to the boil and cook the broad beans for 4–5 minutes, until tender. Cool briefly in cold water and peel off the translucent skins, splitting the beans in half. Dress the beans in a tablespoon of the lemon-fennel oil and set aside.

- To serve, spoon the risotto into warmed shallow bowls. Drizzle some lemon-fennel oil around, then scatter the broad beans and the goat's cheese over each portion.

Watercress, lemon & pine nut risotto with roasted pepper broth

Serving a separate broth with risotto is something we sort of stumbled upon a few years ago in Café Paradiso, while trying to solve what seemed like conflicting issues of appearance and intensity. The classic way to bring the flavours of this pepper broth – spiked with basil and chilli – to the risotto would be to use it as the stock in the cooking process. But the risotto doesn't actually need all that background flavour. It is intended to be fresh and lemony. The broth is really there to provide an extra external flavour, a sweet one to contrast with the lemon and pungent watercress in the rice. It is also there to make the plate look prettier. And don't ever underestimate the importance of a good-looking plate!

Broth is a bit of a misnomer. I just like the word. This is broth with attitude, and it needs to be intensely flavoured and coloured – and richly oily, so that you can pour a little on the plate to big effect. For this to work visually, remember to cook the risotto a little dryer than classic recipes suggest. Don't overcook it; just cook off the last ladleful of stock a little faster. The broth will keep for a day in the fridge, but after that it will lose its intensity.

- First make the roasted pepper broth: roast the peppers over a flame, in the oven or under a grill, until the skin is blackened. Put in a bowl, seal with cling film and leave for 20 minutes. Peel away the skin, stalk and seeds. Chop the flesh coarsely.

- Heat the olive oil in a heavy pan or wok over high heat, add the onions and fry for 3–4 minutes, until beginning to colour. Add the garlic, roasted peppers, tomatoes, chillies and basil, and cook for 10–12 minutes, stirring often. Add 300ml/11fl oz of the vegetable stock, bring it to the boil and simmer for 10 minutes.

- Push the cooked vegetables through a sieve, saving the liquid. Put this in a small saucepan and simmer to reduce and thicken a little. Keep the broth warm or reheat when the risotto is done.

- Make the risotto: bring the rest of the vegetable stock to the boil and keep it at a low simmer.

Continued on following page...

for 4

2 tbsp olive oil
3 garlic cloves, sliced
300g/11oz Carnaroli or
  Arborio rice
125ml/4½fl oz dry white
  wine
150g/5oz watercress,
  coarsely chopped
60g/2½oz pine nuts,
  lightly toasted
4 spring onions, finely
  chopped
finely grated zest of 2
  lemons and juice of 1
60g/2½oz butter
60g/2½oz hard cheese,
  finely grated
salt and pepper

for the roasted pepper broth
2 red peppers
4 tbsp olive oil
2 onions, thickly sliced
4 garlic cloves, sliced
2 ripe tomatoes
2 fresh red chillies,
  deseeded and coarsely
  chopped
1 small bunch of fresh
  basil, coarsely chopped
1.5 litres/2½ pints
  vegetable stock

Continued from previous page...

- Heat the olive oil in a wide, heavy pan over medium heat and sauté the garlic and rice for 7–8 minutes, stirring often. Add the white wine and simmer until it has been absorbed. Add a ladleful or two of the hot stock. Stirring often, let this simmer until it has been absorbed, then add more stock. Continue in this way for about 20 minutes, until the rice is just tender and the liquid is almost all absorbed.

- Stir in the watercress, pine nuts, spring onions, lemon zest and juice, butter and half of the cheese. Season with salt and pepper.

- Serve the risotto on warmed plates with a little of the broth poured around each portion. Sprinkle with the remaining cheese.

Roast parsnip farrotto with pine nuts & citrus-rosemary butter

Farro, the ancient wheat grain, makes wonderful risotto, especially with autumnal or winter ingredients, as its nutty flavour and chewy texture combine beautifully with roasted roots, caramelised onions and dark greens.

The technique is the same as that used for rice, though the farro takes longer to cook – up to twice as long, in fact. However, it has the advantage of having a wider window of 'doneness', in that it doesn't suddenly go from under- to over-cooked in the blink of an eye, and so needs less twitchy attention.

In this version, the butter, which is usually stirred in, is flavoured with citrus and rosemary and added to the dish on the plate. This brings a contrast and a freshness to the earthy parsnip and grain that have melded together in the long cooking process.

- Put the rosemary and citrus rind in a small saucepan with 30g/1¼oz of the butter. Heat gently until the butter begins to sizzle, then remove from the heat and leave to infuse for at least 30 minutes in a warm place. Strain through a sieve and discard the solids. Stir the flavoured butter into the rest of the butter. Keep warm or soften again just before serving.

- Bring the stock to the boil in a large saucepan, then turn down the heat and keep at a low simmer.

- In a wide, heavy pan, heat the olive oil and cook the shallots and parsnip for 2 minutes over medium heat, stirring. Add the thyme, honey and vinegar, then cover with baking parchment, lower the heat and simmer for 10 minutes more. The parsnips should caramelise a little but remain firm.

- Add the farro and garlic, and cook over medium heat for 5 minutes, stirring occasionally. Remove the thyme sprigs. Add the white wine, bring to the boil and simmer until the wine has been absorbed.

- Pour in a ladleful or two of the hot stock and simmer, stirring occasionally, until it has been absorbed. Carry on adding stock in this way for 40–50 minutes, until the grains are soft and chewy. Stir in the cheese and season well with salt and pepper.

- To serve, spoon some farrotto into warmed shallow bowls and drizzle some of the butter over each one. Scatter with pine nuts.

for 4

leaves from 3 sprigs of fresh rosemary
rind of 2 oranges and 2 lemons, in large strips
200g/7oz butter, softened, plus extra to finish
1.5 litres/2½ pints vegetable stock
2 tbsp olive oil
250g/9oz shallots, thinly sliced
400g/14oz parsnips, peeled, woody cores removed, and cut into large dice
2 sprigs of fresh thyme
2 tbsp honey
1 tbsp cider vinegar
300g/11oz farro
4 garlic cloves, sliced
100ml/3½oz dry white wine
75g/3oz hard cheese, finely grated
2 tbsp pine nuts, lightly toasted and chopped
salt and pepper

Chanterelles in hazelnut tarragon butter on a leek & squash farrotto

for 4

250g/9oz peeled and deseeded squash, cut into 2cm/¾in dice
2 tbsp olive oil, plus extra for tossing
1 litre/1¾ pints vegetable stock
2 leeks, well washed, halved lengthways and thinly sliced
200g/7oz farro
2 sprigs of fresh thyme, leaves only
3 garlic cloves, sliced
100ml/3½fl oz dry white wine
50g/2oz butter
4 small shallots, thinly sliced
200g/7oz fresh chanterelles
salt and pepper

for the hazelnut tarragon butter
1 tbsp hazelnuts
50g/2oz butter, softened
1 tbsp chopped fresh tarragon

Chanterelles – if you're lucky enough to have access to fresh ones – are too good to be hidden away inside a risotto or farrotto. In this recipe, the farrotto is really in a supporting role; it is a smaller portion than usual of farrotto, to emphasise just who is the star here.

That said, this is a fine farrotto in itself. To serve it without the chanterelles, increase the farrotto part of the recipe by a third, and douse the finished dish in the hazelnut tarragon butter. You might want to add some finely grated cheese too, which I have avoided here, out of respect for the fungi.

I'm never comfortable giving quantities for fresh wild mushrooms. 'As many as you've got' would be a better measure.

- First prepare the hazelnut tarragon butter: preheat the oven to 180°C/350°F/gas mark 4.

- Roast the hazelnuts on a small oven tray for 10–15 minutes, until lightly coloured. Leaving the oven on, place them in a towel and rub briefly to remove as much of the skins as will come away easily. Grind the hazelnuts as finely as possible in a food processor, grinder or with a mortar and pestle. Put the butter in a bowl and stir in the ground hazelnuts and chopped tarragon.

- To roast the squash, toss it in a little olive oil in an oven dish and roast it for 20 minutes, stirring occasionally, until tender and beginning to colour.

- Meanwhile, bring the stock to the boil in a large saucepan, then turn down the heat and keep at a low simmer.

- In a wide pan, heat the 2 tablespoons of olive oil over medium heat, add the leeks and sauté for 5 minutes, stirring. Add the farro, thyme and garlic, and cook over medium heat for 5 minutes, stirring occasionally. Add all but 2 tablespoons of the white wine, and simmer until it has been absorbed.

- Pour in a ladleful or two of hot stock and simmer, stirring occasionally, until it has been absorbed. Carry on adding stock in this way for 40–50 minutes, until the grains are soft and chewy. Stir in the roast squash and 30g/1¼oz of the butter. Season well with salt and pepper.

- When the farrotto is almost done, heat the remaining butter in a frying pan over high heat. Add the shallots and sauté for 1 minute. Turn the heat up, add the mushrooms to the pan and sauté for 5 minutes, stirring.

- Add the remaining 2 tablespoons of wine, reduce the heat to medium again and simmer for 2 minutes. When the mushrooms are tender, stir in the hazelnut tarragon butter and remove the pan from the heat. Season well.

- Serve the farrotto in warmed shallow bowls, discarding the thyme sprigs. Place some mushrooms on each portion and pour the pan juices over.

Wild garlic & roast cherry tomato risotto with lemon-braised artichokes

for 4

200g/7oz cherry tomatoes, halved
2 tbsp olive oil, plus extra for tossing
1 onion, finely diced
300g (11oz) Carnaroli or Arborio rice
100ml/3½fl oz dry white wine
115g/4oz wild garlic, coarsely chopped
40g/1½oz butter
75g/3oz hard sheep's cheese, finely grated
salt and pepper

for the lemon-braised artichokes
8 small globe artichokes
3 lemons
1.4 litres /2¼ pints vegetable stock
4 tbsp olive oil
100ml/3½fl oz dry white wine
2 sprigs of fresh thyme

The ideal artichokes for this dish are small firm ones with no hairy choke in the centre and long edible stems. The best way to be sure of this is to know their source. If you're not so lucky, you can take a good guess by giving the artichokes a handling test. They should be very firm and elongated rather than round. At the bottom just above the stem – which should also be firm – if there is a distinct rounded rim before the upper leaves taper upwards, then it is likely that the hairy choke is already well developed.

That doesn't mean they are inedible, just that you will have some choke to remove and less flesh and leaf to eat. If you are using larger ones, remove the inedible centres, and quarter before cooking. At a stretch, I would say that you could also use good-quality bottled artichokes, but rinse them really well first. Because the lemony juice from the artichokes is poured over the finished dish, I would cook this risotto a little dryer than usual.

- Preheat the oven to 180°C/350°F/gas mark 4.

- First toss the cherry tomatoes with a little olive oil and salt in an oven dish, then roast them for 10–15 minutes, until softened and beginning to colour. Remove from the oven and set aside.

- Prepare the artichokes: pull away and discard some of the outer leaves and peel the stems back to the edible centres. Cut the tops off the remaining leaves, then slice the artichokes in half lengthways. Squeeze the juice from 1 of the lemons into some cold water, throw in the lemon too and drop in the prepared artichokes.

- Bring the stock to the boil. Remove the artichokes from the acidulated water, add to the stock and boil for 5 minutes. Remove the artichokes and arrange them in another oven dish, cut sides up. Add the olive oil, 200ml/7fl oz of the stock and half of the white wine. Slice the remaining lemons thickly and add them to the artichokes with the thyme. Season with salt, cover loosely with baking parchment and place the dish in the oven to braise for 20 minutes. The artichokes should be tender and the liquid reduced by half. Discard the thyme sprigs and the lemons.

- Meanwhile, cook the risotto. Heat 2 tablespoons of the olive oil in a heavy pan over medium heat and sauté the onion for 5 minutes. Add the rice and toast it for 5 minutes, stirring often. Add the white wine, bring to the boil and simmer until it has been absorbed. Pour in a ladleful or two of the hot stock and simmer, stirring occasionally, until it has been absorbed. Carry on adding stock in this way for about 20 minutes, until the rice is just done. Stir in the wild garlic and roasted cherry tomatoes, the butter and half of the cheese. Season well with salt and pepper.

- Serve the risotto in warmed shallow bowls. Arrange some artichokes on each portion and pour over the juices from the oven dish. Sprinkle the remaining cheese on top.

Soup

Soup

I had the honour in the second year of its life of being put in charge of a 'stone soup' class at the Savour Stratford Food Festival in Ontario. My job was simple – to turn into soup the ingredients that people brought along from their gardens or that they had bought at the farmer's market that was going on at the same time. Even though we inevitably ended up with more than a fair share of courgettes and carrots, I had taken the precaution of bringing along a few staples like olive oil, garlic and a decent stock powder. In the end, we did indeed manage to make a very edible potion. Everyone took a little of the soup home, and the most important ingredient of the dish was achieved – a warm fuzzy feeling brought on by the communal spirit of the act of sharing.

The story is an ancient one that seems to have roots in different cultures all over the world. I think the Irish version has a fairy in it. The version told on the day of the class came from Eastern Europe, I think, and went something like this:

A soldier was wandering through the ravaged countryside at the end of a war that had left the small rural communities in poverty, their land and crops destroyed. During the war, and in the scarcity of the aftermath, people had become frightened and suspicious. They hoarded what food they could scrape together, and hid from their neighbours any sense that they could have something the others might envy. The soldier's trick was to light a fire on the outskirts of a village and set a large pot on it. He filled this with water and chucked in a few large stones. When this drew the curiosity of a few of the villagers, the soldier explained that he was making stone soup, a very fine soup indeed, and that there would be plenty to go around when it was done. However, he admitted, it would be greatly improved by a few onions. One of the locals went off and came back with a handful of onions, which he chopped up and added to the pot. The smell attracted more of the locals to the scene, excited to hear there would be stone soup for all in a little while. Stone soup sounded strange, but it was free and was beginning to smell good. The soldier then said that what the soup really needed now was a head of cabbage or two, and immediately one of the men ran off to fetch them from his stash at home. Meanwhile, the soldier was lamenting the lack of a few pounds of potatoes, and more of the villagers went to draw some from their hiding places. After a few more requests, all answered, the soldier pronounced the soup ready except for the lack of a pinch of salt. No sooner said than done. By now everyone in the area had gathered, all bringing something to add to the pot and all anxiously waiting with their bowls in hand. The soup was shared out, and there was even enough for seconds for the hungriest among them. Everyone agreed it was the best soup they'd ever had, though they'd never had stone soup before. Afterwards there was music and dancing, and the locals went to bed that night happier and more optimistic about the future than for a long, long time.

It's a sweet story but, like all good fables, its power is in the degree of truth at its core.

Like its close relative, the stew – which is really just soup with more stuff and less liquid – soup is for sharing, and the ingredients are less important than the spirit of the thing and the people gathered around it. Probably more than any other dish, we make soup to make others feel better.

The soups in this section of the book could be divided into two types – smooth, blended ones and more rustic chunky ones. Probably because I get bored eating one-dimensional food, I like to add one or two extra elements to a puréed soup, to provide a contrast in flavour and to add texture. Here, you will find salsas, flavoured creams, dumplings and spiced croutons. You will also find soups made in two parts, where a purée acts as supporting stock to some sautéed vegetables, bringing a bit of both soup worlds together.

Chunky, stewy soups need less or no garnishing, and they follow less regimental recipes too. All of those here could be made with very different vegetables, and even different quantities of vegetables, depending on the time of year and what you've got to hand. These soups are the stuff of hearty lunches and second portions, and a fine thick loaf of bread is the best accompaniment.

Black bean soup
with chocolate & chillies
and avocado salsa

This is a rich, intensely flavoured soup with lots of bold Mexican tastes. Although the soup is puréed, it retains a chunky texture by virtue of some of it being coarsely mashed while the rest is blended.

Chipotle chillies have a distinctive smoky flavour. If you can't find them, add another fresh chilli and a teaspoon or two of smoked paprika. On the subject of chillies, it's impossible to give definitive quantities in a recipe, though of course I have to write some number down. The chillies I used to make this soup were very hot. If the ones you have are anything less, you might want to double the quantity. Only you can figure that out, and the only way to do it is to taste them. Check a sliver near the middle – the ends are sometimes milder. And check the seeds too, then decide whether to use them or not.

- Heat the olive oil in a large, heavy saucepan, and sauté the onion for 5 minutes over medium heat. Add the garlic, chillies, oregano, ground spices, red pepper and celery, and simmer for 7–8 minutes more, until the vegetables are soft. Add the beans, tomato purée and stock, bring to the boil, then cover and simmer for 40 minutes.

- Scoop one-third of the soup into a food processor and pulse to get a coarse mash. Use a hand-held blender to make a smooth purée of the rest of the soup, then return the mash to the pan. Melt in the chocolate and season the soup with salt.

- Make the avocado salsa by combining all of the ingredients in a bowl.

- Serve the soup with a spoonful of the salsa and a swirl of soured cream on top.

for 4

2 tbsp olive oil
2 red onions, finely chopped
4 garlic cloves, chopped
1 fresh green chilli, deseeded if you prefer and finely chopped
1 chipotle chilli, finely chopped
1 tsp dried oregano
2 tsp ground cumin
2 tsp ground coriander
1 tsp ground allspice
½ red pepper, deseeded and finely chopped
2 celery sticks, finely chopped
500g/1lb 2oz dried black kidney beans, soaked and cooked, or 800g/1¾lb drained tinned beans
1 tbsp tomato purée
1 litre/1¾ pints vegetable stock
30g/1¼oz dark chocolate, finely chopped
salt
3 tbsp soured cream, to serve

for the avocado salsa
1 avocado, peeled, stoned and diced
2 spring onions, finely chopped
1 tbsp chopped fresh coriander
juice of 1 lime

Love soup

You might read this recipe and think – hang on a sec, that's a variation on ribollita, the Italian bread soup. And you'd be right, it turned out that way, but it came to me as an act of love, though it started out as a cleaning exercise. Well, cleaning is an act of love too, isn't it?

It was time to do a job on the fridge, take stock, use up what was useable and throw away what wasn't, before going to the market. I took everything out of the fridge, cleaned it and put the jars and booze back in. Left on the countertop was an aging bunch of greens, a couple of yellowing leeks, a wrinkly red pepper, a wilting handful of basil and a few heirloom tomatoes so soft they were thinking of becoming soup all by themselves. Soup, I thought, fridge soup. Not very enthusiastically, I have to say, as I was more in cleaning mode than cooking mode.

I started chopping the leeks and, by the time they were simmering in a hefty dollop of olive oil in the pan, I started to think about my girlfriend Maureen at work. She'd gone off without any lunch and I knew she'd be starving when she got home in a few hours. Gradually, as I mulled over whether to go for a blended or chunky soup, my attitude changed from one of making something for the sake of using up old vegetables to wanting to make the best soup she would ever have tasted. I wanted it to be exactly what she wanted and needed when she got home. I couldn't plant a craving for fridge soup in her mind, so somehow I had to make a soup that was more than the sum of its parts, one that would speak for itself, and for me. One that would say, I love you Maureen, this is what you need, though you don't know it yet. I couldn't change the ingredients, so the only thing I could add to the recipe was my love for her, expressed as a deep empathy for her needs at the end of the day.

I would say I always cook with love but I don't think I had ever focused on it as much as that day. Must have had something to do with lack of faith in the ingredients themselves, pigs' ears, silk purses and all that.

Cooking with love is a much-used phrase, often by chefs trying to express their passion for their work.

Sometimes it seems to mean a passion for the act of cooking itself, or an affinity with ingredients. I have felt both of those emotions in the process of designing menus and preparing dishes in a restaurant setting, and I strongly believe that cooking is a means of communication as well as self-expression. This devotion to the process of cooking can create dishes that somehow give intense pleasure to people you don't know at all, nor even set eyes on sometimes. I like to think that the chef is a medium between the produce and the diner, but it is certainly true too that the chef adds part of his or her own love of their role in the process.

To cook with the same devotion for someone you love is a humbler act. It is focused on one very precious person and what you think will bring them pleasure or soothe their troubles. When that comes off, there is no punching the air or high-fiving, but a profound communion of two souls. Over a bowl of soup, no less.

You'll be wanting to know what happened next, I suppose. Perhaps Maureen arrived home already satiated, having stopped for a quick beer and pizza on the way? No chance, the simmering soup was wafting signals across town... 'save your appetite, hurry home, the answer to all your cravings awaits'... something like that. It's hard to translate soup-speak, a language of impenetrable subtlety, whispers, signs and allusions, understood only by that part of us where appetite meets emotion.

I send out signals like that all the time, but it took a soup to hit the target. She didn't come home craving fridge soup, nor even love soup if truth be told. But when I placed the bowl before her, I swear she melted into it.

I've never repeated the exact recipe, but I've learnt how to conjure up the essence of it. With occasional exceptions when I get bogged down in the mechanics of a new recipe, the first ingredient of dinner is always a question – what would make Maureen happy today?

The technical stuff – greens, tomatoes, olive oil and bread – are the core ingredients here. Squash, potato or other roots would be good too.

Continued on following page...

for 4–6

3 thick slices of stale bread
100ml/3½fl oz olive oil
2 leeks, halved lengthways,
  well washed and chopped
4 garlic cloves, thinly sliced
1 fresh red chilli, deseeded
  and thinly sliced
1 handful of cavolo nero
  (black kale) or rapini,
  shredded
4 tomatoes, diced
1 bunch of fresh basil
1 red pepper, deseeded and
  diced
1 litre/1¾ pints vegetable
  stock
200g/7oz fresh or frozen
  cooked borlotti beans, or
  drained tinned beans
leaves from 2–3 sprigs
  of fresh oregano
salt and pepper

Continued from previous page...

- Preheat the oven to 130°C/250°F/gas mark ½.

- Cut the crusts off the bread, place the slices on an oven tray and bake in the oven for 10–15 minutes, until they are crisp but not coloured.

- In a large saucepan, heat 2 tablespoons of the olive oil. Add the leeks, garlic and chilli, and stew them for 10 minutes, stirring occasionally.

- Add the greens and stew for 5 minutes more. Next add the tomatoes, basil and red pepper, and stew again for 10 minutes, until the vegetables are soft.

- Add the stock and beans, bring to the boil and simmer, covered, over low heat for 30 minutes. Season with salt and pepper.

- At this point, the soup can be served or left, off the heat, for a number of hours. Before serving, break the bread into chunks and stir them into the soup with the oregano leaves. Reheat gently, stirring. The bread should break up a little, thickening the soup, but not completely.

- To serve, spoon the soup into bowls and drizzle a tablespoon of olive oil over each portion.

Roasted aubergine & pepper soup with honeyed cabbage & leeks and chilli oil

Aubergines, while having a wonderful ability to carry flavour, can end up making hopelessly bland soup unless roasted to the point where they are charred to some extent. This smoky flavour is essential to the soup, which is why the skin is left on the aubergine even after being almost blackened in the oven. Make sure you blend the roasted vegetables to a very fine purée. While the finished soup is richly flavoured, the honey sweetness balanced by the cabbage and oven intensity, the addition of acidic yoghurt and hot chilli oil adds more levels of complexity at the table.

- Grind the chillies to a fine powder, stir them into the olive oil and leave to stand for an hour or more.

- Preheat the oven to 200°C/400°F/gas mark 6.

- In a large oven dish, toss the onions, aubergine and red pepper in some olive oil and roast in the oven for 15 minutes. Add the tomatoes and garlic, cover loosely with baking parchment and continue roasting for 15–20 minutes more, until the vegetables are soft and browned.

- Put the roasted vegetables in a large saucepan with enough of the stock to cover them and simmer for 10 minutes. Blend to a purée, return to the pan and add more stock as necessary to get a rich but not too thick soup consistency.

- While the vegetables are roasting, prepare the honeyed cabbage and leeks: heat the olive oil in a wide pan over medium heat and fry the leek, cabbage and spices for 5 minutes. Add 3–4 tablespoons of the stock and the honey. Cover the pan, lower the heat and cook for 20 minutes until the vegetables are soft.

- Stir the cabbage and leeks into the puréed soup, season with salt and pepper and heat through.

- Serve the soup with a spoonful of yoghurt on top and a drizzle of the chilli oil.

for 4

4 dried bird's eye chillies
100ml/3½fl oz olive oil, plus extra for tossing and cooking
2 red onions, coarsely chopped
1 large aubergine, cut into large dice
1 red pepper, deseeded and coarsely chopped
2 tomatoes, coarsely chopped
6 garlic cloves, peeled
600–800ml/1 pint–29fl oz vegetable stock

for the honeyed cabbage and leeks
1 tbsp olive oil
½ leek, halved lengthways, well washed and thinly sliced
50g/2oz green cabbage, finely sliced about 2cm/¾in long
1 tsp cumin seeds, ground
1 tsp coriander seeds, ground
1 tsp fennel seeds, ground
2 tbsp honey
3 tbsp thick natural yoghurt

Celeriac soup with walnut & green pepper salsa and goat's cheese cream

for 4

30g/1¼oz butter
1 leek, well washed and
  finely chopped
4 garlic cloves, chopped
1 celeriac root, about
  500g/1lb 2oz, peeled and
  diced
1 medium potato, peeled
  and diced
2 sprigs of fresh thyme
100ml/3½fl oz dry white
  wine
800ml/29fl oz vegetable
  stock or water
large pinch of freshly
  grated nutmeg
salt and pepper

*for the walnut and green
pepper salsa*
2 tbsp finely chopped
  walnuts
½ green pepper, deseeded
  and finely diced
1 tbsp chopped fresh
  parsley
1 tbsp olive oil

for the goat's cheese cream
50g/2oz soft fresh goat's
  cheese
125ml/4½fl oz double
  cream

Celeriac, walnuts and goat's cheese crop up together in many dishes, like gratins and salads. And you might well imagine reinventing this soup as a pancake filled with leeks and roasted celeriac, garnished with the walnut and green pepper salsa and a drizzle of goat's cheese cream. By adding some of the ingredients at the table, you get the same effect here in a bowl of soup. The celeriac purée is comfortingly and quietly delicious, the salsa adds a lively uplift and the cream a mildly sharp but rich note. If you don't like lumpy bits in your soup, leave out the salsa.

• Melt the butter in a heavy saucepan over medium heat, and sauté the leek and garlic for 5 minutes. Add the celeriac, potato, thyme and wine. Cover with baking parchment, lower the heat and simmer for 10 minutes.

• Add the stock and bring to the boil, then cover the pan and simmer over low heat for 30–40 minutes, until the vegetables are soft. Blend to a smooth purée, and season with salt and pepper and the nutmeg.

• While the soup is simmering, prepare the walnut and green pepper salsa by mixing together all of the ingredients.

• Prepare the goat's cheese cream by mashing or blending the goat's cheese with a little of the cream, then stir in the rest, to get a thick pouring consistency.

• Serve the soup in shallow bowls with some goat's cheese cream swirled on top and a spoon of salsa in the centre.

Spiced cabbage & garlic soup with rice noodles and fried tofu

This is the kind of soup I like to make when the winter chill is getting into my bones. It's a soup you can make in bulk and have all day long when you don't feel like eating anything else. Essentially a cleansing, pick-me-up broth with all the goodness of cabbage, garlic, ginger and chillies, I've added some noodles for body and a little fried tofu just for the oily protein kick.

- Place the leek and cabbage in a large saucepan with 300ml/11fl oz of the stock. Cover with baking parchment and simmer over medium heat for 15 minutes.

- In another saucepan, bring the remaining stock to the boil, then add the garlic, ginger, chillies, coriander and parsley. Simmer for 15 minutes, then strain through a sieve, saving the liquid.

- Add this to the cabbage pan and bring to the boil. Break the rice noodles into short pieces and drop them into the soup. Simmer gently for 5–7 minutes, until the noodles are tender.

- While the soup is simmering, heat the vegetable oil in a wok or frying pan over high heat. Add the tofu cubes and stir-fry for a minute, until they are beginning to brown. Add a tablespoon of the soy sauce and continue to cook for a few seconds more to coat the tofu, then remove from the heat. Stir the remaining soy sauce into the soup.

- Serve the soup in deep bowls, and scatter the tofu and spring onions over the top.

for 4

1 leek, halved lengthways, well washed and thinly sliced
150g/5oz Savoy cabbage, shredded
1.5 litres/2½ pints vegetable stock
2 heads of garlic, cloves separated and peeled
100g/3½oz fresh ginger, thickly sliced
4 fresh green chillies
1 small handful of fresh coriander
1 small handful of fresh parsley
75g/3oz wide rice noodles
1 tbsp vegetable oil
200g/7oz firm tofu, cut into 2cm/¾in dice
100ml/3½fl oz soy sauce
3 spring onions, thinly sliced

Chard, white bean & potato in chilli, basil & tomato broth

for 4

olive oil, for cooking
2 red onions, thinly sliced
4 garlic cloves, sliced
1 large bunch of fresh basil
1.2 litres/2 pints vegetable stock
300g/11oz potatoes, peeled and diced
6 medium chard leaves
4 tbsp soaked and cooked dried cannellini beans
salt

for the chilli, basil and tomato broth
1kg/2lb 2oz tomatoes, quartered
2–4 fresh red chilles, thinly sliced
olive oil, for coating

Here, broth and vegetables are cooked separately and brought together only at the end of the cooking. This is partly to better control the cooking of the vegetables, and partly for aesthetic reasons. You can make quite a pretty picture in the serving bowls, with an island of vegetables in the middle of a small lake of broth.

You can easily turn it into a more substantial stew by increasing the quantities of vegetables, or adding others. One or two at a time of kale, broad beans, green beans, courgettes and squash would all be very welcome.

I haven't included any cheese in the recipe, but I would definitely be inclined to grate some over this soup. Try your favourite hard cheese for pasta.

• Preheat the oven to 200°C/400°F/gas mark 6.

• First make the broth: toss the tomatoes and chillies in an oven dish with enough olive oil to coat. Season with salt and roast for 20 minutes, until the tomatoes are beginning to colour.

• Heat 2 tablespoons of olive oil in a saucepan over medium heat and sauté the onions and garlic for 7–8 minutes. Chop the basil coarsely, add it to the pan and cook for 2 minutes more. Add the roast tomatoes and 400ml/14fl oz of the stock. Bring to the boil and simmer for 5 minutes. Blend to a purée and pass through a sieve, saving the liquid and discarding the solids. Return the liquid to the pan, add the rest of the stock and bring back to a boil, then simmer for 10 minutes. Season well with salt.

• Bring a small saucepan of water to the boil, add the potatoes and simmer for 10–12 minutes, until almost done. Drain.

• Cut the chard leaves at the base and discard the stalk ends. Strip the leaves from the remaining stalk. Slice the stalks thinly and chop the leaves coarsely.

• Heat 2 tablespoons of olive oil in a heavy saucepan over high heat. Add the chard and sauté, stirring, for 5–7 minutes, until tender. Add the potatoes and beans and a ladle of the broth. Simmer for 5 minutes, until the potato is cooked and the stock absorbed.

• Ladle some broth into shallow bowls and pile some of the vegetables in the centre.

Leek & potato soup
with watercress pesto

I know, I know… leek and potato?… We can all make leek and potato soup, I hear you cry. Well, apparently not. And besides, you can use this recipe as a prototype for most root vegetable soups by simply replacing all or some of the potato with turnips, carrots or parsnips, or a combination of all three to create that classic pub sustenance known as 'vegetable soup'.

You can get nostalgic for anything if you wait long enough, and if the replacement is bad enough. I can't remember exactly when Irish country pubs started offering tomato and basil soup and mozzarella paninis, but I'm fairly sure that if we'd had a referendum it would have been voted down. One of the great pleasures of driving aimlessly around the countryside was knowing that you would, just in time, come across a nice little pub to stop into for a pint. If you were hungry, it was likely they could feed you. And the menu du jour? Soup and toasted sandwiches. What kind of soup? Leek and potato, of course, sometimes 'vegetable'. What kind of sandwiches? Whatever you want! Sorted.

I have a mental map of places that still know how to make toasted sandwiches. The research can be a minefield of panini, but I have developed a keen ability to tell from the outside which pubs are likely to be up to scratch. It goes without saying that the same places still know how to make leek and potato soup too.

Leek and potato soup is not hard to make, but it is easy to get horribly wrong. The recipe overleaf isn't a family traditional recipe, nor do I claim that it is definitive, only that it makes a decent soup by paying attention to the few details you have to get right.

Potato soup can take on the texture of wallpaper paste if there isn't enough onion and/or leek in it. It is also not a good idea to blend it forever, which is why the vegetables are cut into small pieces that blend quickly.

It is a scientific fact that eight out of ten people prefer their potato soups just a little bit lumpy. Of the other two, one likes it really lumpy and the other is French.

Again, the combination of small chunks of vegetables and brief blending will ensure you leave some of those delicious pieces of potato and leek somewhat intact. And despite it being so unfashionable that we have to search the back of our mothers' cupboards to find any, white pepper works better here than black. I don't think that's just nostalgia.

I like to finish the soup by enriching it with yoghurt or soured cream, some in the blended soup to cut the sweetness of the leeks and a little more on top of each bowlful. The combination of yoghurt or soured cream and watercress pesto makes for a lovely contrast as you spoon your way through the soup.

• Melt the butter in a heavy saucepan over medium heat, add the onions and sauté for 5 minutes, stirring occasionally. Slice the leeks into quarters lengthways almost to the root, wash them under cold running water and then finely chop. Add to the pan with the garlic and parsley, and cook for 10 minutes more, stirring occasionally.

• Chop the potatoes into small dice and add to the pan with the stock. Bring to the boil, then lower the heat and simmer for 20–30 minutes. Blend with a stick blender or in a liquidiser. Return the soup to the pan, whisk in half of the yoghurt and season well with salt and the white pepper.

• To make the pesto, put the watercress, garlic and walnuts in a food processor and finely chop them. Add the olive oil and pulse briefly to get a pouring consistency.

• Serve the soup in deep bowls and top each with a teaspoonful of yoghurt and a generous swirl of watercress pesto.

for 4

25g/1oz butter
2 white onions, finely chopped
2 leeks
4 garlic cloves, finely chopped
1 small bunch of fresh parsley, finely chopped
500g/1lb 2oz potatoes, peeled
1 litre/1¾ pints vegetable stock
150ml/5fl oz natural yoghurt or soured cream
¼ tsp white pepper
salt

for the watercress pesto
100g/3½oz watercress
1 garlic clove, peeled
30g/1¼oz walnuts
150ml/5fl oz olive oil

Roast pumpkin soup with chickpeas, leeks & spiced croutons

The texture of what I think of as a North African spiced soup comes from the roast squash that is added to the pot as a coarse mash and then breaks up some more, bringing body and depth of flavour to the background stock. As you can imagine, this is a keeper, a soup that gets better for hanging around for a day or two.

Any dense, orange-fleshed pumpkin or squash will do the trick here. The rather rustic but highly spiced croutons bring a lot of flavour to the soup too, as well as texture – at first crunchy, then chewy as they melt into the liquid. They are no bother to make and you could easily make a lot more than you need here, as they keep very well. If you make the soup without the croutons, add some of their spicing to the soup instead – just not the eight chillies!

- Preheat the oven to 190°C/375°F/gas mark 5.

- Cut the pumpkin or squash in half and scoop out the seeds. Brush the flesh with olive oil and place the halves, cut side down, in an oven dish. Pour in 200ml/7fl oz of the stock and place in the oven to roast for 30–40 minutes.

- While the pumpkin is roasting, make the spiced croutons. Chop or tear the bread into small pieces and toss them in an oven dish with the spices, chillies and olive oil. Season with salt and roast in the oven for 10–12 minutes, until crisp. Remove from the oven and leave to cool.

- In a saucepan, heat the 4 tablespoons of olive oil over medium heat. Add the shallots and fennel, and sauté for 2 minutes, stirring. Add the garlic, ginger, leeks and chickpeas, and continue to sauté for 5 minutes more. Add the white wine, then cover with baking parchment, reduce the heat and simmer for 15 minutes.

- When the pumpkin is tender, scoop out the flesh and chop it to get something like a coarse, lumpy mash. Add this to the soup pan with the remaining stock. Bring to the boil and simmer, uncovered, for 5 minutes. Stir in the lemon juice and season with salt and pepper.

- Serve the soup with a generous pile of croutons on top.

for 4

1 small or ½ medium pumpkin or squash, about 1kg/2lb 2oz
4 tbsp olive oil, plus extra for brushing
800ml/29fl oz vegetable stock
4 small shallots, finely diced
½ medium fennel bulb, finely diced
4 garlic cloves, thinly sliced
2 tbsp grated fresh ginger
3 leeks, well washed and thinly sliced
250g/9oz soaked and cooked dried chickpeas
100ml/3½fl oz dry white wine
juice of ½ lemon
salt and pepper

for the spiced croutons
4 slices of day-old bread
1 tsp ground cumin
1 tsp fennel seeds, ground
8 dried bird's eye chillies, ground
sprinkling of olive oil

Cauliflower & leek soup with hazelnut gougères

for 6 as a starter

15g/½oz butter
2 leeks, well washed and
  finely chopped
4 garlic cloves, finely
  chopped
100ml/3½fl oz dry white
  wine
100g/3½oz potato, peeled
  and diced
500ml/18fl oz vegetable
  stock
1 medium cauliflower,
  about 575g/1lb 5oz
2 sprigs of fresh thyme
2 sprigs of fresh parsley
4 bay leaves
400ml/14fl oz milk
3 tbsp double cream
¼ tsp freshly grated
  nutmeg, plus extra to
  serve
1 tbsp finely chopped fresh
  chives
salt and pepper

for the hazelnut gougères
25g/1oz hazelnuts, toasted
115g/4oz strong white
  flour
60g/2½oz butter
2 eggs
75g/3oz Gabriel cheese, or
  other hard cheese, grated
vegetable oil, for
  deep-frying

This is a rich soup with an even richer garnish, bringing together cauliflower, hazelnuts and cheese – very good company indeed. Resist the temptation to turn it into a dish of pastries in a cream sauce. When you get the balance right, it is a lovely elegant starter. Serve it in shallow bowls, with about 200ml/7fl oz of soup each and three small gougères. The gougère mix is the same one you would use if making choux pastry to be baked in the oven, except this time it is fried in scant teaspoonfuls, to get tiny crisp dumplings.

• Melt the butter in a saucepan over medium heat. Add the leeks and garlic, and sauté for 5 minutes, stirring. Add the white wine and potato, then cover with baking parchment, reduce the heat and simmer for 10 minutes. Add the vegetable stock, bring to the boil and simmer, covered, for 20 minutes.

• While that simmers, chop the cauliflower florets into small pieces, discarding the central stalk. Put the cauliflower in a pan with the thyme, parsley, bay leaves, milk and cream. Bring to the boil and simmer, uncovered, over low heat for 7–8 minutes, until the cauliflower is tender. Discard the herbs and add the cauliflower and milk to the leeks and potato. Blend to a smooth purée and season with salt and pepper and the nutmeg.

• Meanwhile, make the hazelnut gougère mix: put the hazelnuts in a food processor and chop them finely. Add the flour and pulse to mix. Put 175ml/6fl oz water and the butter in a small saucepan and bring to a rapid boil. With the food processor running, pour in the water and butter in one go and leave to blend for 30 seconds.

• With the motor still running, add an egg and beat until well incorporated, then repeat with the second egg and then the cheese. Season with salt and pepper, and transfer the mix to a bowl.

• Heat enough vegetable oil for deep-frying in a deep-fryer or heavy saucepan to 170°C/325°F. Take teaspoons of the gougère mix, slide them into the oil and fry for 3–4 minutes, turning once if necessary. You may need to do 2 batches. Drain on kitchen paper.

• Reheat the soup gently and ladle it into bowls. Place 3 gougères in each bowl and sprinkle the chives over the soup. Grate a little more nutmeg on top and serve.

Summer squash, borlotti bean & roasted pepper soup with basil chilli oil

Somewhere between a soup and late summer stew, this dish comes together in three parts – the broth, the vegetables and the basil chilli oil, which delivers quite a lot of the final flavour. Basil-flavoured oil is best used on the day it is made, after an hour or so infusing. If you want to keep it longer, store it in the fridge overnight, then pass it through a sieve to remove the solid particles. The colour will be less intense, but the flavour will keep. I've included here fresh borlotti beans, which are briefly marinated in lemon juice before joining the rest of the vegetables. Tinned beans will work too – warm them up before marinating.

- First prepare the basil chilli oil: drop the basil into boiling water for a few seconds, drain it immediately through a sieve and cool in cold water, then squeeze it dry. Put the basil, ground chillies and olive oil in a food processor and blend. Leave to stand for an hour or more.

- Preheat the oven to 200°C/400°F/gas mark 6.

- Put the peppers on an oven tray and roast them for 10–15 minutes, turning occasionally, until the skins are blackened. Transfer the peppers to a bowl and cover tightly with cling film. When cool, peel the peppers, discard the seeds and chop the flesh.

- While the peppers are roasting, in an oven dish, toss the tomatoes and onions in a little olive oil and roast them for 20 minutes, until browned.

- Put the tomatoes, onions and peppers in a saucepan with the vegetable stock, bring to the boil and simmer, uncovered for 10 minutes. Blend to a purée and season with salt.

- Cook the borlotti beans in boiling water for 10–15 minutes, until tender. Remove from the heat, drain and stir in the marjoram, lemon zest and juice and 2 tablespoons of olive oil. Season with salt.

- Heat the remaining 2 tablespoons of olive oil in a pan over medium heat. Add the courgettes, squash and garlic, and sauté for 5–6 minutes, until tender. Stir in the spring onions and the borlotti beans, and simmer for 1 minute. Season with salt.

- Spoon the vegetables into serving bowls and pour the pepper broth over. Drizzle some basil chilli oil over the vegetables and serve.

for 4

4 red peppers
4 tomatoes, quartered
2 red onions, thickly sliced
4 tbsp olive oil, plus extra for coating
800ml/29fl oz vegetable stock
200g/7oz podded fresh borlotti beans
2 tbsp fresh marjoram leaves
finely grated zest and juice of 1 lemon
200g/7oz small courgettes, thinly sliced
200g/7oz small scallopini or Patty Pan squash, halved and thinly sliced
4 garlic cloves, thinly sliced
4 spring onions, thinly sliced
salt

for the basil chilli oil
100g/3½oz fresh basil leaves
8 dried bird's eye chillies, ground
200ml/7fl oz olive oil

Spiced lentil soup
stock & two variations

for 4

2 tbsp vegetable oil
1 onion, finely chopped
6 garlic cloves, chopped
3 tbsp grated fresh ginger
1 tbsp coriander seeds,
  ground
1 tbsp cumin seeds,
  ground
4 cloves, ground
1 star anise, ground
1 tsp turmeric
250g/9oz red lentils, well
  rinsed
1 tbsp tamarind
  concentrate
1 tsp tomato purée
2 litres/3½ pints vegetable
  stock
salt and pepper

The idea for this came about when my son, Tom, and I were living over Café Paradiso after the floods that destroyed the restaurant and closed it for a month in November 2009. Having no cooking facilities, we ate out a lot for the first week or so, our budgets and the quality of food we were eating sinking by the day. He tired of it sooner than I did and set up a two-burner stove in the office. One of his favourite things to make was based on a tin of lentil soup. He would fry up a few vegetables and spices, and tip in the contents of the tin, sometimes adding stale bread, making a wonderfully satisfying meal in minutes. Being a bit sniffy about tins of soup, I thought – why not make our own lentil base for the soups? When we got a proper kitchen back, of course. Until then, tins were a lifesaver.

The recipe below makes a lot of soup, about 10 portions, as the base for two or three different soups. It is well flavoured but subtly spiced – having no chillies, for example – and is meant to act as a background stock for any variety of soups you want to make from it later. Make double the quantity if you have the ingredients and the space. Divide it into batches of about 700–800ml/24–29fl oz and freeze them, though they will also keep in the fridge for a few days.

The two soups that follow illustrate two different ways to use the stock. The first is as simple as it gets, where some vegetables are fried briefly before the lentil stock is added. The second is more elaborate, in which another flavour – in this case roasted aubergine – is added to the stock, with other vegetables giving body to the soup. Again, it lends itself to endless variation.

• Heat the vegetable oil in a saucepan over medium heat, and fry the onion for 5 minutes, stirring. Add the garlic and spices, and cook for 2 minutes more. Add the lentils, tamarind and tomato purée, stir to combine with the spices, then add the stock. Bring to the boil and simmer, covered, over low heat for 30 minutes.

• Use a hand-held blender to blend the soup, and then season with salt and pepper.

lentil soup with smoked aubergine, chickpeas & lime yoghurt

- Prick the aubergines all over with a fork and char them in one of two ways – either by turning over a flame or by placing on an oven tray in a very hot oven – until the skin is crisped and the insides are very soft. Leave to cool for a few minutes, then cut them in half and scoop out the flesh. Chop this finely and set aside.

- Bring the lentil soup stock to the boil in a saucepan. Stir in the aubergine and paprika, and keep the soup on a very low simmer.

- In a wide pan, heat the olive oil over medium heat. Add the leek, chillies and chickpeas, and fry for 5 minutes, stirring. When the leek is soft, stir in the coriander and remove the pan from the heat.

- Ladle the soup into bowls and spoon some of the chickpeas into each portion, but don't stir it.

- Make the lime yoghurt by mixing the ingredients together and drizzle some on each bowl of soup.

for 4

2 medium aubergines
1 litre/1¾ pints Spiced Lentil Soup Stock (see opposite)
1 tsp smoked paprika
2 tbsp olive oil
1 leek, well washed and diced
2 fresh green chillies, thinly sliced
200g/7oz soaked and cooked dried chickpeas
2 tbsp fresh coriander, chopped

for the lime yoghurt
juice and finely grated zest of 1 lime
4 tbsp natural yoghurt

lentil, potato & kale soup

- Halve the leek lengthways, wash well and chop into 1cm/½in slices.

- In a saucepan, heat the vegetable oil over medium heat. Fry the leek, kale and chillies for 5 minutes, stirring.

- Dice the potatoes about 1cm/½in thick and add them to the pan with the tomatoes. Cook for 1 minute, then add the lentil stock.

- Bring to the boil and simmer over low heat, covered, for 10–12 minutes, until the vegetables are tender.

for 4

1 small leek
2 tbsp vegetable oil
200g/7oz cavolo nero (black kale), stalks discarded and leaves finely chopped
2 fresh red chillies, thinly sliced
300g/11oz potatoes, peeled
2 tomatoes, deseeded and diced
800ml/29fl oz Spiced Lentil Soup Stock (see opposite)

Mash

Mash

I can hardly think the words 'comfort food', never mind speak or hear them, without thinking about potatoes, and specifically mash. There, it just happened again. I tried to start typing that sentence and my mind wandered off to busy itself visualising a bowl of mash with spicy lentils and a little cheese grated over the top. Yum, tonight's dinner is forming in my mind as I write. More than that, it always surprises me when people give other answers to the question – what is your comfort food? I hear answers like rice, eggs, pasta, specific soups and stews, broths and noodles, and I think... well, fine, but what about a plate of spuds?

There are dishes that we all recognise as being in the territory of comfort food, usually autumnal gratins, stews and thick soups, which relate to one shared understanding of the phrase. Coming down off a long traipse across a mountain as the cold sun disappears from an early winter's evening, I think we would all agree that a big bowl of stew and thick bread amounts to proper comfort food. But when I ask the question, or hear it asked, I'm thinking of the dish that you would make for yourself when you're feeling fragile, whether that be from excessive partying, disappointment or simply being under the weather and in need of self-administered pampering.

It must be a cultural thing. I've got spuds in my blood where others, half the world or more, have rice. Some appear to have baked beans, strangely. I imagine that a lot of Italians would say pasta. Not just pasta in general, I'm sure, but a specific dish and probably one that mama used to make for them, if that's not overdoing the cultural cliché. More of them might say risotto, which, for all its current glamour, is not much more than a bowl of rice. And I say that as a fan.

All of which is by way of beginning to explain why I feel a little aggrieved for the humble potato. Other cultures have had their particular comfort foods elevated to internationally recognised iconic status, many of which I happily embrace. Noodles in broth, dal and bread, pizza, tortilla both Spanish and Mexican, pasta and risotto. There is a mystique around the Italian way of cooking their comforting rice dish that I envy for the potato. Imagine if the same sense of awe and respect had spread across the world over a bowl of steaming, fluffy mash, rich in butter so that it melts in your mouth having absorbed the flavours of a few other simple ingredients. Debates would then rage over which potato to use, how much butter was needed, about the use of mashers versus ricers and whether anyone outside of Ireland – or France, if they had claimed it first – could truly claim to make 'authentic' mash.

It's a fantasy, for sure, but we can dream. In Ireland, the potato is the only ingredient that garners serious analysis around the dinner table. Or used to, at least. People would switch from one variety to the next and change suppliers frequently through the year, to make sure that, whatever else was on the table, the spuds would be decent. Even now, my mother will ask me if I have access to good potatoes, as if in having that supply secured I should have the basis of good food.

Recently, I was asked to take part in a radio documentary about heritage varieties of Irish potatoes. My role was to test 10 of them, giving marks on their flavour, colour, skin condition and texture. Unsure if I was qualified for the job, I enlisted the help of Regina Sexton, the food historian at Cork University. The potatoes were all of a type, in that they aspired to the Irish ideal of a good spud, namely one with a dry, floury texture, good for mashing. As well as the historically interesting Buffs and Bloomers – the latter from County Clare and a favourite of the great de Valera – there were the prettily named Catriona and a couple sporting the cocky name of Champion.

Having boiled one of each in separate pots, we set about tasting them unadorned by even a speck of salt.

They were given the kind of attention usually reserved for fine wines, without the spitting, and we found ourselves using the language of wine tasters to describe these humble almost-forgotten spuds. The colours ranged from buttercup yellow through straw to translucent off-whites. Surprisingly, though, all were at the far floury end of the texture spectrum; some were dry and cloying, while others melted perfectly in the mouth and more became watery after a few chews. The flavours were just as varied. Not only did we pick up, amongst other things, hazelnut, earthy sweetness and buttermilk, but these were sometimes mild and other times very powerful. Most wine-like of all, which made us laugh at the recognition of it, some flavours were short and simple, more started out interesting but became overly sweet when swallowed, and others lingered and improved for a long, long time. The winner, by a unanimous decision, was the Skerry Champion, a spud that was, in the early 20th century, the biggest seller in the country but which has somehow lost its way.

The potato probably last had a place as the main item of dinner when people had nothing else to eat. Maybe we've moved on far enough from that to give it another chance, and to rediscover the complex character and wide-ranging versatility of the formerly powerful but currently humble spud. There are so many ways to make dinner from a potato or three. But now, simply because it is my comfort food, I want to use the next few pages to promote the idea of mash as dinner. Put away your bags of pasta and risotto once a week and give this simple notion a go.

The recipes, while giving the impression of being very specific, are actually quite loose. They can be taken as instruction or as guidelines to inspire you to try out your own combinations. The essential element is a soft, comforting mash complemented by a highly flavoured side dish that produces a delicious juice or gravy to be soaked up by the mash. Often the side dish is spiked with chillies; other times the mash is intensely flavoured and the side dish is the softener. I haven't put it in any of the recipes, but if you feel like sprinkling a little grated hard cheese over the finished dish, go right ahead. Potato risotto aficionados aren't nearly as snooty as their rice counterparts.

Leek & wasabi mash with oyster mushrooms and choi in coconut tamarind sauce

for 4

100g/3½oz butter
2 leeks, well washed and
  finely chopped
1.2kg/2½lb floury
  potatoes, peeled and
  chopped into large
  chunks
150ml/5fl oz milk
2 tsp wasabi powder
300g/11oz oyster
  mushrooms
4 small heads of bok choi,
  quartered
1 tbsp grated fresh ginger
1 fresh green chilli, thinly
  sliced
salt

for the coconut tamarind
sauce
1 tbsp tamarind pulp
200ml/7fl oz coconut milk
1 tbsp soy sauce

Mash goes East! And why not? Potatoes didn't start out in Europe – they haven't even been there very long. So why would they not take a trip to exotic Southeast Asia if they had a mind to? I'll admit this wasn't my idea. My own tastes in mash accompaniments are adventurous enough, but they didn't previously include coconut milk.

There is a mainstay dish on the Café Paradiso menu that involves highly spiced tofu, poached greens, noodles and a lemongrassy coconut broth. One of the dining room staff, young Dave, was very fond of having it for staff dinner, but with mash instead of noodles. 'Savage!' was how he would describe it, which I think is a compliment among the youth of Cork.

This went on for a bit, a few others started to ask for it too, so eventually I felt I had to try it for myself. To be honest, while I could see what he liked about it, it didn't quite work for me. The coconut broth was just too sweet for the relatively bland potato mash. I let the notion stew in the back of my mind for a while, simply because I loved the idea of mash going on a world tour.

Next time it bubbled up in my mind, tamarind seemed the way to go to cut the sweetness of the broth and to bring a deeper richness to it. The earthy taste and texture of a few mushrooms would help that depth too.

Wasabi always brings its own very dramatic qualities to a dish, in the way its mustardy pungency hits you hard and fades quickly, leaving your mouth clean but your brain reeling. This is partially muted when wasabi is used in rich foods like mayonnaise, cream sauces or, here, in the buttery mash. It still has a punch, but one that lingers in a more even way.

• Heat 15g/1½oz of the butter in a saucepan over medium heat. Add the leeks and stew them in the butter, stirring often, for 10–12 minutes, until tender.

• Steam the potatoes until soft, then drain. Add a little of the milk to the wasabi powder to create a paste. Put the remaining milk and all but 15g/½oz of the butter in the pan, and warm gently until the butter softens. Return the potatoes to the pan and mash them. Stir in the leeks and the wasabi paste, and season well with salt.

- While the potatoes are cooking, start preparing the coconut tamarind sauce: put the tamarind in a heatproof bowl and pour over 100ml/3½fl oz boiling water. Leave for 10 minutes, then push the mixture through a sieve, saving the liquid and discarding the pulp.

- Heat the remaining butter in a frying pan or wok over high heat. Add the mushrooms and fry for 2 minutes, stirring. Add the bok choi and ginger, and continue to stir-fry for 2–3 minutes, until the choi is tender. Stir in the tamarind water, coconut milk and soy sauce, bring to the boil and simmer for 30 seconds.

- Serve the mash in shallow bowls with the vegetables in their sauce on the side.

Basil mash with olive
& caper peperonata

Because we tend to save our comfort foods for the colder evenings, mash doesn't get as many outings in the summer. However, this recipe puts two of my favourite dishes together and, when the craving strikes, I'll eat it any time or any place I can get decent peppers and potatoes at the same time.

  The herby mash is a wonderful way to mop up the oily juices of slow-cooked peppers, spiked with the heat of chillies and the fruity saltiness of olives and capers. And this is definitely a mash dish that is calling out for a dusting of finely grated cheese.

- Steam the potatoes until soft and drain them. Chop the basil and put it in the pan with the milk, butter and spring onions. Warm gently until the butter softens, then return the potatoes to the pan and mash them. Season well with salt and pepper.

- While the potatoes are steaming, make the caper peperonata: heat the olive oil in a frying pan, add the peppers, garlic and chilli, and fry for 2 minutes. Cover, lower the heat and simmer for 15 minutes. Stir in the olives and capers, and simmer for 2 minutes more. Check the seasoning and add a little salt if necessary – the capers may have brought enough salt to the dish.

- Spoon some mash on serving plates, place some peperonata beside each portion and pour the pan juices over the peperonata.

for 4

1.2kg/2½lb floury
  potatoes, peeled and
  chopped into large
  chunks
1 small bunch of fresh
  basil leaves
150ml/5fl oz milk
100g/3½oz butter
2 spring onions, finely
  chopped
salt and pepper

for the caper peperonata
3 tbsp olive oil
3 red peppers, deseeded
  and thickly sliced
4 garlic cloves, sliced
1 fresh red chilli, deseeded
  and thinly sliced
12 black olives, stoned and
  quartered
1 tbsp small capers, rinsed

Roast garlic & fennel mash with lemon-braised chickpeas & aubergine

for 4

2 heads of garlic
olive oil, for brushing and
  cooking
150ml/5fl oz milk
½ large fennel bulb, cored
  and chopped into small
  dice
1.2kg/2½lb floury
  potatoes, peeled and
  chopped into large
  chunks
115g/4oz butter
2 tbsp finely chopped fresh
  flat-leaf parsley
1 red onion, diced
1 medium aubergine,
  chopped in 2cm/¾in
  cubes
1 tsp cumin seeds
250g/9oz soaked and
  cooked dried chickpeas
100ml/3½fl oz dry white
  wine
½ red pepper, deseeded
  and finely diced
finely grated zest and juice
  of 1 lemon
15g/½oz butter
salt and pepper

A gentle autumnal dish with subtle Mediterranean flavours, this lemony chickpea stew is nicely balanced by the sweetness that roasted garlic and fennel bring to the mash. On another day, I might be tempted to throw a couple of hot chillies into those chickpeas, or a handful of chopped fresh coriander leaves. Then there are those evenings when you just want your comforts without thrills. Adjust this one to suit your mood.

- To prepare the roast garlic: preheat the oven to 180°C/350°F/gas mark 4.

- Snip the top off the garlic bulbs. Brush with olive oil and place on an oven tray. Roast for 15–20 minutes, until the garlic is soft. When cool enough to handle, squeeze the flesh from the skins into a food processor. Add the milk and blend to a purée.

- In a small saucepan, heat a tablespoon of olive oil and sauté the fennel over low heat for 10–12 minutes, stirring often, until soft.

- Steam the potatoes until soft and drain them. Put the garlic milk purée into the pan with 100g/3½oz of the butter and warm gently until the butter softens, then add the potatoes back to the pan and mash them. Stir in the fennel and parsley, and season well with salt and pepper.

- In a wide pan, heat 2 tablespoons of olive oil and fry the onion, aubergine and cumin seeds over high heat until the aubergine is soft and lightly browned. Add the chickpeas and white wine, and continue cooking for 5 minutes more. Add the red pepper, lemon zest and juice and the remaining butter. Remove from the heat. Season with salt and pepper.

- Spoon some mash on serving plates and place some of the chickpeas and aubergine on to each portion, then pour the pan juices around the plates.

Wild garlic mash with grilled asparagus & citrus tarragon-dressed Puy lentils

for 4

60g/2½oz Puy lentils
1 tbsp olive oil, plus extra
   for drizzling
2 shallots, finely diced
2 tbsp chopped fresh
   tarragon
30g/1¼oz butter
finely grated zest of
   1 orange and 1 lemon,
   the juice of ½ lemon and
   1 tbsp orange juice
12–16 asparagus spears
salt and pepper

for the wild garlic mash
1.2kg/2½lb floury
   potatoes, peeled and
   chopped into large
   chunks
150ml/5fl oz milk
100g/3½oz butter
4 tbsp chopped wild garlic

Spring mash. New potatoes are still a month or more away, and the wild garlic is fading as the asparagus crop begins to appear. You have to seize these little moments in the year, and some of the nicest combinations are in the meetings of crops that are oppositely waning and rising. The meeting of winter squash and spring greens is a favourite of mine, and the combination of rhubarb and strawberries is much loved. If you can't get wild garlic, try watercress in this recipe, or a good old-fashioned combination of chives and spring onion.

- First prepare the citrus tarragon-dressed Puy lentils: bring a small saucepan of water to the boil, add the lentils and then simmer for 15–20 minutes until just tender. Drain them through a sieve and set aside.

- Make the wild garlic mash: steam the potatoes until soft and drain them. Put the milk and butter in the pan, warm gently until the butter softens, then add back the potatoes and mash them. Stir in the wild garlic and season with salt and pepper.

- In a small saucepan, heat the olive oil over medium heat. Fry the shallots for a minute, then add the tarragon and cook for a few seconds more. Add the lentils with the butter and the citrus zests and juices. Wait for the butter to melt, then remove the pan from the heat and season the contents with salt and pepper.

- At the same time, preheat a hot grill or heat a griddle pan over high heat. Snap the ends off the asparagus spears. Drizzle the spears with olive oil, sprinkle with salt and grill them for a few minutes, until just tender and lightly coloured.

- Serve the mash on warm plates, with 3–4 asparagus spears beside each portion. Spoon some of the lentils and their pan juices over the asparagus.

Roast parsnip mash with sage-grilled portobello & caramelised red onion

for 4

400g/14oz parsnips,
  peeled, cored and diced
olive oil, for tossing
800g/1¾lb floury potatoes,
  peeled and chopped into
  large chunks
150ml/5fl oz milk
100g/3½oz butter
1 tbsp chopped fresh chives
salt and pepper

for the caramelised red onion
1 tbsp olive oil
2 red onions, halved and
  thinly sliced
1 tbsp balsamic vinegar
1 tsp soft brown sugar

for the sage-grilled mushrooms
30g/1¼oz butter
10 fresh sage leaves, thinly
  sliced
4 large portobello
  mushrooms

Parsnip doesn't really mash. Yes, you can physically mash it but it won't have the fluffy texture of potato mash. So, to make a parsnip-flavoured mash, I roast the parsnips to concentrate their flavour, then purée them to a fine paste and fold this into a classic potato mash. Hey presto – the texture of mash with the flavour of parsnip. You have to love cooking, really.

This works very well with celeriac too, another winter root that, when roasted and puréed, brings a lovely earthy sweetness to the dish. Like all the mash dishes in this book, the essence of this one is that the mash is there to mop up the juices from the side dish. Most of the rich liquid in this case comes from the butter-roasted mushrooms. Just before serving, check that there is enough juice in the pan, and add a little more butter or olive oil if necessary.

- Preheat the oven to 200°C/400°F/gas mark 6.

- Toss the parsnip in a little olive oil in an oven dish, cover loosely with baking parchment and roast in the oven for 15 minutes, until soft. Blend the parsnips to a purée in a food processor.

- Steam the potatoes until soft and drain them. Put the milk and butter in the pan, warm gently until the butter softens, then add back the potatoes and mash them. Stir in the parsnip and chives, and season with salt and pepper.

- Meanwhile, prepare the caramelised red onion: in a small saucepan, heat the olive oil and fry the onions over medium heat for 5 minutes, stirring. Add the vinegar and sugar, cover loosely with baking parchment and lower the heat. Simmer for 10–15 minutes, until the onions are tender and caramelised.

- Meanwhile, prepare the sage-grilled mushrooms: soften the butter and stir in the sage. Spread the butter on the portobello mushrooms, season with salt and pepper and place them on an oven tray. Roast in the oven, or place under a hot grill, for 8–10 minutes, until the mushrooms are tender. Pour the mushroom juices into the onion pan.

- Spoon some mash on each serving plate. Cut the mushrooms in half and place beside the mash. Scatter over the onions, then pour on the pan juices.

Smoked mash with tomato & maple-braised Brussels sprouts

No, the mash isn't actually smoked. It has smoky flavours added to it. If you've got a smoking kit at home – for food, I mean – you might try passing the potatoes over it after steaming. Or you could try the Café Paradiso occasional accidental method, which goes something like this.

Steam the peeled potatoes over furiously boiling water that evaporates just about at the same time as the potatoes are cooked. Forget to notice this until you get a faint whiff of burning pot. Quickly whip the potatoes out of the steamer into another pot and gather everyone around to decide if they are going to taste clean, slightly smoky or scorched. If slightly smoky, carry on with the mashing process and change the menu to read 'smoked mash'.

- Steam the potatoes until soft and drain them. Add the milk and butter to the pan, warm gently until the butter softens, then add back the potatoes and mash them. Stir in the cheese, paprika and chives, and season with salt and pepper.

- Make the maple-braised Brussels sprouts: heat the olive oil in a wide pan, and fry the onion and garlic for 2 minutes over medium heat. Add the Brussels sprouts and continue to fry for 5 minutes. Add the tomatoes, orange zest, soy sauce and maple syrup, cover and simmer for 2 minutes.

- Spoon some mash on serving plates and place some sprouts beside it, pouring the juices around the plate.

for 4

1.2kg/2½lb floury potatoes, peeled and chopped in large chunks
150ml/5fl oz milk
100g/3½oz butter
100g/3½oz lightly smoked cheese
1 tsp smoked paprika
1 tbsp chopped fresh chives
salt and pepper

for the maple-braised Brussels sprouts
2 tbsp olive oil
1 red onion, halved and thinly sliced
2 garlic cloves, sliced
300g/11oz Brussels sprouts, halved and parboiled
115g/4oz cherry tomatoes, halved
finely grated zest of 1 orange
1 tbsp soy sauce
1 tbsp maple syrup

New potato crush with courgettes, broad beans & cherry tomatoes

for 4

1.2kg/2 ½lb new potatoes, washed
115g/4oz butter
2 tbsp finely chopped fresh chives
4 spring onions, finely chopped
200g/7oz podded fresh broad beans
4 tbsp olive oil
500g/1lb 2oz small courgettes, quartered lengthways
1 red onion, halved and thinly sliced
4 garlic cloves, thinly sliced
1 tbsp fresh marjoram leaves
2 tbsp finely chopped fresh basil
200g/7oz cherry tomatoes, halved
salt and pepper

Using a classically waxy new potato, this recipe will still give you a nice 'crush' finish, and if you've got a floury new potato, it will be heaven on a plate. The most important thing is that the potatoes are proper early spuds with little or no skin. A quick wash will remove some of the papery skin anyway, but the little that is left clinging to the potatoes is part of the pleasure of this dish. I suggested earlier that any of these mash dishes would happily take a dusting of finely grated hard cheese as a finishing touch, and this recipe is certainly one that would love it.

• Steam the new potatoes until tender. Put them in a wide bowl and use a knife, slice, spoon or whatever is handy to break them into small pieces.

• Heat the butter in a wide pan over medium heat. Add the chives and spring onions, and fry for 1 minute. Now add the potatoes. Use a slice, and occasionally a masher if needed, to fold and crush the potatoes into the butter until you have a coarse, lumpy mash. Season well with salt and pepper.

• While the potatoes are steaming, cook the broad beans in boiling water for 5–7 minutes, until tender. Drain and set aside.

• Heat 2 tablespoons of the olive oil in a wide frying pan over medium heat. Fry the courgettes for 2 minutes, then add the red onion and cook for 2 minutes more. Add the garlic, herbs and cherry tomatoes. Fry for 1–2 minutes, until the tomatoes are breaking down. Add a little water and the remaining olive oil to mingle with the tomatoes to make a nice pan juice. Season with salt and pepper.

• If you have a moulding ring to hand, use it to make a loose but orderly circle of crushed potato on the plate, and serve the vegetables beside, with their pan juices poured over. Alternatively, serve generous portions of the mash in shallow bowls and simply pour the vegetables on top.

Dilled mash with braised celery in maple & blue cheese broth

for 4

1.2kg/2½lb floury
  potatoes, peeled and
  chopped into large
  chunks
150ml/5fl oz milk
125g/4½oz butter
2 tbsp chopped fresh dill
1 head of green celery,
  trimmed and cut at an
  angle into slices
  1cm/½in thick
100ml/3½fl oz dry white
  wine
200ml/7fl oz vegetable
  stock or water
2 tbsp maple syrup
50g/2oz blue cheese
salt and pepper

I got this idea from a pub conversation with an architect who loves to cook and eat. Starting with his beloved but much maligned celery, we were trying to verbally construct a dish that would do it justice. At the time, we were thinking of a more elaborately constructed dish, but next day my mind was fixated on mash. We were definitely agreed on the ingredients – celery, potato, maple syrup, blue cheese. Yes, I know, we were in a pub.

The scribbled note in my pocket the next morning suggests that the celery recipe conversation was a tangent from his explanation of the notion of 'the golden section', a concept that is used as a tool or sometimes occurs naturally in architecture, music and art. It's all about the beauty of proportions. Here's one definition: 'In mathematics and the arts, two quantities are in the golden ratio if the ratio of the sum of the quantities to the larger quantity is equal to the ratio of the larger quantity to the smaller one.'

I admit the conversation lost me until we got around to deciding whether to go with honey or maple syrup. I've checked the numbers below, and there is no golden section in their ratio. Maybe it's in the way you arrange the dish on a plate? Your homework this evening is to make it and see.

- Steam the potatoes until soft and drain them. Put the milk and 100g/3½oz of the butter in the pan, warm gently until the butter softens, then add the potatoes back and mash them. Stir in the dill and season with salt and pepper.

- While the potatoes are steaming, melt 15g/½oz of butter over medium heat in a wide pan. Add the celery and sauté for 5 minutes, then add the wine and stock. Cover and simmer for 10 minutes, until the celery is tender. If the braising liquid has evaporated, add a few tablespoons of water and bring back to the boil. Add the maple syrup, blue cheese and remaining butter, and boil briefly to form a slightly thickened sauce.

- Serve the mash in shallow bowls with the celery alongside and the juices poured over.

All wrapped up

All wrapped up

Probably the most challenging aspect of creating vegetarian restaurant menus is the knife-and-fork issue – quite literally, food that insists you take a knife and fork to it. It's not so much that we have a sadistic urge to make people work harder for their dinner. The intention is really focused on creating dishes with complex layers of flavour and texture, and these inevitably end up as ones to which you need to give a little attention, rather than eating absent-mindedly with a trowel. Structure and texture are the means to arrange flavours in such a way that they are delivered to you exactly as we would want you to experience them. That sounds arrogant, but you have paid us a fair bit of cash to make your dinner, so let's assume you trust us.

Layering, stacking, stuffing and otherwise corralling ingredients on a plate are all ways to achieve this effect. Arranging separate tiny elements on a plate – as was fashionable for a bit – works too, if the intention is for the separate items to be eaten one at a time. God, I've just remembered the pinnacle of that trend, where the waiter told you which direction to go around the plate. Clockwise might give you the pleasure of increasing flavour and intensity, while driving the wrong way round would result in a crashed palate. Scooping a couple of the morsels into the previously mentioned trowel would cause plate and mouth carnage in one swoop.

When teaching a cooking class, I occasionally like to deconstruct something like a carefully layered gratin or timbale. Mostly this is to emphasise how the separate elements might be useful in so many other ways in your kitchen, but it's also true that the deconstructed version, all elements slopped on to a plate, has lost two of its best qualities – its aesthetic beauty and the pleasurable symmetry of each mouthful having the right balance of each ingredient.

With all of this in mind – a heavy burden, yes, but we must soldier on – I am always looking for ways to wrap things up. Making a parcel is one of the best ways to arrange an unruly bunch of flavours into a coherent whole. The wrapping material – whether it is a vegetable, a flower or a concoction made from grain flours – as well as creating a textured structure always brings its own flavour to the dish too. A finishing touch to elevate the filling inside beyond the simple stirred-together mélange of flavours it may have once been.

So, by forcefully arranging the ingredients into a particular order on the plate, cooks use texture and structure to deliver their fantasies, or even to make their fantasies yours. Hmmm... yes, it is a nice job.

Not all restaurant food is quite so structured, nor should it be. A simple risotto with a glass of wine in good company can be the greatest of pleasures. Most of the recipes in this book happily acknowledge that good food can be made quickly and relatively simply, and can be eaten with trowels, spoons, forks, fingers or anything else you have free while doing something else. But every now and again, you will want to present dinner on a plate in a way that makes someone go 'Wow, look at that!'... 'Thank you for taking the trouble to make such a pretty picture!'

Rice paper parcels of asian greens with lime, chilli & coconut dip

for 4

for the lime, chilli and coconut dip
1 x 400ml/14fl oz tin of coconut milk
100g/3½oz sugar
100ml/3½fl oz rice vinegar
4 whole dried bird's eye chillies
juice of 1 lime

for the rice paper parcels
150g/5oz pak choi, coarsely chopped
150g/5oz mixed rocket leaves, mustard leaf, mizuna etc, coarsely chopped
4 spring onions, thinly sliced
4 slices of pickled ginger, chopped
1 handful each of fresh coriander, mint and basil, chopped
1 pack of rice paper sheets

Rice paper can be daunting the first time you use it. There are varying ideas on how best to moisten the paper to make it pliable. The idea is to soak it in water so that it becomes soft enough to roll, but not so soft that it falls apart. Some recipes will tell you to use hot water for a short time, others suggest lukewarm water to give you more time to get the soaking part right. I've drifted from the first to the second method, but I have seen others make these parcels a lot faster than I can do it – by getting the paper ready faster. It can also help to place the soaked rice paper on a fine linen or cotton napkin before filling it. So, the best advice is to get some practice in and work out which works best for you.

The filling is essentially a combination of salad leaves flavoured with pickled ginger and a lot of fresh herbs. When dunked in the sweet spicy dip, the result is a highly flavoured mouthful, and definitely my favourite way to eat salad.

• First make the lime, chilli and coconut dip: in a small saucepan over low heat, simmer the coconut milk until reduced by half, about 8–10 minutes.

• At the same time, in another saucepan, simmer the sugar, vinegar and chillies for 8–10 minutes, until reduced by half and syrupy. Strain out the chillies and then stir in the reduced coconut milk and the lime juice. Leave to cool.

• To make the rice paper parcels: combine the pak choi, mixed leaves, spring onions, ginger and herbs.

• Fill a wide bowl with hand-warm water. Place a rice paper in it and gently hold submerged until the paper is soft all over. Remove it from the water and place it on a chopping board (which has been covered with a linen or cotton napkin, if you like).

• Place a generous handful of filling just above the near end of the rice paper, and fold that end over the filling. Roll up halfway, keeping the parcel very tight. Fold in the sides, again keeping it very tight, then roll to the end. Set the finished parcel aside on a plate covered with a lightly dampened cloth while you make the rest.

• Just before serving, cut the parcels in half at a slight angle. Serve 3 halves per person, or on a communal platter.

Potato crêpes of asparagus & brie with tarragon butter and warm beetroot & Puy lentil salsa

for 4

for the potato crêpes
3 eggs
300ml/11fl oz milk
200ml/7fl oz soured cream
150g/5oz plain flour
300g/11oz peeled potatoes, cooked and mashed
large pinch of cayenne pepper
2 tbsp finely chopped fresh chives
melted butter, for brushing
salt and pepper

for the asparagus
24 asparagus spears
160g/5½oz Brie, thinly sliced
melted butter, for brushing

for the tarragon butter
2 tbsp finely chopped fresh tarragon
2 tsp lemon juice
60g/2½oz butter, softened

for the warm beetroot and Puy lentil salsa
75g/3oz Puy lentils
200ml/7fl oz vegetable stock or water
2 sprigs of fresh thyme, leaves only
4 garlic cloves, finely chopped
1 medium beetroot, washed, cooked and peeled (about 200g/7oz)
2 spring onions, thinly sliced
1 tbsp maple syrup
1 tbsp balsamic vinegar

There are a few good reasons to put potato in a crêpe batter. The very coincidence that you fancy making crêpes for dinner and that there is some leftover mash in the fridge is good enough on its own. Perhaps suggesting that potatoes taste good in anything might sound a bit Irish, but I have yet to hear a good argument against it. In the case of this recipe, the best reason is simply that asparagus loves potato, and potato – so easy to get on with – loves dear old asparagus back. Asparagus is quite set in its ways, most of its foibles being well known, and this recipe could be seen as asparagus pampering – covering it with Brie, wrapping it in potato, dressing it with warm butter and tarragon, and finishing with earthy beets and lentils.

The potato gives the crêpes a rich, soft texture, but it can make them a little tricky to cook. Just a little tricky, though; every stage is straightforward except that moment where they have to be flipped. Do it carefully but confidently, like you do everything else. The quantities below will give you 10–12 crêpes, and you only really need 8, so you've got room for error. Not that I'm encouraging sloppiness, mind. Nor am I suggesting you only use these crêpes with asparagus. They bring their own potatoey wonderfulness to any filling because, well, potatoes love just about everything.

The number count for asparagus spears assumes you are using long thick ones. Get a few extra if you're not sure.

- First make the potato crêpe batter: in a large mixing bowl, whisk the eggs, milk and soured cream together, then whisk in the flour, followed by the mashed potato, cayenne pepper, chives and a large pinch of salt. Leave this batter to chill in the fridge for 15–30 minutes.

- While it chills, prepare the asparagus: bring a saucepan of water to the boil. Trim the asparagus spears to about 20cm/8in long and peel the tougher ends. Drop the spears into the boiling water and boil for 3–4 minutes, until tender but still crisp. Drain and cool in cold water, then drain and pat dry with kitchen paper.

- Then make the tarragon butter: stir the tarragon and lemon juice into the softened butter and keep in a warm place so that the butter remains soft but not quite melted.

- To make the crêpes: heat a 20cm/8in crêpe pan over medium-high heat and brush it with melted butter. Pour in enough batter to make a thinnish crêpe, and cook it for 2–3 minutes. Flip the crêpe over and cook the other side for a minute, until lightly coloured. Repeat with the rest of the batter, brushing the pan with more melted butter each time.

- Place a crêpe on a work surface. Put a line of Brie slices across the centre and 3 spears of asparagus on top. Fold over the crêpe to make a tight parcel. Repeat with the other crêpes to make 8 in total. Place these on a baking parchment-lined oven tray, so that the Brie is above the asparagus. Brush with melted butter and store in the fridge until needed.

- Preheat the oven to 180°C/350°F/gas mark 4.

- Make the warm beetroot and Puy lentil salsa: put the lentils in a saucepan with the stock or water, thyme and garlic. Bring to the boil and simmer, uncovered, for 20 minutes, until the lentils are just tender. Drain off any remaining stock and return the lentils to the pan. Dice the beetroot and add it to the pan with the spring onions, maple syrup and balsamic vinegar. Season with salt and pepper.

- When the lentils are almost tender, put the crêpes in the oven for 5–7 minutes, until the Brie is beginning to melt.

- Place 2 crêpes close together on each plate and spoon some of the tarragon butter over them. Add some of the warm salsa on top and serve.

Corn pancakes of courgettes, pine nuts & roasted onion with warm Sungold tomato & caper salsa

for 4

for the corn pancakes
a few saffron threads, crumbled
100g/3½oz fine cornmeal
50g/2oz plain flour
½ tsp paprika
pinch of cayenne pepper
½ tsp salt
ground black pepper
2 eggs
300ml/11fl oz milk
butter for brushing
olive oil, for cooking

for the filling
2 red onions, halved and thinly sliced
olive oil, for tossing and brushing
40g/1½oz pine nuts
500g/1lb 2oz small courgettes
4 garlic cloves, sliced
1 tbsp chopped fresh marjoram
30g/1¼oz sheep's cheese, such as Cratloe Hills (or pecorino), finely grated
salt and pepper

for the warm Sungold tomato and caper salsa
250g/9oz Sungold tomatoes, halved
1 fresh green chilli, deseeded and thinly sliced
1 tbsp small capers, rinsed
2 tbsp olive oil
pinch of salt

Pancakes or crêpes… I'm never sure which word to use, but in the summer I usually find myself reaching for the bag of fine cornmeal – or ground maize, as it is sometimes labelled – or fine polenta, but definitely not 'cornflour', the thickening powder that won't bring anything useful to the pancake party. Corn and sunshine go together like, well, courgettes and tomatoes, making this dish a lovely way to parcel up a little bit of summer.

Sungold tomatoes are orange-skinned cherry tomatoes, that deliver a full complex balance of sweet, tart and savoury tomato flavours. If you can't get them, the salsa still works well with any small tomato, as the capers will bring their own sharp and salty character to it. Boiled new potatoes make a good accompaniment to this dish.

• First prepare the corn pancake batter: soak the saffron in a tablespoon of boiling water for 5 minutes. Sift the cornmeal, flour, paprika, cayenne, salt and pepper into a large mixing bowl. Beat the eggs and milk together briefly, add the saffron water, then whisk this into the flours to produce a smooth batter. This batter can be used as soon as it is made. In fact, you should whisk it well before pouring each time, as the cornmeal tends to sink.

• Heat a 20cm/8in crêpe pan over medium-high heat and brush it with melted butter. Pour in enough batter to make a thin crêpe, and cook it for 2–3 minutes. Flip the crêpe over and cook the other side for a minute. Repeat with the rest of the batter, brushing the pan with more melted butter each time.

• Preheat the oven to 200°C/400°F/gas mark 6.

• To prepare the filling: in an oven dish, toss the red onions with a little olive oil and a pinch of salt. Roast for 15 minutes, until the onions are browned. Add the pine nuts for the last 5 minutes of roasting. Leave the oven on when you remove them.

• While the onions are roasting, slice the courgettes in half lengthways and again in half across. Then slice them into sticks about 5mm/¼in thick. Just before adding the pine nuts to the onions in the oven, heat a tablespoon of olive oil in a wide, heavy pan over medium heat and sauté the courgette, garlic and marjoram, stirring often, for 5–6 minutes. Stir in the roasted onion and pine nuts, then remove from the heat and allow to cool. Stir in the cheese, and season with salt and pepper.

- Place a crêpe on a work surface. Put some of the courgette filling in a line across the centre and roll up the crêpe to make a tight parcel. Repeat with the other crêpes to make 8 in total.

- Place these on a baking parchment-lined oven tray, brush with olive oil and put in the oven for 5 minutes to heat through.

- While the crêpes are heating, make the warm Sungold tomato and caper salsa: put the tomatoes, chilli and capers in a small saucepan with the olive oil and salt. Heat gently until the tomatoes soften. Just before serving, add a splash of water to make the salsa more moist.

- Serve the crêpes with the salsa.

Chard dolmades of quinoa, carrot & currants with saffron cashew butter sauce

Chard is my green of choice when it comes to wrapping things up, the leaves being thinner and more pliable than those of cabbage, but with much more strength and substance than spinach. That is, if you use decent-sized leaves. Unlike the time I made a team of chefs make dolmades for 50 people using the last thinnings from chard plants gone to seed over winter, and using two – and sometimes three – leaves for each parcel. Don't try this at home, folks. It's best to wait for the leaves to be bigger than your hand at least.

The quantity of water used to cook the quinoa is a little more than it would be if you were planning to serve it in a salad or pilaf. This is to ensure that the filling is soft enough to be pressed into shape to make the rolling easier. For the same reason, it's best to cook the carrots until they are soft enough to break up a little when they are pressed.

Years ago, I used to make a sauce from cashews, but I never really worked on refining it and eventually I let it slip out of my repertoire and my memory. Recently, my friend Ultan told me he was making a saffron cashew sauce, so I decided to revisit it using his version as a starting point. This one is better than I remember mine being: more of an elegant sauce and less of a nut purée.

The initial stage of frying the cashews in butter until they are golden is important for the richness, colour and toasty depth of flavour in the sauce. Grinding the nuts to a very fine paste is also vital, to make sure the result is a smooth, unctuous sauce without any coarse nutty bits.

As well as making a rich sauce for these tartly fruity parcels, the cashew sauce is also good with pasta, especially on a ravioli of strong greens. Or you might try adding coconut milk and some spices to take it off in another direction entirely.

If you make the sauce in advance – and you can, up to a day before – it will thicken while it sits and you will need to add some more water with the cream at the final stage.

I would serve these dolmades with a simple side dish of green beans or courgettes in summer, or braised fennel in colder months.

- First make the saffron cashew butter sauce; heat the butter in a heavy frying pan, add the cashews and fry over low-to-medium heat, stirring often, for 10–15 minutes, until golden. Grind the cashews to a fine paste in a food processor. Return them to the pan with the saffron, lemon juice and 150ml/5fl oz water. Bring to the boil, remove from the heat and leave to infuse.

- Prepare the chard dolmades: heat a teaspoon of olive oil in a saucepan over medium heat. Add the quinoa and toast it for 5 minutes, stirring. Add 300ml/11fl oz boiling water and stir once, then reduce the heat to very low, cover the pan and simmer for 12 minutes. Test that the grain is cooked and all the water is absorbed. If not, remove the lid and increase the heat to boil off the residual water.

- At the same time, bring another saucepan of salted water to the boil, add the carrots and simmer for 5–7 minutes, until the carrots are tender. Drain well.

- In a wide pan, heat 2 tablespoons of olive oil over medium heat. Fry the onion in it for 5 minutes, stirring. Add the garlic and cumin seeds, and cook for 2 minutes more. Add the carrot and currants, and continue cooking for 5 minutes, until the carrot is soft. Stir the vegetables into the quinoa with the herbs, lemon zest and juice and the cayenne pepper. Season to taste with salt.

- Bring another saucepan of water to the boil. Cut the stalk from the chard leaves at the base, and drop the leaves into the water. Boil for 3–4 minutes, until tender. Cool in a bowl of cold water, then pat the leaves dry with kitchen paper.

- Preheat the oven to 180°C/350°F/gas mark 4.

- Place a chard leaf on a work surface. Put a tablespoon of the filling at the wide end. Roll the leaf up one full turn from that end, fold in the sides tightly and continue rolling to make a cylindrical parcel.

- Repeat with the remaining leaves.

Continued on following page...

for 4

for the saffron cashew butter sauce
30g/1¼oz butter
100g/3½oz cashew nuts
large pinch of saffron
  threads
juice of ½ lemon
100ml/3½fl oz double
  cream
salt

for the chard dolmades
olive oil, for cooking and
  brushing
140g/4¾oz quinoa
500g/1lb 2oz carrots,
  peeled and finely diced
1 red onion, finely diced
2 garlic cloves
1 tbsp cumin seeds
40g/1½oz currants
2 tbsp chopped fresh
  parsley
2 tbsp chopped fresh mint
finely grated zest of
  1 lemon, plus the
  juice of ½ lemon
large pinch of cayenne
  pepper
12 medium chard leaves
100ml/3½fl oz vegetable
  stock or water (optional)

Continued from previous page...

- Generously brush an oven dish with olive oil and place the dolmades in it, not too close together (use 2 dishes, if necessary).

- Brush the tops of the dolmades with olive oil and sprinkle over about 100ml/3½fl oz water or vegetable stock. Bake in the oven for 12–15 minutes, until the dolmades are warmed through and sealed.

- When ready to serve, finish the sauce by adding the cream, bringing it to the boil and simmering for a minute. You may need to add some more water at this stage to get a smooth pouring consistency. Season with salt.

- Pour some cashew sauce on to plates and arrange 3 dolmades on top of each.

Maple-seared king oyster mushrooms on a leek & smoked cheese crêpe with sage cream

Although similar in flavour, king oyster – 'royal trumpet' – mushrooms are at the other end of the texture spectrum from the more common oyster mushrooms. While the latter are delicate and wide-headed, the kings are solid and consist almost exclusively of a thick stem. Sliced into thick slabs, these hold their shape really well when cooked, making them one of the best mushrooms for marinades and, as in this recipe, for glazing. Fried in butter, the mildly earthy flavour of the mushrooms is nicely balanced with the almost savoury notes in the maple syrup. This is best with a strong maple syrup, one that is robust enough to add character to the combination of mushrooms and a rich smoky pancake.

- First make the sage cream: in a small saucepan, simmer the cream gently with the sage leaves for 15 minutes. Remove the leaves. Turn up the heat and reduce the cream by half. Remove from the heat and stir in the crème fraîche and the salt. The sauce should have a thick pouring consistency. It can be gently warmed through or served at room temperature.

- Preheat the oven to 180°C/350°F/gas mark 4.

- Make the crêpes: sift the flour with the salt. Whisk the eggs and milk together, then whisk into the flour. Leave to sit for a few minutes. Heat a 20cm/8in crêpe pan over medium-high heat and brush it with melted butter. Pour in enough batter to make a thin crêpe, and cook it for 2–3 minutes. Flip the crêpe over and cook the other side for a minute. Repeat with the rest of the batter, brushing the pan with more melted butter each time.

- Prepare the mushrooms: chop 2 of them into small dice and keep for the filling. Slice the others lengthways about 5mm/¼in thick. Heat a frying pan over medium heat, add the butter and allow it to melt. Add the sliced oyster mushrooms and salt and cook for 5 minutes on each side, until tender and lightly browned.

- Pour in the maple syrup and stir to coat the mushrooms, then remove from the heat.

Continued on following page...

for 4

for the sage cream
200ml/7fl oz double cream
12 fresh sage leaves
3 tbsp crème fraîche
pinch of salt

for the crêpes
75g/3oz plain flour
large pinch of salt
2 eggs
150ml/5fl oz milk
melted butter, for brushing

for the mushrooms
10 king oyster mushrooms
30g/1¼oz butter
pinch of salt
1 tbsp maple syrup

for the filling
15g/½oz butter
600g/1lb 6oz leeks,
    quartered lengthways,
    well washed and finely
    diced
2 garlic cloves, finely
    chopped
3 tbsp dry sherry
1 sprig of fresh thyme,
    leaves only
1 tbsp chopped fresh
    parsley
1 tsp hot mustard
120g/4¼ oz smoked
    semi-hard cheese, diced

Continued from previous page…

- Prepare the filling: place a large pan over high heat and add the butter, leeks, garlic and reserved diced mushrooms. Cook, stirring, for 10 minutes, then add the sherry, thyme, parsley and mustard. Cook for 2–3 minutes more, then transfer to a bowl to cool. When the mixture is cool, stir in the smoked cheese.

- Fill 4 of the crêpes with the leek mixture, making tight rectangular parcels. Place on a baking parchment-lined oven tray and brush lightly with butter.

- Place the crêpes in the oven for 5–7 minutes, until warmed through and lightly golden.

- Spoon some sage cream onto 4 warm plates and place a crêpe on each. Arrange the oyster mushrooms on the crêpes and drizzle a little more cream on top.

Egg roll pancakes of roasted Brussels sprouts & sweet potato with green onion, tamarind & coconut sauce

for 6

for the egg roll pancakes
110g/3¾ fl oz plain flour
large pinch of salt
4 eggs, beaten
vegetable oil, for brushing
2 tbsp melted butter, for
  brushing

*for the green onion,
tamarind and coconut
sauce*
1 tbsp tamarind pulp
1 star anise, broken up
1 x 400ml/14fl oz tin of
  coconut milk
4 spring onions, finely
  chopped
1 fresh green chilli,
  deseeded and thinly
  sliced

for the filling
500g/1lb 2oz sweet
  potatoes, peeled
500g/1lb 2oz Brussels
  sprouts
15g/½ oz butter, melted
1 tbsp vegetable oil
1 bunch of spring onions,
  chopped
2 tbsp grated fresh ginger
1 tbsp coriander seeds,
  toasted and crushed

Egg rolls, or pancake rolls, as distinct from the smaller spring rolls, obviously make me think of Chinese food, so that's where I started out with this. Then I looked in the fridge to see what I might put in them, and the long-ignored bag of Brussels sprouts literally pleaded to be given a shot at it. That's how I heard it anyhow. Having taken a sharp turn like that, it was only a short hop, skip and jump to recruit the sweet potatoes, tamarind and coconut, so the finished article ended up with southern Asian flavourings and a northern European interloper. I wouldn't have it any other way now, but if you don't have a pleading bag of sprouts to hand, try replacing them with broccoli, cabbage or green beans.

Unlike most pancakes, these are best cooked over low heat, so that they set without browning, which would give them a fried egg flavour. Not that I would throw one away for being a little coloured, but the ideal is soft and pale yellow. Try to make them as thin as possible so that they are pliable enough to roll up.

Because the sauce is served at room temperature, it can be made first or at any time during the cooking.

• First make the pancake batter: sift the flour and salt together in a bowl, then whisk in the eggs. Stir in 120ml/4¼fl oz water to make a pouring batter.

• Warm a heavy frying pan, or a crêpe pan, over low heat. Brush with a little vegetable oil and pour in enough batter to make a thin pancake. Cook over low heat for a few minutes, then flip the pancake over and cook the other side for a minute more. Do not let the pancake colour. Repeat with the rest of the batter to make 6 pancakes. Stack the pancakes on a plate to cool.

• While they cool, prepare the green onion, tamarind and coconut sauce: put the tamarind and star anise in a heatproof bowl and pour 100ml/3½fl oz boiling water over them. Leave to stand for 20 minutes.

• Meanwhile, put the coconut milk in a saucepan and simmer slowly over low heat to reduce it by half. Add the spring onions and chilli, and simmer for 5 minutes more. Transfer to a bowl or jug. Push the tamarind paste through a sieve and discard the solids. Add the tamarind juice to the coconut milk mix and leave to cool to room temperature.

- Preheat the oven to 200°C/400°F/gas mark 6.

- Make the filling: chop the sweet potatoes into 1cm/½in dice. Peel away and discard the outer leaves of the Brussels sprouts, snip off the ends, then cut the sprouts into slices about 5mm/¼in thick. Toss the vegetables with the melted butter and vegetable oil in an oven dish. Roast in the oven for 20 minutes, turning once. Mix in the spring onion, ginger and coriander seeds, return the dish to the oven and roast for 10 minutes more, until the sprouts are beginning to colour and the potatoes are soft. The sweet potatoes breaking up a bit helps make a stable filling for the pancakes.

- Remove the filling from the oven, keeping it on. Place a pancake on a work surface and put 2 tablespoons of filling in an oblong shape in the centre. Fold the near end over the filling, then fold in the sides and roll the pancake up to get a tight parcel. Repeat with the remaining pancakes and place the filled ones on a baking parchment-lined oven tray, with the seal side down. Brush with melted butter, and place in the oven for 7–8 minutes, until beginning to crisp.

- Drizzle some sauce on the plates and place a pancake on each one, then drizzle some more sauce over the top.

Braised chard timbale of haloumi, roast tomato & Puy lentils with citrus fennel butter

for 4

8 large tomatoes
olive oil, for drizzling,
  cooking and oiling
150g/5oz Puy lentils
1 leek, well washed and
  finely diced
3 garlic cloves, chopped
2 sprigs of fresh thyme,
  leaves only
15g/½oz butter
250g/9oz haloumi cheese,
  cut into 6 slices
1 tbsp chopped fresh mint
8 medium chard leaves
salt and pepper
vegetable stock or water,
  for moistening

for the citrus fennel butter
120g/4¼oz butter,
  softened
finely grated zest of
  1 orange and juice of ½
finely grated zest and juice
  of 1 lemon
1 tbsp finely chopped
  fresh chives
1 small fennel bulb

A timbale, that is to say – in my kitchen language – an individual, drum-shaped parcel with layered fillings, is a lovely way to show off the pretty veining of chard leaves. Because chard leaves are thin, you can be generous with them as a wrapping for timbales, doubling up and overlapping as you see fit, in a way that you can't when using a more substantial leaf like cabbage.

This looks like a daunting recipe with a lot of stages, but most can be done ahead. In fact, the timbales are best made earlier in the day and refrigerated to firm up before cooking. So, when it comes to dinner time, you simply need to pop them in the oven.

You will need four metal rings 7–8cm/2¾–3¼in in diameter and 3–4cm/1¼–1½in high.

Serve these timbales with new potatoes and green beans or asparagus – all of which will go very well with the butter sauce.

- Discarding the tops and ends, slice the tomatoes thickly, getting 3 slices from each one. Place the tomato slices on baking parchment-lined oven trays, drizzle with olive oil and season with salt and pepper. Roast in the oven for 15–20 minutes, until the tomatoes are beginning to colour.

- While the tomatoes are in the oven, in a saucepan of boiling water, simmer the Puy lentils for 20 minutes, until just done but still firm. Cool briefly in a colander under cold running water. Leave to drain.

- While the lentils are simmering, in a wide pan, heat 2 tablespoons of olive oil over medium heat. Add the leek and garlic, and sauté for 5 minutes, stirring often. Add the thyme and cook for 3–4 minutes more, until the leeks are tender. Stir in the drained lentils, season with salt and pepper and remove from the heat.

- Heat a tablespoon of olive oil and the butter in a frying pan over medium heat. Cut the haloumi slices in half diagonally and fry the pieces for 5–6 minutes, turning once, until coloured on both sides. Add the mint at the end, turning the cheese once or twice more so that the mint sticks to it. Transfer the cooked haloumi to a plate lined with kitchen paper.

- Preheat the oven to 200°C/400°F/gas mark 6.

- Brush one of the metal rings with olive oil and line it with 2 chard leaves so that there is enough leaf overhanging to form a closed parcel on top later. Put 3 slices of roast tomato in the bottom and a tablespoon of lentils on top of that. Next, put in a layer of 3 half slices of haloumi, followed by another tablespoon of lentils and another layer of tomato. Fold over the leaves to make a closed parcel, and press down firmly. Repeat to make 4 timbales in all. Place a sheet of baking parchment on top and weigh the timbales down with a plate. Chill in the fridge for at least 30 minutes.

- Preheat the oven to 180°C/350°F/gas mark 4.

- Place the timbales on a baking parchment-lined oven tray. Drizzle generously with olive oil and splash a little stock or water on top. Bake in the oven for 12–15 minutes, until the chard is crisping a little on top.

- While they are in the oven, make the citrus fennel butter; put 25g/1oz of the butter in a small saucepan over low heat. Stir the citrus zests and juices together with the chives into the remaining butter. Quarter the fennel bulb, discard the core and stalk and finely dice the rest. Add this to the butter in the pan and increase the heat to medium. Sauté the fennel, stirring, for 5–6 minutes, then stir in the citrus butter and remove the pan from the heat. Season with salt and pepper and keep warm.

- To serve, turn the timbales out on to plates, sealed side down. Leave to rest for a minute in the rings, then gently pull the rings off. Spoon the citrus fennel butter over and around the timbales.

Aubergine, leek & tofu parcels on sesame cabbage with gingered pumpkin sauce

Probably the most frequently asked question about the ingredients I work with is the favourite vegetable issue. Now, that's like asking a mother about her favourite child. Of course I love them all equally, goes the common protest. But then you start to think... well... those little green broad beans are so cute; asparagus is a handsome lad in the short time he bothers to poke his head out; or you remember that you haven't given a moment's thought to a parsnip for months, the poor neglected ragamuffin. Some are all sunshine and laughs, while others hide their virtues and need a lot of nurturing.

A slightly less frequent question is the one about versatility and all-round usefulness. Now, that's easy. If aubergines were kids, they'd bring you breakfast in bed, vacuum willingly, and pour your wine just before you thought of needing a refill... all the while being brainy and sporty without being a nerd or a jock. The aubergine... maybe not the favourite, but how the hell would the place run without him? Right, that's that metaphor well and truly worn out.

Perhaps because of their innate blandness, aubergines have an amazing ability to absorb flavours and to be assimilated into any style of cooking from any part of the world. Perhaps even more importantly for vegetarian cuisine, an aubergine has a wide range of textural uses. Tiny dice, large chunks, thin circles or fat ones all deliver their own character to a dish, not to mention the fun you can have with halved aubergines or the soft, gooey inside when they are roasted whole and the skin discarded. But the most useful cut of all is the lengthways slice. A roasted slice of aubergine has so often for me been the jumping-off point and the foundation of many dishes.

After you've made this recipe, and the one that follows it, try a freestyle approach. Roast some aubergine slices, then look around your kitchen to see what you might put in them. If the results are delicious, and there's a good chance they will be, send me the recipe. Or invite me round for tea.

- Start preparing the tofu for the filling: combine the honey, vinegar, chilli, soy sauce and 2 tablespoons of water to make a marinade. Add the tofu and leave for 15–30 minutes.

- Preheat the oven to 220°C/425°F/gas mark 7.

Continued on following page...

for 4

for the tofu filling
3 tbsp honey
1 tbsp rice vinegar
1 tsp chilli powder
1 tbsp soy sauce
225g/8oz firm tofu, cut into 12 slices about 5mm/¼in thick
vegetable oil, for brushing

for the aubergine and leek wraps
2 large aubergines
olive oil, for brushing
1 leek, white part only, halved lengthways and well washed

for the gingered pumpkin sauce
200g/7oz pumpkin or squash, peeled, deseeded and diced
olive oil for tossing and cooking
2 tbsp grated fresh ginger
1 fresh green chilli, finely chopped
2 garlic cloves, finely chopped
200ml/7fl oz vegetable stock
3 tbsp coconut milk
salt

for the sesame cabbage
2 tbsp olive oil
200g/7oz Savoy cabbage, inner leaves only, shredded
1 tsp coriander seeds, crushed
1 tsp mustard seeds
1 tsp black onion seeds
1 tbsp tahini
1 tbsp lemon juice
1 tbsp orange juice
salt

Continued from previous page...

- Prepare the aubergines: slice them lengthways to get 12 slices, each about 5mm/¼in thick. Brush these on both sides with olive oil and place on a baking parchment-lined oven tray. Roast for 10–12 minutes, until lightly coloured on both sides, turning once if necessary. When done, remove them from the oven, leaving it on, and trim the skin off each slice.

- At the same time, prepare the leeks. Bring a small pan of water to the boil. Separate the leaves of the leek and drop them into the water. Simmer for 10 minutes until soft. Drain and cool in cold water.

- Prepare the gingered pumpkin sauce: toss the diced pumpkin in a little olive oil in an oven dish. Season with salt and roast in the oven for 12–15 minutes, until tender and slightly caramelised.

- Heat a tablespoon of olive oil in a saucepan and fry the ginger, chilli and garlic over medium heat for 5 minutes. Add the stock and the roasted pumpkin, bring to the boil and simmer for 5 minutes. Blend to a purée, then add the coconut milk and a little salt. Set aside and reheat when required.

- Now finish the tofu for the filling: heat a wok or large frying pan and brush it with vegetable oil. Drain the tofu well, reserving the marinade. Put the pieces of tofu in the wok or pan and fry over medium heat for 2 minutes on each side, until browned.

- Add all but 2 tablespoons of the marinade and continue cooking until it has been absorbed.

- To assemble: lay the aubergine slices on a work surface and cover each with a layer of leek. Place a slice of tofu in the centre and fold up the ends of the aubergine slices to make neat parcels. Place on an oven tray, drizzle with the remaining marinade, and heat through in the oven for 5 minutes.

- Meanwhile, prepare the sesame cabbage: heat the olive oil in a wide pan or wok and stir-fry the cabbage with the 3 types of seeds for 2 minutes, then remove from the heat.

- Whisk together the tahini and citrus juices, then add some water to give it a thin pouring consistency. Stir the dressing into the cabbage and season with salt.

- Place some cabbage in the centre of each plate and pour some sauce around it. Arrange the aubergine parcels on top.

Pumpkin, courgette & cashew roti with fennel & mango salsa

for 6

for the curry filling
600g/1lb 6oz pumpkin or squash, peeled and deseeded and cut into 2cm/¾in dice
vegetable oil, for tossing and cooking
300g/11oz potato, peeled and cut into 2cm/¾in dice
1 red onion, thinly sliced
4 garlic cloves, sliced
2–4 fresh green chillies, deseeded and thinly sliced
1 tbsp grated fresh ginger
1 tbsp coriander seeds, ground
4 cloves, ground
1 tsp turmeric
½ tsp ground cinnamon
300g/11oz courgette, halved and cut into 2cm/¾in-thick slices
75g/3oz cashew nuts
1 tbsp tamarind paste or juice of 1 lime
200ml/7fl oz coconut milk
salt

for the fennel and mango salsa
2 tbsp mango chutney
½ medium fennel bulb, finely diced
2 spring onions, finely chopped
½ red pepper, deseeded and finely diced
juice of 1 lime
2 tbsp olive oil

for the roti
250g/9oz plain flour
2 tsp baking powder
large pinch of salt
2 tbsp melted butter
vegetable oil, for brushing

I don't know where roti have been all my life, but I got to 50 without eating one. What a disaster. I'll have to make up for that in the next 50. Maybe I've been holidaying in the wrong places. Roti, this unleavened flat bread rather like a thicker chapati, might have its origins in India, but it seems to have found a home in the laid-back Caribbean, where the simple pleasures of life are a notch or two higher on the daily agenda. I first ate one in St. Lucia, on a lazily blissful romantic holiday. The next that I ate was one I made myself a week later in the Ontario Snow Belt. Mine was better – ahem! – and what it lacked in idyllic surroundings was made up in the pleasure of making it from scratch. Like making a snowman in St. Lucia... you can see how that might be fun.

Curry and bread are great together, right? Well, somehow, wrapping the curry in the bread not only turns it into knife-and-fork food, but it also seems to intensify the pleasure of eating the two. Maybe it's the hungry way you devour parcelled food. Or maybe it's just one of those happy food accidents best left unanalysed.

You can make roti using any curry recipe and some thin flour tortillas, but the breads are fun to make, and shop-bought bread never tastes as good as your own. It's best to have the curry ready when you begin to cook the breads, as they don't remain fully pliable for very long. Alternatively, if you make the bread a little earlier, you can soften them again by dampening them with water and warming them for a few seconds in the oven.

Roti are usually served with a sweet chutney, often made from mango. The salsa in this recipe is a fresher, zingier way to bring those classic flavours to the dish.

- Preheat the oven to 180°C/350°F/gas mark 4.

- First make the curry filling: in an oven dish, toss the pumpkin or squash in a little vegetable oil and then roast for 20 minutes, until tender and beginning to caramelise.

- Bring a saucepan of water to the boil and drop in the diced potato. Boil for 5 minutes to partly cook the potato, then drain in a colander and set aside.

- Heat 2 tablespoons of vegetable oil in a heavy saucepan over medium heat. Add the onion and fry for 2 minutes, stirring. Add the garlic, chillies and all the spices, and cook for 2 minutes more, stirring often. Add the courgette and cashews, and fry for 5 minutes. Add the potato, pumpkin, tamarind and coconut milk. Bring back to the boil and simmer for 10 minutes, until the potato is tender and the sauce has reduced to a barely moist consistency. Season to taste with salt.

- While the curry is cooking, make the fennel and mango salsa by combining all of the ingredients in a bowl.

- Make the roti: sift the flour and baking powder together with the salt. Stir in the butter. Add 160ml/5½fl oz water and knead for a minute to make a soft dough. Cut this into 6 pieces and shape each into a ball. Leave to stand for 10 minutes.

- Place a wide, heavy pan or griddle pan over medium heat. Roll out a piece of dough very thinly to a diameter of about 24cm/9½in. Brush the top with vegetable oil and place on the pan, oiled side down. Cook for a minute, brush the top again with oil and then flip the roti over to cook for 1 minute more. Roll the next one while the first is cooking, and continue until all are cooked. Store the cooked roti under a moist towel.

- Place a warm roti on a work surface and put a generous amount of the curry filling in the centre. Fold up the near end of the roti, then fold in the sides and fold over again to make a tight parcel.

- Warm the filled roti in the oven for a minute or 2, then serve with some salsa spooned over them.

Socca crêpe of roast squash, caramelised red onion, kale & pine nuts, with tomato coriander salsa & goat's cheese cream

Socca is a flat bread from southeastern France around Nice made from gram flour, or chickpea flour, which is perhaps better known for its role in Indian cooking. Across the border, the Italians make a version called farinata. Both are street food snacks, and both vary in recipe and in thickness from place to place and source to source. I have included a version of farinata on page 251, which doesn't stray too far from its origins, while below we take a more radical approach to the French prototype.

This version marries the socca to a classic French crêpe to get a softer pancake, pliable enough to fold around a filling, in this case an autumnal combination of roast squash and kale.

I use two contrasting sauces to flavour this dish, partly for the aesthetic reason of making pretty contrasting patterns on a plate. But I also like the way that this deconstructs how the flavours come together. Instead of, say, putting goat's cheese into the filling, it is an external flavour to be taken in varying degrees with each forkful. The same goes for the tomatoes and herbs of the salsa, which gives a zingy fresh finish to what is otherwise a comfortingly intense dish.

- Preheat the oven to 180°C/350°F/gas mark 4.

- First make the socca batter: mix the flours together with the toasted cumin seeds. Add the egg and then gradually add the milk, olive oil and enough water to get a creamy pouring consistency, about 125ml/4½fl oz. Season well with salt and pepper and set aside.

- Start preparing the filling: peel the squash and discard the seeds. Chop the flesh into small dice, toss with a little olive oil and roast in the preheated oven for 15–20 minutes, until browned.

- While the squash is roasting, heat a little olive oil in a frying pan and fry the onion for 8–10 minutes, until caramelised.

- Chop the kale and add it to the pan with the ginger, and cook for 5 minutes over medium heat.

Continued on following page...

for 4

for the socca crêpes
100g/3½oz gram (chickpea) flour
50g/2oz plain flour
1 tsp cumin seeds, toasted
1 egg, lightly beaten
5 tbsp milk
1 tbsp olive oil, plus extra for brushing
salt and pepper

for the filling
¼ medium squash, such as Crown Prince, kabocha or butternut
olive oil, for tossing, brushing and cooking
1 large red onion, halved and thinly sliced
500g/1lb 2oz kale, cooked and squeezed as dry as possible
1 tbsp grated fresh ginger
1 tbsp pine nuts, toasted and coarsely chopped
salt and pepper

for the tomato coriander salsa
2 tomatoes, skinned and diced
1 spring onion, finely chopped
1 fresh green chilli, finely chopped
2 tbsp chopped fresh coriander
2 tbsp olive oil

for the goat's cheese cream
125g/4½oz fresh goat's cheese, crumbled
1 garlic clove, crushed
2 tbsp natural yoghurt
single cream, for thinning (optional)

Continued from previous page...

- Add the pine nuts and roast squash, and cook for a few minutes more, stirring to break the squash a little. Add some water if necessary to keep the filling moist. Season with salt and pepper.

- Make the socca: heat a crêpe pan over medium heat and brush it with olive oil. Pour in some of the batter and swirl to get an even covering a little thicker than a traditional crêpe. Cook for 2 minutes, until the bottom is lightly coloured, then flip the crêpe over and cook the other side for a minute, until lightly coloured. Repeat to make 4 crêpes in total.

- Place a crêpe on a work surface and put a quarter of the filling over the bottom half. Fold the top half over, then fold again to get a triangle. Repeat with the others. Place these on a baking parchment-lined oven tray and brush lightly with olive oil. Bake in the oven for 5 minutes, just to warm through.

- Make the tomato coriander salsa by combining all of the ingredients in a small bowl.

- Make the goat's cheese cream: in a food processor, blend the cheese with the garlic and yoghurt. Transfer to a bowl and stir in enough water or cream to give a pouring consistency.

- To serve, drizzle some goat's cheese cream on a plate, place a crêpe on top and spoon some of the salsa over it.

Aubergine involtini of almonds, capers, currants & sheep's cheese with cardamom-green chilli pesto

Like the previous aubergine recipe, this is based on the idea of wrapping a filling in some roasted aubergine slices. Involtini is an Italian word suggesting – as distinct from meaning – something thinly sliced and rolled around a filling. The flavouring in this version moves the dish further eastwards along the Mediterranean a little, or so it seems to my mind anyway.

- Preheat the oven to 200°C/400°F/gas mark 6.

- Cut the ends off the aubergines, and remove a slice from 2 sides of each. Cut the remaining flesh lengthways to get 12 slices about 5mm/¼in thick. Brush the slices on both sides with olive oil and place on baking parchment-lined oven trays. Roast for 12–15 minutes, until well done on each side, turning once if necessary.

- While these roast, soak the currants in the wine for 15 minutes.

- In a heavy frying pan, heat a tablespoon of olive oil over medium heat and sauté the leek for 5 minutes, until tender. Add the currants, almonds, capers and breadcrumbs, stir well and then leave to cool. Add the cheeses and season with pepper.

- Remove the aubergine slices from the oven, leaving it on, and place them on a work surface. Take a generous tablespoon of the filling, squeeze it into a cylindrical shape with your hands and place this at the base of one of the slices. Roll the slice up to form a tight parcel. Repeat with the other slices, then place them, seal side down, in an oiled oven dish.

- Make the cherry tomato sauce: heat the olive oil over low heat in a small saucepan. Add the tomatoes and garlic, and cook gently for 2–3 minutes, until the tomatoes are beginning to soften. Add 2 tablespoons of water, bring to the boil and pour this sauce over the involtini. Bake for 10–12 minutes, until warmed through.

- Meanwhile, make the pesto: put the chillies, herbs, cardamom seeds and orange zest in a food processor and blend to a fine paste. Add the olive oil and pulse briefly to get a pouring consistency.

- Serve 3 involtini per person with some of the tomato sauce clinging to them and the pesto drizzled over.

for 4

for the involtini
2 large or 3 medium aubergines
olive oil, for brushing, cooking and oiling
30g/1¼oz currants
2 tbsp dry white wine
1 leek, well washed and finely diced
75g/3oz whole blanched almonds, toasted and coarsely chopped
2 tbsp small capers, rinsed
100g/3½oz breadcrumbs, toasted
250g/9oz sheep's milk ricotta
50g/2oz hard sheep's cheese, grated
black pepper

for the cherry tomato sauce
2 tbsp olive oil
250g/9oz cherry tomatoes, quartered
2 garlic cloves, finely chopped

for the cardamom-green chilli pesto
2 fresh green chillies, deseeded and chopped
50g/2oz fresh parsley
50g/2oz fresh coriander
20 green cardamom pods, seeds only
finely grated zest of 1 orange
150ml/5fl oz olive oil

Savoy cabbage terrine of potatoes, leeks, apple & smoked cheese with balsamic beetroot syrup

The bumpy texture of Savoy cabbage leaves can make them seem an indelicate wrapping material. But when rolled flat, the inner leaves are as light as any leaf, and still have that wonderfully sweet Savoy flavour.

This is a robust, earthy terrine of winter flavours, and much more a main course loaf than delicate starter. It can be made well in advance, and reheated by placing slices flat on a baking parchment-lined oven tray in a low oven.

- At least 2 hours before you want to serve, preheat the oven to 180°C/350°F/gas mark 4.

- Cut off the green part of the leeks and trim the root ends. Slice the white parts in half lengthways. Check for dirt in the leaves and wipe clean if necessary. Place the leeks in a single layer in an oven dish. Drizzle generously with olive oil, pour over the wine and season with salt and pepper. Cover with baking parchment and bake in the oven for 20 minutes until tender.

- Meanwhile, discard the dark green outer leaves of the cabbage. Take enough of the next layers of leaves comfortably to line a 900g/2lb loaf tin with a generous overhang. Cut out any large stalk from the rest of the cabbage, halving the leaves if necessary. Bring a saucepan of water to the boil and drop in the leaves. Cook for 7–8 minutes, until quite tender. Cool the leaves in cold water, drain and dry on kitchen paper. Flatten them gently with a rolling pin and set aside.

- Bring the water back to the boil, add the potato slices and boil for 5 minutes, then transfer them to a bowl and toss with half of the butter and some salt and pepper.

- Chop 100g/3½oz of the remaining cabbage finely. Heat the remaining butter in a saucepan over medium heat. Add the cabbage and garlic, and sauté for 5 minutes, stirring often.

- Add the thyme and dill, and cook for 5 minutes more. Add the cream, bring to the boil and then remove from the heat.

Continued on following page…

for 6

8 leeks
olive oil, for drizzling
125ml/4½fl oz dry white wine
1 head of Savoy cabbage
600g/1lb 6oz potatoes, peeled and cut into slices 3mm/⅛in thick
30g/1¼oz melted butter, plus extra for greasing
3 garlic cloves, chopped
2 sprigs of fresh thyme, leaves only
1 tbsp chopped fresh
100ml/3½fl oz double cream
2 eggs, lightly beaten
100g/3½oz smoked cheese, grated
2 medium-tart apples, cored and thinly sliced
salt and pepper

for the balsamic beetroot syrup
250g/9oz beetroot, washed, cooked and peeled
200ml/7fl oz balsamic vinegar
2 tbsp maple syrup

Continued from previous page...

- When the cabbage has cooled, stir in the eggs and cheese.

- Brush the loaf tin with butter. Place a strip of baking parchment along the base of the tin and up the 2 short sides. Line the sides with cabbage leaves, overhanging the top. Cover the base with a layer of overlapping leaves.

- Place a layer of potato slices in the bottom, followed by a layer of leeks, then one of apple slices, followed by half of the cabbage and egg mixture. Repeat the layers and finish with a layer of potato. Cover this with another layer of cabbage leaves, fold over the overhanging leaves and press down firmly. Place another strip of baking parchment on top and weight it down with a plate.

- Place the loaf tin in a deep oven dish. Bring a saucepan of water to the boil and pour it into the oven dish to come halfway up the loaf tin. Put the dish in the oven to bake for 50–60 minutes. Test to make sure that the terrine is firm before removing the dish from the oven.

- While the terrine is cooking, make the balsamic beetroot syrup: chop the beetroot into small dice and put in a large saucepan with the water. Bring this to the boil and simmer for 5 minutes. Blend the beetroot and 250ml/9fl oz water to a fine purée, pass this through a fine sieve and return to the pan. Add the balsamic vinegar and maple syrup, bring to the boil and simmer until the sauce has thickened slightly. This may take 20–30 minutes. Leave the sauce to cool, when it will thicken a little more.

- When the terrine comes out of the oven, leave it to rest for 10 minutes before turning it out on to a board. Carefully cut it into slices about 2cm/¾in thick.

- To serve, drizzle some beetroot syrup on each plate and place a thick slice of terrine on top.

Roast squash flowers with feta, currants & capers in a tomato, thyme & orange sauce

I'm not a flower eater. I've never been keen on flowers in my salad, unless they are an integral part of the dish – as opposed to a garnish, in which case I'll probably order something else, thanks. I do make exceptions, out of curiosity or politeness, but the only flower I actually look forward to eating is the blossom of summer squash. If you grow courgettes, scallopini or any other such varieties, then you have a second very useful ingredient sitting on the end of each squash. Not to mention the proud male flowers standing to attention in the middle of the plant; all edible, and much more versatile than their fragile appearance would suggest.

There is some debate about whether the males or females are better to eat, and another about which it is better to eat from the point of view of the crop. In the second argument, I am neutral, waiting for permission to pick. In the first, it depends on the condition of the flowers, to some extent. Sometimes it seems the males hold up better and are easier to work with. But, as a chef, I would always opt for the females with small courgettes attached, simply because they look so good on the plate and there is a second element to their flavour and structure.

Also, while it's true that the flowers are useful in soups, risotto, frittata and summer stews, I think they are far too beautiful to be hidden away or hacked up. Stuffed with soft cheese, or feta as in this recipe, they can be deep- or shallow-fried, poached in stock or... roasted.

Serve with a little lemon-flavoured risotto, slices of grilled polenta or buttered new potatoes.

- Preheat the oven to 200°C/400°F/gas mark 6.

- Prepare the flowers by opening them gently and pulling out the stamen – if there is one in there.

- Make the filling by mixing together all of the ingredients.

- Stuff each flower about two-thirds full with the filling and twist the strands on top to close it over. Roast them on an oven tray for 7–8 minutes, until warmed through.

Continued on following page...

for 4

8–12 courgette flowers

for the filling
250g/9oz feta cheese, crumbled
100g/3½oz ricotta
2 tbsp currants
2 tbsp tiny capers, rinsed
2 tbsp finely ground almonds

for the tomato, thyme and orange sauce
6 tomatoes
100ml/3½fl oz olive oil
3 garlic cloves, finely chopped
finely grated zest of 1 orange
2 sprigs of fresh thyme, leaves only
2 sprigs of fresh oregano, leaves only
1 tbsp tomato passata
100ml/3½fl oz water or vegetable stock
salt and pepper

Continued from previous page...

- Meanwhile, make the tomato, thyme and orange sauce: bring a saucepan of water to the boil. With a sharp knife, score the base of the tomatoes with a cross and drop them into the water for 30 seconds or so. Transfer them to a bowl of cold water, then peel off the skins. Deseed the tomatoes and finely dice the flesh.

- Heat the olive oil in a small saucepan over medium heat. Add the diced tomato and garlic, and cook for 1 minute. Add the orange zest and herbs, and cook for 1 minute more. Add the passata and water or vegetable stock. Simmer for 1 minute, then remove from the heat and season with salt and pepper.

- Place the roast squash flowers in shallow bowls and spoon some of the sauce over each.

Bowls

Bowls

As much as we all need to make the effort now and then to create what I've referred to elsewhere in this book as knife and fork food, there is a very modern need too for dinner, lunch or that charming meal often referred to as supper to sometimes be a simple bowl of delicious food. It might be eaten at the family dining table, or sitting at stools around the kitchen counter. And it also has to be acknowledged that increasingly our meals are eaten while doing something else, whether that be watching the news, a favourite TV show or huddled on the couch with the lights down low as a movie begins. In comfortable company, or happily alone.

It is pointless to rail against the changes in the way people live or to insist rigidly that there is only one right way to share food. Right now, I'm starving. I've been working all day on recipes, in a borrowed house on the side of a stunningly beautiful valley in Kerry. For the last half hour or so, my stomach has been telling my mind to get to the part of the day where I feed it something comforting and rewarding. The prize at the end of the day. It's likely to be pasta with greens, tomatoes, chillies and olive oil, and I don't know yet whether I will eat at the table while staring at the mountains, half reading a book, or distracting myself with some downtime TV nonsense. I wouldn't want dinner tonight to be a challenge to make or to eat, but I do want it to taste like something I deserve, and to be nutritionally sound. I'd also like it to go well with a bottle of Malbec into which I intend to make a decent dent.

The recipes in this chapter range across the spectrum from comforting pasta through Asian-influenced noodle dishes and North African pilafs to vegetable stews and curries from here and there and nowhere very specific. Some are simple to make, while others take a bit more time. They all fulfil the brief of a meal that requires little enough attention in the eating from anything other than your tastebuds. I would go so far as to say that cradling a warm bowl in your hand, as you slurp up some highly flavoured vegetables and grains, is one of the most pleasurable ways to feed your body and soul. Primal is a word that comes to mind, in a good way. Whether you are alone or surrounded by loved ones, similarly slurping, is irrelevant. Bowl food is alright on the night... some nights.

By their very nature, the recipes are essentially flexible prototypes. With a few exceptions, once you retain the basic flavourings, spicing and seasoning, the other ingredients can be adapted to what you have to hand. No rice noodles available? Use basic egg noodles or commandeer a pasta such as tagliatelle to be Asian for a night. There are a couple of recipes featuring millet, one with wild rice and one with couscous – try swapping them around, or use rice, buckwheat or quinoa instead.

Vegetables aren't as flexible as that awful phrase 'mixed veg' on menus suggests. But you can swap one green for another, replace a cauliflower with broccoli or maybe even some roots and play around with beans, courgettes and asparagus. Just don't throw so many of them at a dish at one time that they get lost and become 'mixed'. Increase or decrease the amounts of vegetables too, or shift the emphasis from one to another as the star of a dish.

Pasta recipes, even where they specify a particular shape, are very adaptable. Making your own is always recommended, for the pleasure of doing it as much as anything, but I would counter that by trotting out the butcher, baker and candlestick-maker argument. Every traditional and vibrant community has always existed on the basis of trading, or effectively bartering, specialised skills. If you are lucky enough to live near someone who makes good pasta, support them as you would a cheesemaker or baker. That might run counter to the idyllic notion of everyone learning to make bread and jam, keep hens, grow vegetables, churn butter from the goat in the yard and knit their own socks. Ugh, did I just suggest goat butter?

A healthy food community should always have specialists. The idea of a farmer's market or any other kind of market in an old town square assumes that someone does his thing better than anyone else, and that gives him his role in the community. The collection of specialists creates the town and the town is the focal, social, cultural and economic centre of the countryside. I was brought up in a small town that is struggling now to survive against the invasion of international chain 'super' markets. The town is really too small for huge companies to be bothered with, but their model is so cheap now they could open in the back room of a country pub.

The people making a difference in the battle, and it is a very real battle, are not those trying to sell the cheap goods as cheaply as the big guys, but the one-off local artisans – a new generation trying its hand on the old main street where rents have fallen. They look like traditionalists but they are in fact ultra modern, and vital to the culture of the town. Support your local sherrif, as it were, and the baker, pasta maker, vegetable farmer, sock knitter and butter maker... so long as they use cow's milk.

(End of speech for the Macroom Urban District Council, moving smartly along through a couple more points of order, towards my dinner time. Definitely craving sprouting broccoli and chilli now.)

I haven't been very specific regarding cheese in the pasta dishes. Most will benefit from a little finely grated hard cheese or crumbled soft cheese. Completely up to you whether you do or not, and which ones you use. Occasionally, I have specified sheep's cheese because I think it works particularly well with a dish. I find myself very drawn to sheep's cheese these days. It's got something to do with the clean, sweetly sharp flavour in general, and more to do with having access, in Ireland, to Cratloe Hills mature hard cheese and Knockalara fresh cheese; and, in Canada, to Monforte's amazing Toscana. Outside of those jurisdictions, try to find a local equivalent before reverting to imported pecorino or manchego; both damn fine cheese styles, it has to be said. Same goes for cow's cheese. Find a local suitable cheese before opting for Parmesan, unless you live in northern Italy, in which case you probably have loads of alternatives anyway.

One last goat reference before I make dinner. I'm starving, but a trooper for finishing work before eating. To indicate the milk source of cheese, I use the phrase 'sheep's cheese' etc. Café Paradiso once got involved in a marketing organisation catering event, and the company asked us to use the phrase 'ewe's milk cheese' (pronounced 'yo's' by the cognescenti) rather than 'sheep's cheese'. Pondering the ludicrousness of it, I wondered what we might call goat's cheese then. The answer to which is nanny's milk, of course. My mother, a granny known as Nanny, wasn't amused. You should have seen her nose wrinkle.

Fresh pasta ribbons in walnut & sheep's cheese sauce with maple-braised endive

What the British and Germans call chicory and everyone else knows as Belgian endive is a peculiar vegetable that comes from a weird growing process. Basically, it is a shoot that sprouts from the roots of a chicory plant after it has been dug up and buried again in loose soil in a dark place. The shoots that sprout on the second growth are allowed only a tiny peak at faint light, resulting in white leaves with a hint of green or purple at the tips. The flavour is milder and less bitter than that of the dark green leaves of the original chicory, but the dominant characteristic is still a slightly bitter one.

The endive is a good foil for what is a very rich, but simple, pasta sauce. Although you can serve it with any pasta you like, I think it's best with a short, wide fresh noodle. The best way to get these, besides making your own, is to buy some pappardelle or lasagne sheets and cut them into strips.

- Prepare the maple-braised endive: cut the chicory in half lengthways, remove the cores and slice the leaves into pieces about 2cm/¾in wide and 4cm/1½in long.

- Heat the butter in a wide, heavy pan over medium heat. Add the leaves and sauté for 1 minute, then cover with baking parchment and simmer for 10–15 minutes, until the chicory is tender. Check occasionally and add a little water if necessary to prevent sticking. Add the maple syrup, orange zest and parsley, remove the pan from the heat and season with black pepper.

- Meanwhile, make the sauce: heat the olive oil in a wide, heavy pan over medium heat. Add the onion and sauté for 5–7 minutes, stirring, until it is beginning to caramelise. Add the garlic and cook for 2 minutes. Stir in the walnuts and ricotta and remove from the heat.

- At the same time, bring a large saucepan of water to the boil. Cut the pasta into short pieces about 1cm/½in wide and 4cm/1½in long, and drop these into the water. Simmer for a few minutes, until tender. Drain, leaving some of the cooking water clinging to the pasta. Stir the pasta into the sauce, and season with salt and pepper.

- Serve the pasta in shallow bowls, with some braised endive on top and the grated cheese sprinkled over each portion.

for 4

400g/14oz fresh
  pappardelle or lasagne
  sheets
40g/½oz hard sheep's
  cheese, finely grated
salt and pepper

for the maple-braised endive
2 heads of chicory (Belgian
  endive)
30g/1¼oz butter
2 tbsp maple syrup
finely grated zest of
  1 orange
2 tbsp chopped fresh
  parsley

for the walnut and sheep's cheese sauce
1 tbsp olive oil
1 red onion, halved and
  thinly sliced
3 garlic cloves, sliced
100g/3½oz walnuts, finely
  chopped
200g/7oz sheep's milk
  ricotta

Orecchiette with broad beans & baby courgettes

for 4

600–800g/1lb 6oz–1¾lb
  broad beans
500g/1lb 2oz orecchiette
salt and coarsely ground
  black pepper
30g/1¼oz butter
100g/3½oz small
  courgettes, thinly sliced
4 medium shallots, finely
  chopped
2 garlic cloves, finely
  chopped
2 tbsp marjoram leaves
60g/2½oz hard sheep's
  cheese, finely grated

The only labour in this simple but classic summer pasta is in podding and peeling the broad beans. Seeing as it's such a lovely evening, do the first part outside in the sunshine with a glass of something cold and bubbly.

Now that you've gone to the trouble of peeling fresh broad beans, do also make sure to get some small courgettes, about as thick as your big finger, or your thumb at a stretch.

Sliced into very thin discs, they will be full of sunshine taste rather than loaded with water.

- Pop the broad beans out of their pods. Bring a large saucepan of water to the boil, drop in the beans and simmer for 1 minute. Remove the beans and drop them into a bowl of cold water. The skins can now be easily slipped off and the beans will split in half.

- Bring the water back to the boil. Add some salt and drop in the orecchiette. Simmer for 10–12 minutes, until almost tender.

- Meanwhile, in a deep, wide pan, melt half of the butter and add the broad beans, courgettes, shallots and garlic. Sauté for 2–3 minutes, until the vegetables are almost tender.

- When the pasta is almost done, strain it into a colander and quickly add it to the vegetable pan with some of its cooking water still clinging to it. Add the marjoram and simmer for 2–3 minutes more, until the pasta is tender and the water has almost evaporated.

- Add the cheese and remaining butter, and season well with salt and coarsely ground black pepper. Stir briefly to melt the cheese.

Spaghettini with cime di rapa, garlic, chillies, orange, feta & breadcrumbs

Although this dish brings together one of my favourite flavour combinations – dark greens, chillies, a touch of sweetness and a sharp cheese – it does so in a slightly unusual way. The spices are delivered in a crunchy crumb mixture sprinkled on top, giving a lively contrast with the greens, pasta and feta. Any greens will work here, but the stronger ones will stand up best to the spices and cheese. Try kale, sprouting broccoli or Brussels sprouts, if you can't get cime di rapa (the leaves of a turnip relative, also known as broccoli rabe). The instructions are for fresh, very thin pasta, so adjust the timing if using dried instead.

• Bring a large saucepan of water to the boil for the pasta and keep it at a simmer.

• In a wide pan, heat a tablespoon of the olive oil over low heat and fry the garlic and chillies for 2 minutes, stirring, until the garlic is lightly coloured. Remove from the pan and set aside.

• Put the bread in a food processor and pulse to get coarse breadcrumbs. Heat another tablespoon of olive oil in the pan and fry the crumbs over medium heat until crisped. Stir into the garlic and chilli mix.

• Add the remaining 2 tablespoons of olive oil to the pan and add the cime di rapa. Fry over medium heat, stirring and occasionally adding a little of the pasta water, for 4–5 minutes, until tender.

• When the greens are almost done, drop the pasta into the water and simmer for 2–3 minutes, until just done.

• Drain and add the pasta to the greens with the orange zest and half of the crumbled feta. Stir briefly so that the feta partly melts, then serve in shallow bowls. Top each with some of the spiced breadcrumbs and finish with the remaining feta.

for 4

450g/1lb fresh spaghettini
4 tbsp olive oil
8 fat garlic cloves, thickly sliced
2 fresh red chillies, halved lengthways, deseeded and sliced at an angle
2 thick slices of day-old bread, crusts removed
500g/1lb 2 oz cime di rapa, coarsely chopped
finely grated zest of 2 oranges
200g/7oz feta cheese, crumbled

Linguine in shallot & tarragon pesto with shredded artichokes, aubergine & almonds

for 4

250ml/9fl oz olive oil, plus
   extra for brushing
4–6 small shallots, finely
   chopped
50g/2oz whole blanched
   almonds
50g/2oz fresh tarragon
50g/2oz fresh parsley
60g/2½oz hard sheep's
   cheese, finely grated
1 medium aubergine
4 medium globe
   artichokes, prepared and
   cooked (see page 98)
450g/1lb fresh linguine
2 tomatoes, deseeded and
   finely diced
salt and pepper

I could say that this dish is a great way to use up leftover artichokes, but who has leftover artichokes lying around? Restaurants do, that's who. I made this one Sunday night while raiding the Café Paradiso kitchen. The artichokes and pesto were just sitting there begging to be eaten, so I obliged. It's rather hard work but worth the trouble, even if you have to start from scratch with the artichokes. At a stretch, and after a good rinsing, I think it's safe to say you could also use good-quality bottled artichokes.

- Heat a tablespoon of the olive oil in a small frying pan over medium heat and sauté the shallot for 2 minutes, stirring. Cover with baking parchment, lower the heat and stew for 10 minutes.

- Put the almonds in a food processor and pulse until roughly chopped. Remove half of the almonds and set aside.

- Add the cooked shallots and herbs to the almonds left in the food processor and blend to a smooth paste. Add 200ml/7fl oz olive oil and blend briefly. Transfer to a bowl and stir in 40g/1½oz of the cheese.

- Preheat the oven to 200°C/400°F/gas mark 6.

- Slice the aubergine in half lengthways, then cut each half into semi-circles about 5mm/¼in thick. Brush lightly with olive oil and place on a baking parchment-lined oven tray. Roast for 10–12 minutes, turning once if necessary, until browned and crisp. Set aside.

- In a deep wide pan, heat the remaining olive oil over medium heat. Slice the cooked artichokes thinly lengthways, add them to the pan and fry, stirring, for 5 minutes. Stir in the reserved almonds and lower the heat.

- While the artichokes cook, bring a large saucepan of water to the boil and cook the pasta for 3–4 minutes, until just tender. Drain in a colander and add it to the artichokes, along with the aubergine and diced tomato. Add enough pesto to coat the pasta generously. Stir to mix everything well, season with salt and pepper and serve immediately, with the remaining cheese sprinkled on top.

Pappardelle with Brussels sprouts, leeks & truffle cream

Whole Brussels sprouts are here sliced into discs, and when these are sautéed some break up into separate leaves and mingle with the sauce while more remain whole. It's a nice effect, if you enjoy that sort of detail.

Truffle oil gets some bad press, but it is a wonderfully intense flavour source to have in your cupboard, and not at all expensive when you factor in how many servings you get from a bottle. Make sure you buy a light oil, such as sunflower or a delicate olive, which has been flavoured with white truffle. Learn to use just enough to give the intensity of flavour you want without doing too much tasting from the pan, as this will usually result in overkill and some turned-up noses at the table.

The recipe calls for fresh pasta, but you can, of course, use dried too, allowing for the longer cooking time needed.

- Bring a large saucepan of water to the boil.

- In a wide pan, melt the butter and sauté the leek, Brussels sprouts and garlic for 5–7 minutes, stirring often, over medium heat.

- Drop the pasta into the boiling water, stirring until the water comes back to the boil, then reduce the heat and simmer for 3–4 minutes, until the pasta is just tender. Drain the pasta into a colander and shake off most of the water.

- Meanwhile, add the white wine to the sprouts pan and cook for a minute or 2, then add the cream. Bring to the boil and simmer for a minute. Stir in the cheese, nutmeg, truffle oil and some salt and coarsely ground black pepper. Remove from the heat. The sauce should be quite moist. Check for seasoning and strength of truffle flavour, and adjust if necessary.

- Divide the pappardelle between 4 warmed bowls and top with some of the vegetables and sauce. Use tongs to combine the sauce and pasta, and serve immediately.

for 4

15g/½oz butter
1 leek, halved, well washed and sliced at an angle
200g/7oz Brussels sprouts, cut into 5mm/¼in-thick slices
2 garlic cloves, sliced
450g/1lb fresh pappardelle
100ml/3½fl oz dry white wine
200ml/7fl oz double cream
30g/1¼oz hard sheep's cheese or Parmesan, finely grated
large pinch of freshly grated nutmeg
2 tsp truffle oil
salt and pepper

Pasta with aubergines, honey, dates, pistachio & feta

for 4

2 tbsp olive oil
2 long Asian aubergines
1 red onion, thinly sliced
2 garlic cloves, thinly sliced
1 tsp cumin seeds
1 fresh red chilli, deseeded
  and thinly sliced
2 tbsp shelled pistachio
  nuts
200g/7oz dried pasta, such
  as farfalle or broken
  strips of pappardelle
4 dried dates, halved and
  thinly sliced
1 tbsp honey
100g/3½oz feta cheese
1 lime, for squeezing
salt and pepper

Despite occasional attempts to make it part of my regular behaviour, I've never quite taken to blogging. When I feel like making an excuse for that, I tell myself it has to do with the sense of whistling your sweetness to the desert air, as a primary teacher used to put it when he felt he was dispensing knowledge in the presence of disinterested heathens. Somehow, that pretty phrase has stuck in my head.

One of my irregular blogs on the Café Paradiso website turned out not to be desert whistling. I had written about my nascent interest in bees and honey, and particularly my interest in working with honey in savoury dishes. This time, someone whistled back, and in a very inspiring way, suggesting I try aubergines with honey. It was news to me, though I have since learnt that it is a common pairing in parts of the Eastern Mediterranean.

Storing the suggestion away at the back of my mind for months, it bubbled up one evening when a friend of my girlfriend Maureen, going temporarily by the name of 'Eggplant Lady', brought over three different varieties of aubergine. We ate a few small courses, each based on aubergine, over a couple of hours, finishing with this dish. It was inspired by the memory of the suggestion, by the need to eat a carbohydrate course and by Maureen's search through the cupboards for more things that might, just might, go with aubergine.

It is an incredibly rich dish with soft textures and salty, spicy, sweet and savoury flavours. Use any wide, flat but not too long type of pasta – we used farfalle because we had it, but torn pappardelle is even better. A small portion goes a long way, each bite offering long, intense and surprisingly balanced taste sensations. The feta tones down the sweetness of the honey and dates, and the chilli cuts through the richness.

If you can't get long, thin aubergines, use any aubergine cut into strips. There will be pieces with no skin to hold them together, but the flavour will be the same.

• Heat the olive oil in a wide pan or wok over medium heat. Cut the aubergines in half lengthways and then into strips about 5cm/2in long. Toss these in the oil with the onion and fry for 1 minute. Add the garlic, cumin and chilli, and continue frying, stirring often, for 7–8 minutes, until the aubergine is browned and softened. Add the pistachios and fry for 1 minute more.

- At the same time, bring a saucepan of water to the boil and cook the pasta until it's just tender, about 3–4 minutes, then drain in a colander.

- Add the pasta to the vegetables with the dates, honey, a pinch of salt and a generous sprinkling of coarsely ground black pepper. Stir briefly and divide between 4 bowls. Crumble the feta over each, squeeze a little lime juice on top and serve.

Rigatoni with green onion, capers, fennel & courgette

for 4

500g/1lb 2oz dried rigatoni
4 tbsp olive oil
1 medium fennel bulb
2 medium courgettes
2 garlic cloves, sliced
6 spring onions, thinly
   sliced at a sharp angle
1 tbsp tiny capers, rinsed
50g/2oz hard cheese, finely
   grated
salt and pepper

In a way, this is what you might call a 'pull-back' dish. Throwing these ingredients together for a quick supper, I would be very likely to add a green chilli too and then ruin the elegant and coolly pale green effect by chucking in a few cherry tomatoes as well. The chilli would add a sprightly kick, so go right ahead if you're that way inclined, but the tomato would take the dish off in another direction. Resist: if I can, you can too. I've included in the ingredients a little hard cheese, to be served with the finished dish. A sprinkling of finely crumbled feta is also great with this.

- Bring a large saucepan of water to the boil, add some salt and drop in the pasta. Bring back to a simmer and cook until the pasta is tender, about 12 minutes usually. Drain into a colander and shake off most of the water.

- Meanwhile, heat 2 tablespoons of the olive oil over medium heat in a deep, wide pan. Saving the green fennel fronds, quarter the fennel bulb, cut out the core and slice the rest thinly. Add the fennel to the pan and sauté for 3 minutes, stirring often.

- Slice the courgettes into matchsticks, add them to the pan with the garlic and sauté for 2 minutes more. Then add the spring onions, fennel fronds, capers and remaining olive oil. Season with salt and pepper and remove from the heat.

- Stir the pasta into the vegetables and serve in shallow warmed bowls, with the cheese sprinkled over.

Maple-glazed tofu
with rice noodles &
kai-lan in a miso broth

The preparation of this highly spiced but clean-flavoured dish is essentially in two parts – the earlier leisurely making of broth and marinade, followed by a pot-juggling exercise as everything comes together at the end. This kind of activity is the bread and butter of restaurant kitchens, but it can be a cause of stress at home. The main difference is that while you might serve 10 or 20 of these in an evening's service from a restaurant kitchen, you are usually only making one or two at a time, and it becomes a routine exercise to get the timing right.

The kai-lan (Chinese kale) and noodles set the timing. Before you cook the greens, make sure everything else is definitely going to be ready when they are. If you don't have a pan large enough to hold all the tofu slices at once, preheat an oven to medium heat and fry the tofu in batches, holding the cooked ones in the oven. You might even want to cook them all before you start on the greens, but don't get too far ahead of yourself. If you can't get kai-lan, use another sprouting green, such as broccoli or rapini, or even one of the choi family.

Out of long habit, I would use sambal oelek, the Indonesian chilli and garlic sauce, in the marinade. Any commercial chilli sauce will do the job, so use the one you are used to. Miso too is a personal issue. I tend to favour a medium dark one, usually made from rice. Although full-flavoured and salty, it's not quite as strong as the darker barley miso.

for 4

200g/7oz flat rice noodles
1 tbsp vegetable oil
300g/11oz kai-lan
  (Chinese kale)
3 spring onions, thinly
  sliced at an angle

for the broth

1 large onion, chopped
2 carrots, peeled and
  chopped
2 celery sticks, chopped
60g/2½oz fresh ginger,
  thinly sliced
1 whole fresh chilli
4 garlic cloves, peeled
1 bunch of fresh coriander,
  including stalks
2 tbsp soy sauce
3 tbsp red miso

for the maple-glazed tofu

3 tbsp maple syrup
4 tbsp soy sauce
2 tsp rice vinegar
1 tbsp chilli sauce
250g/9oz firm tofu
vegetable oil, for brushing

- First make the broth: in a large saucepan, bring 1 litre/1¾ pints of water to the boil. Add the onion, carrot, celery, ginger, chilli, garlic and coriander. Simmer gently, uncovered, for 30 minutes. Leave to stand for a further 30 minutes.

- While it is standing, prepare the maple-glazed tofu: mix together the maple syrup, soy sauce, vinegar and chilli sauce.

- Slice the tofu into 16 slices about 1cm/½in thick. Place the tofu in the liquid and leave to marinate for 20 minutes.

Continued on following page...

Continued from previous page…

- Heat a heavy frying pan over medium heat or preheat a medium grill and brush the pan or the tofu slices lightly with vegetable oil. Add the tofu slices and fry for 2–3 minutes on each side, until lightly coloured. Pour in most of the marinade and continue frying, swirling the pan to make sure that the tofu is coated with the marinade, which will stick to the tofu as a glaze. Add more marinade as you see fit.

- At the same time, bring a saucepan of water to the boil and cook the noodles according to the packet instructions. This usually means simmering over very low heat for 8–10 minutes. Drain in a colander.

- Finish the broth: strain out the vegetables through a sieve, returning the broth to the pan. Add the soy sauce.

- Put the miso in a bowl and stir in a few tablespoons of the broth to get a smooth pouring consistency. Bring the broth back to the boil, whisk in the miso and hold the broth at a low simmer.

- Heat 1 tablespoon of vegetable oil in a wide pan over high heat. Add the kai-lan and sauté for 4–5 minutes, occasionally adding a splash of the broth.

- To serve, place some noodles in warmed bowls. Using tongs, lift the kai-lan from the broth and place on top of the noodles. Ladle some broth over each portion, top with the slices of glazed tofu and finally sprinkle over the spring onions.

Grilled ravioli of cavolo nero & almonds in sweet spiced citrus butter

for 4–6 as a starter or 2–3 as a main course

for the pasta
200g/7oz very fine durum
 wheat flour
¼ tsp salt
1 egg, plus 2 extra egg
 yolks

for the filling
4 tbsp whole blanched
 almonds
250g/9oz cavolo nero
 (black kale)
50g/2oz ricotta
60g/2½oz hard cheese,
 finely grated
½ tsp paprika
salt and pepper

*for the sweet spiced citrus
butter*
rind of 1 lemon and
 1 orange, in large strips,
 plus the juice of ½ the
 lemon and ½ the orange
125g/4½oz butter,
 softened
¼ tsp ground cinnamon
¼ tsp freshly grated
 nutmeg

Because I often find spinach ravioli disappointing, in that they seem to be more about the creamy cheese element than the green, I've tried in this recipe to reverse that effect. It's a simple dish, focused on the pasta filling, which is all about the cavolo nero – black kale – a densely chewy and highly flavoured green, not easily dominated by a little cheese. Then the ravioli are served in a citrus butter, subtly flavoured with the sweet spices, cinnamon and nutmeg. To get the desired concentration of kale, squeeze it as dry as possible after boiling and chop it as finely as you would a bunch of herbs. For the hard cheese, use a mature, well-flavoured and slightly sweet one, either from cows' or sheep's milk.

- First make the pasta: sift the flour into a bowl with the salt, add the egg and extra yolks with 1–1½ tablespoons water and bring them all together. Knead for a minute, then leave the dough to rest for 10 minutes under a cloth.

- While the dough is resting, make the filling: put the almonds in a food processor and chop finely. Set aside 1 tablespoon of the almonds.

- Pull the cavolo nero leaves from their stalks. Bring a saucepan of water to the boil and cook them for 5 minutes. Drain and cool in cold water. Drain again and squeeze dry. Add to the almonds in the food processor and blend to chop finely. Transfer to a bowl and stir in the ricotta and half of the hard cheese. Season with the paprika and a little salt and pepper.

- Pass the dough through a pasta machine, then fold it and pass it through again. Repeat 2–3 more times, each time lowering the setting to get a thinner sheet of dough, finishing on the second-lowest setting.

- Place a sheet of dough on a work surface. Take a teaspoon of the filling, squeeze it into a tight ball and place it on the dough. Repeat with more filling, spacing them about 2cm/¾in apart. Brush the pasta with water and place another sheet on top. Press this down, making sure there are no air bubbles and that the 2 sheets are well joined. Use a ravioli cutter or knife to cut out square ravioli. Store these under a damp towel until needed.

- Make the sweet spiced citrus butter: put the citrus juices in a small pan with 100ml/3½fl oz water. Bring to the boil, add the rind and simmer to reduce the liquid by half. Discard the rind and pour the juices into a shallow, heatproof bowl. Stir in the butter, cinnamon and nutmeg.

- Preheat a grill to high. Bring a large saucepan of water to the boil and drop in the ravioli to simmer for 5 minutes. Place the bowl of flavoured butter on top of the pan while the ravioli cook. As the ravioli are cooked, lift them out of the water and put into the butter to keep warm.

- Place the ravioli on plates, pouring some of the butter over each portion. Sprinkle on the remaining cheese and put the plates under the grill for a minute or 2, until the cheese melts. Serve the ravioli with the reserved finely chopped almonds scattered over.

Broad bean & feta mezzaluna in wild garlic butter with roasted asparagus, red onion & hazelnuts

for 4

for the broad bean and feta filling
400g/14oz podded fresh broad beans
75g/3oz feta or fresh sheep's cheese, crumbled
1 tbsp chopped fresh basil
50g/2oz breadcrumbs
freshly ground pepper

for the pasta
200g/7oz very fine durum wheat flour, plus extra for dusting
¼ tsp salt
1 egg, plus 2 extra egg yolks

for the wild garlic butter
1 handful of wild garlic leaves
115g/4oz butter, softened

for the roasted vegetables
2 tbsp hazelnuts
2 red onions, halved and thinly sliced
olive oil, for tossing and drizzling
pinch of salt
12 asparagus spears
2 tsp sherry vinegar

This is indeed exactly what it looks like – an excuse to put broad beans, asparagus and wild garlic together in a dish. Not for the first time and not for the last. They're easy company; you start a sentence with one of them in the room and before you know it you've written that combination out again and they're all having a grand old time.

Mezzaluna is ravioli in the shape of a half-moon. Mezzaluna, literally. This time I've given a recipe for making your own pasta, as I think mezzaluna or ravioli are best with a fairly thin pasta. If you can buy one locally, go ahead; otherwise, buy a pasta machine.

The weight for broad beans assumes you've podded enough whole beans to get 400g/14oz, probably about 1kg/2lb 2oz of whole pods. And, yes, of course you can use frozen ones if you need to.

- First make the filling: bring a saucepan of water to the boil, drop in the broad beans and simmer for 5 minutes. Drain and cool in a bowl of cold water. Drain again, then peel off the skins.

- Put the peeled broad beans in a food processor with the feta and basil. Pulse to get a coarse mash. Transfer to a bowl and stir in enough breadcrumbs to get a firm texture. Season with black pepper and keep in the fridge until needed.

- Make the pasta: sift the flour into a bowl with the salt, add the egg and extra yolks with 1–1½ tablespoons of water and bring them all together. Knead for a minute, then leave the dough to rest for 10 minutes under a cloth.

- Pass it through a pasta machine, then fold it and pass it through again. Repeat 2–3 more times, each time lowering the setting to get a thinner sheet of dough, finishing on the second-lowest setting.

- Cut circles of dough 6cm/2½in in diameter. Place a teaspoon of filling in the centre of each circle. Brush the edges with water and fold the pasta to make a half-moon shape, ensuring there is no air pocket inside and pressing the edges to form a seal. Place the mezzaluna on a lightly floured tray and cover with a damp cloth until ready to cook.

- Prepare the wild garlic butter: bring a saucepan of water to the boil and drop in the wild garlic for a few seconds. Drain in a sieve, cool under cold running water and squeeze the garlic dry. Chop it finely and stir it into the softened butter.

- Preheat the oven to 150°C/300°F/gas mark 2.

- Roast the hazelnuts on an oven tray for 10–15 minutes. Put them in a tea towel and rub vigorously to remove as much of their skin as possible. Chop the peeled hazelnuts to a coarse crumb texture in the food processor.

- Turn the oven up to 200°C/400°F/gas mark 6.

- Toss the red onions with a little olive oil and a pinch of salt on an oven tray. Roast for 10–12 minutes, until beginning to colour and crisp.

- Snap the tough ends off the asparagus and cut the rest into pieces about 4cm/1½in long. Lay the asparagus on top of the onion, drizzle over a little more olive oil and roast for 5 minutes more, until the asparagus is tender but still crisp. Stir in the sherry vinegar and remove the tray from the oven.

- While the vegetables are roasting, bring a large saucepan of water to the boil. Drop in the mezzaluna to simmer for 3–4 minutes. Place the butter in a shallow, heatproof bowl over the pan. When the pasta is cooked, lift them out with a slotted spoon and slide them into the melting butter.

- To serve, put the mezzaluna in shallow bowls or rimmed plates and place some roasted vegetables on top. Sprinkle over some of the chopped hazelnuts and spoon a little more melted wild garlic butter over each dish.

Caraway-roasted roots & millet in maple & apple cider butter with spiced pecan salsa

Roasted root vegetables braised in apple cider harks back to what seems like very old English flavours... a winter stew for cold evenings. Caraway, a perennially unfashionable spice that must have once been the essence of exotica, emphasises that sense. I like my comfort food with an edge, and I like my traditions alive and singing, so I've added a crunchy mix of chillies, pecans and herbs to give this one a kick. The millet is cooked separately and stirred into the cooked roots. You could also serve the grain under – rather than in – the stew.

- Preheat the oven to 200°C/400°F/gas mark 6.

- Toss the red onion in a little olive oil in an oven dish, and roast for 5 minutes. Remove from the oven.

- Bring a large saucepan of water to the boil. Peel the vegetables and chop them at an angle into bite-size chunks. Put the swede in the boiling water and simmer for 5 minutes, then add the carrots. Simmer for 2 minutes, then add the parsnips and simmer for 2 minutes more.

- Drain in a colander and stir the vegetables together with the roast onion. Add the 2 tablespoons of olive oil, garlic, thyme and caraway seeds, and season well with salt.

- Put the dish back in the oven and roast the vegetables for 20 minutes, until they are beginning to caramelise. Add the cider vinegar and cider, cover the vegetables loosely with baking parchment and continue to roast for 10–15 minutes more, until the they are tender and the sauce has reduced a little. Remove from the oven, discard the thyme sprigs and stir in the maple syrup and butter.

- At the same time, for the millet: heat the olive oil in a small saucepan over medium heat. Add the millet and toast it, stirring often, for 5 minutes. Add 280ml/10fl oz boiling water and the salt, cover the pan, lower the heat and simmer for 15 minutes.

- Make the salsa by combining all of the ingredients.

- Stir the millet into the roots and serve immediately in individual bowls. Spoon some of the salsa over each portion.

for 4

1 red onion, halved and thinly sliced
2 tbsp olive oil, plus extra for tossing
400g/14oz swede
400g/14oz carrots
300g/11oz parsnips
8 garlic cloves, halved
2 sprigs of fresh thyme
1 tbsp caraway seeds
2 tbsp cider vinegar
150ml/5fl oz apple cider
2 tbsp maple syrup
45g/1¾oz butter
salt

for the toasted millet
1 tbsp olive oil
140g/4¾oz millet
pinch of salt

for the spiced pecan salsa
100g/3½oz pecans, thinly sliced
2 fresh red chillies, deseeded and thinly sliced
2 spring onions, thinly sliced
2 tbsp chopped fresh coriander
2 tbsp chopped fresh parsley
finely grated zest and juice of 1 lime

Samphire in lemon–saffron butter with celeriac & hazelnut ravioli and roast cherry tomatoes

for 4

300g/11oz samphire
12 cherry tomatoes, halved

for the filling
200g/7oz peeled celeriac
50g/2oz hazelnuts, lightly
   toasted in a dry pan
50g/2oz ricotta
large pinch of freshly
   grated nutmeg
salt and pepper

for the pasta
200g/7oz very fine durum
   wheat flour
¼ tsp salt
1 egg, plus 2 extra egg
   yolks

for the lemon-saffron butter
1 lemon
100ml/3½fl oz dry white
   wine
large pinch of saffron
   threads
75g/3oz unsalted butter,
   softened

Due to its growing popularity on restaurant menus, samphire is becoming a high-value crop that can be bought at market stalls during its short season in the early months of summer. It is a unique vegetable, with characteristics of both the sea and the land, and it grows wild in the marshy parts of certain beaches. As much as I'd like to say go pick your own, I'd be on weak ground – marshy, even – as I've never had to do that. Nor do I know where to find it. My only source of the stuff doesn't divulge such valuable information. So get hold of it any way you can.

Because samphire is quite salty – in a good way – it works well with rich accompaniments. That alone is a good characteristic of a green vegetable – one that encourages you to eat rich food with it. So, while this is very much a recipe to show off the samphire, it would also work well with asparagus if samphire eludes you. Or, in winter you could flip the whole dish around and think of it as a celeriac ravioli recipe that could be garnished with a few rocket leaves.

- Trim the samphire of any woody stem ends, and put it in a large bowl of cold water to soak for 20–30 minutes.

- Meanwhile, preheat the oven to 180°C/350°F/gas mark 4.

- Make the filling: chop the celeriac into 2cm/¾in dice and boil or steam it until tender. Place the cooked celeriac on an oven tray and place in the oven to dry out for 10–15 minutes. Leaving the oven on, mash the celeriac and put it in a bowl to cool.

- Chop 1 tablespoon of the hazelnuts coarsely and reserve. Put the rest in a food processor, chop them finely and stir them into the celeriac. Add the ricotta and nutmeg and season with salt and pepper.

- To make the pasta: sift the flour into a bowl with the salt, add the egg and extra yolks with 2 teaspoons of water and bring them all together with your hands to form a dough. Knead for a minute, then leave the dough to rest under a cloth.

- Prepare the lemon saffron butter: pare the rind of the lemon in wide strips. Squeeze the juice of the lemon into a small saucepan, add the wine and bring to the boil. Drop in the lemon rind and saffron, and simmer for 30 seconds. Remove and discard the rind. Put the softened butter in a heatrproof, shallow bowl and whisk in the lemon juice and wine.

- Pass the dough through a pasta machine with the rollers at the widest setting, then fold it and pass it through again. Do this 3–4 times, reducing the machine setting each time.

- Place a sheet of dough on a work surface. Put teaspoonfuls of the filling on the dough, spaced about 2cm/¾in apart. Brush the pasta with water and place another sheet on top. Press this down, making sure there are no air bubbles and that the 2 sheets are well joined. Use a ravioli cutter or knife to cut out square ravioli. Store these under a damp towel until needed.

- Bring a large saucepan of water to the boil. Drop in the ravioli and simmer for 3–5 minutes, until the pasta is just done. Place the butter bowl on top of the pan to keep it warm. Remove the ravioli and drop them into the lemon butter to keep them warm.

- Bring the water back to the boil and cook the samphire for 30 seconds.

- While the ravioli are cooking, put the tomatoes on an oven tray, sprinkle with olive oil and salt and place in the oven to roast for 5 minutes.

- To serve, place 3 or 4 ravioli in each of 4 rimmed plates or shallow bowls. Pile some samphire on each portion and dress with a generous amount of the warm butter. Place a few tomato halves and their juices on top, and garnish with the reserved chopped hazelnuts.

Chestnut & sheep's cheese ravioli with kale in pumpkin broth

for 4 as a starter or 2 as a main course

250g/9oz pumpkin or squash, peeled, deseeded and diced
4 garlic cloves, peeled
olive oil, for tossing
1 tbsp maple syrup
800ml/29fl oz vegetable stock
1 sprig of fresh rosemary
rind of 1 lemon, in large strips
large pinch of cayenne pepper
100g/3½oz kale
nutmeg, for grating
salt and pepper

for the ravioli
100g/3½oz very fine durum wheat flour
2 egg yolks

for the filling
150g/5oz chestnuts, cooked and chopped
2 tbsp sherry
115g/4oz fresh sheep's cheese or ricotta
25g/1oz hard sheep's cheese, grated

For the purpose of this dish and any other where the chestnuts will be mashed, chopped, puréed or turned into stuffings, the best way to buy chestnuts – weighing up all the pros and cons – is to get those little vacuum packs of peeled and cooked ones. I'm not generally one to be advocating that people buy prepared products when there is so much fun to be had preparing your own. However, buying fresh chestnuts is a badly stacked lottery. I still take a gamble on fresh ones once in a blue moon.

I have an alter ego who is a really good gambler. He can see around corners, and makes a living by knowing when to hang tough and when to throw a big stash at the pot. My innate small town shopkeeper mentality prevents me joining him in his glamorous lifestyle. But I test out the theory by occasionally investing some money in casinos, and at other times buying fresh chestnuts at a farmer's market. Let me tell you that I have a lot more success in the casinos.

There is no way to tell how much chestnut you will get from a kilo bag of 'chestnuts'. Some of the mouldy ones you will find as you cut your fingers off trying to get them out of their shells. Others you may not discover until you're on stage three of the process, whether that be boiling or roasting. The good ones are wonderful, but the skin will stick mockingly to those. If you insist on buying fresh, I didn't tell you to, OK? And buy a truckload, just in case.

- To make the ravioli: sift the flour into a bowl with a good pinch of salt, add the egg yolks and 2 teaspoons of water, and bring them all together with your hands to form a dough. Knead for a minute, then leave the dough to rest under a cloth while you make the filling.

- For the filling: put the chestnuts in a saucepan with the sherry and a tablespoon of the vegetable stock. Simmer over low heat for a few minutes, until the liquids have evaporated. Mash the chestnuts, leave to cool a little, and stir in the cheeses. Season with salt and pepper.

- Pass the rested pasta dough through a pasta machine with the rollers at the widest setting, then fold it and pass it through again. Do this 3–4 times. Cut the dough in half and fold it until you have 2 equal-sized pieces about 2x10cm/¾x4in. Continue to pass these through the pasta machine, reducing the thickness of the sheet each time by adjusting the rollers. After the lowest setting you should have two sheets of equal length and about 7cm/2¾in wide.

- Arrange 12 separate teaspoons of filling on 1 sheet with about 3cm/1¼in between each teaspoon of filling. Dampen the uncovered pasta with water. Place the other sheet of pasta on top, pressing down around the mixture to form rough ravioli shapes. Make sure not to leave any air pockets. Cut into 12 individual ravioli and cover them with a damp cloth while you make the sauce.

- Preheat the oven to 200°C/400°F/gas mark 6.

- In a roasting tray, toss the pumpkin and garlic in a little olive oil. Roast for 15–20 minutes, until softened. Add the maple syrup for the last minute of roasting.

- Meanwhile, simmer the stock in a large saucepan with the rosemary and lemon rind for 10 minutes. Remove the rosemary and lemon rind, and slice the latter thinly to use as a garnish. Add the roasted pumpkin and garlic to the stock. Blend to a purée, then pass this through a sieve to get a thin but well-flavoured broth. Season with salt and the cayenne pepper.

- Cook the kale in a saucepan of boiling water for 4–5 minutes, drain it and cool it in a dish of cold water. Squeeze it dry and slice it into thin strips.

- Bring the broth back to the boil, add the ravioli and simmer until cooked through, about 4–5 minutes. Remove the ravioli with a slotted spoon and place in shallow bowls. Scatter over some of the cooked kale. Ladle over some of the broth and dust each portion with a grating of nutmeg. Sprinkle the lemon rind slices on top.

Blue cheese & walnut ravioli with maple-glazed shallots

for 4

for the filling
200g/7oz blue cheese, crumbled
100g/3½oz ricotta, crumbled
50g/2oz walnuts, finely chopped
1 tbsp finely chopped fresh chives
salt and pepper

for the pasta
200g/7oz very fine durum wheat flour, plus extra for dusting
¼ tsp salt
1 egg, plus 2 extra egg yolks

for the maple-glazed shallots
8 long shallots, peeled
45g/1¾oz butter
1 tbsp sherry vinegar
3 tbsp maple syrup
salt and pepper

for the spinach
1 tbsp olive oil
300g/11oz baby spinach leaves
pinch of freshly grated nutmeg
salt and pepper

One of the most popular starters on the Café Paradiso menus over the winter, this dish is all about the combination of blue cheese and maple syrup, and the rest of the ingredients are there merely as support players to this lovely meeting of sweet, creamy, acidic and toasty vanilla flavours.

Without the work involved in making pasta, this is a simple dish, and, if you make pasta regularly, that won't be much of a chore to you either. Three ravioli will make a generous starter, while five or six constitute a very filling main course.

- First make the filling: stir together the blue cheese, ricotta, walnuts and chives. Season with black pepper.

- Make the pasta: sift the flour into a bowl with the salt, add the egg and extra yolks with 1–1½ tablespoons of water and bring them all together. Knead for a minute, and leave the dough to rest under a cloth.

- Pass it through a pasta machine, then fold it and pass it through again. Repeat 2–3 more times, each time lowering the setting to get a thinner sheet of dough, finishing on the second-lowest setting.

- Cut circles of dough 6cm/2½in in diameter. Place a teaspoon of filling in the centre of each circle. Brush the edges with water and fold the pasta to make a half-moon shape, ensuring there are no air pockets inside and pressing the edges to form a seal. Place the ravioli on a lightly floured tray and cover with a damp cloth until ready to cook.

- Prepare the maple-glazed shallots: quarter the shallots lengthways. Heat 15g/½oz butter in a frying pan, add the shallots and fry over medium heat for 2 minutes. Add the vinegar and 1 tablespoon of the maple syrup, reduce the heat, cover loosely with baking parchment and leave to simmer for 15 minutes. Just before serving, add the remaining butter and maple syrup, stir and remove from the heat. Season with salt and pepper.

- About halfway through the shallot cooking time, bring a large saucepan of water to the boil and drop in the raviloli. Keep the water simmering for 5–6 minutes, until the pasta is cooked, then drain and put the ravioli on a warmed plate.

• While the ravioli are cooking, cook the spinach: heat the olive oil in a saucepan, add the spinach and stir over high heat for 1–2 minutes until the spinach is wilted. Season with salt and pepper and the nutmeg.

• To serve, put some spinach on 4 warmed plates, and then place the ravioli on top with some shallots scattered over, spooning their juices over too.

Squash, okra & chickpea tagine with apricots & cherries

for 4

400g/14oz butternut
squash, peeled, deseeded
and cubed
4 tbsp olive oil, plus extra
for tossing and cooking
200g/7oz courgettes,
halved lengthways and
thickly sliced
1 large red onion, halved
and thickly sliced
4 garlic cloves, sliced
1 tbsp grated fresh ginger
1 tsp ground cinnamon
1 tsp ground cumin
1 tsp ground coriander
6 green cardamom pods,
seeds only, lightly
crushed
1 x 400g/14oz tin of
chopped tomatoes, juice
included
200ml/7fl oz vegetable
stock
rind of 2 oranges, in large
strips
10 dried apricots, thickly
sliced
2 tbsp dried cherries
1 x 400g/14oz tin of
chickpeas, drained
115g/4oz whole fresh okra
2 fresh green chillies,
deseeded and thinly
sliced
2 tbsp chopped fresh
parsley
2 tbsp chopped fresh
coriander
2 lemons, for squeezing

With the classic Moroccan tagine flavours of both hot and fragrant spices combining with sweet and sour fruit, this stew also has the contrast of slow-cooked vegetables and the quickly stir-fried okra added at the end. There's a lot going on, so it needs little or no accompaniment. You might serve it with a chunk of fresh or grilled bread on the side, or, more traditionally, put a little couscous in the bottom of the bowl to soak up the juices. Okra divides people like few vegetables can. Love it or hate it, there is no convincing the doubters. If you're not a fan, try some green beans or broccoli instead.

- Preheat the oven to 200°C/400°F/gas mark 6.

- In an oven dish, toss the squash in a little olive oil and roast in the oven for 30 minutes, until tender and beginning to caramelise. In a separate dish, do the same with the courgette, but roast for just 10–15 minutes.

- Reduce the oven temperature to 170°C/325°F/gas mark 3.

- Heat 2 tablespoons of olive oil in a large, heavy flameproof casserole dish and sauté the onion for 5 minutes over medium heat. Add the garlic and spices, and cook, stirring, for 2 minutes more. Add the tomatoes with their juice, the stock, orange rind, dried fruit and chickpeas. Bring to the boil, cover the pan and place it in the oven to simmer for 40–50 minutes.

- Heat the remaining 2 tablespoons of olive oil in a frying pan over high heat. Add the okra and chillies, and fry for 2 minutes, until the okra is tender but still firm and lightly coloured.

- Remove the pan from the oven and stir in the chopped herbs. Serve the tagine with some lemon juice squeezed over each portion.

Mussaman curry of new potatoes, cauliflower, chickpeas & green beans with cucumber coriander salsa

for 4

for the curry paste
1 tbsp fennel seeds
1 tbsp coriander seeds
2 tsp cumin seeds
1 tsp white peppercorns
5 cloves
5 green cardamom pods,
  seeds only
⅓ cinnamon stick
1 tsp turmeric
2 dried bird's eye chillies
115g/4oz shallots
2 garlic cloves, peeled
10g/⅓oz fresh ginger
1 fresh green chilli,
  deseeded if preferred
2 lemongrass stalks
1 large bunch of fresh
  coriander
vegetable oil, for cooking
1 x 400ml/14fl oz tin of
  coconut milk, plus extra
  for thinning
200g/7oz firm small new
  potatoes, washed and
  quartered or sliced
½ medium cauliflower,
  broken into florets
200g/7oz green beans
200g/7oz soaked and
  cooked dried chickpeas
vegetable stock or water,
  for thinning

*for the cucumber
coriander salsa*
½ cucumber, deseeded and
  finely diced
2 spring onions, finely
  chopped
1 tomato, deseeded and
  finely diced
1 bunch of fresh coriander,
  coarsely chopped
2 limes, for squeezing

rice, to serve

Mussaman, massaman... how do you like to spell it? Or season it, for that matter? Although now commonly associated with Thai cuisine, this aromatic stew has clearly wandered around Southern Asian bit, picking up flavours here and there to the extent that it would be foolhardy to put a stop sign on it saying 'definitive version, no more meddling!' I once saw a menu with it in a Thai restaurant where it was described as being flavoured with cloves, cardamom and potato. That's the version I want, I thought... imagine flavouring something with potato... right up my street. Then I moved the potato centre stage, but kept that core spicing combination of cloves and cardamom. You can use any vegetables here, so long as you keep the spuds. There we have it – that's the golden rule of mussaman/massaman.

Don't, however, get too subtle with it. If it is too lightly spiced, it can seem bland and heavy, so getting the chilli heat level right is important. There is a little dried chilli in the initial paste, and one fresh green chilli added later. If the latter isn't fairly hot, add a few more, or double the dried chillies.

The cucumber salsa certainly isn't from Thai cuisine or any other part of Southern Asia either. But it does do something that I think the stew needs, and that is to add a light crisp herby contrast. With that balance sorted, I think the dish can be eaten alone, with a slab of Indian flat bread on the side.

- First make the curry paste: grind all of the dry spices together.

- In a food processor, chop the shallots, garlic, ginger, fresh chilli, lemongrass and the stalks of the fresh coriander to a fine paste. Add a little water if necessary.

- Heat a little vegetable oil in a large saucepan over medium heat and fry the paste for 5 minutes. Add 2 tablespoons of the dry spice mix and cook for 2 minutes more. Add the coconut milk and bring to the boil.

- Meanwhile, steam the potatoes until just tender.

- In a wide pan or wok, stir-fry the cauliflower and green beans in a little vegetable oil for 3–4 minutes, until tender but still firm.

- Add to the curry sauce with the potato and chickpeas. Cover and simmer for 15–20 minutes over very low heat. Add a little stock, water or more coconut milk, if necessary, to maintain a richly wet sauce.

- While the curry is cooking, make the salsa by stirring together the cucumber, spring onions, tomato, coriander and the juice of 1 lime.

- Serve the curry in shallow bowls with freshly cooked rice. Spoon some salsa over each portion and squeeze some more lime juice over the top.

Rice noodles & cabbage in gingered honey almond sauce with spring onion omelette & spiced cucumber

for 4

2 tbsp vegetable oil
1 onion, halved and thinly
  sliced
¼ Savoy cabbage, shredded
225g/8oz wide rice noodles

for the spiced cucumber
1 large cucumber
1 tbsp salt
2 tbsp sambal oelek

*for the gingered honey
almond sauce*
100g/3½oz almond butter
2 tbsp grated fresh ginger
1 tbsp honey
1 tbsp soy sauce
juice of 1 lemon

*for the spring onion
omelette*
4 eggs
4 spring onions, finely
  chopped
2 tbsp finely chopped fresh
  coriander
vegetable oil, for brushing
salt and pepper

My joint favourite things about rice noodles are that they are a great way to eat 'pasta' without guilt when you've been up to your eyes in pasta, and they are also a great way to eat rice when you feel you should but you'd rather twirl a fork than shovel a spoon. I might give honorary mention to the lovely way the wide rice noodles have of seeming to resist a sauce yet still pick up just enough of it. Separate and a little stand-offish, yet quietly co-operative. You have to admire such appealing qualities. One thing I'm not crazy about in rice noodles is how long they often are. Then, slightly sinisterly, you occasionally come across references to superstitions about breaking rice noodles. What's that about? Ignore them without a second thought. Shorten them any way you can, unless you like to slurp 15-inch slippery things.

With this honey, ginger and almond sauce, you should aim for the consistency of pouring cream. It might seem a little thin, but even the slightest contact with heat will thicken it enough to coat the noodles and cabbage. It is a quietly seductive sauce that leaves room for some highly spiced cucumber to bring drama to the finished dish. If you're not inclined to make the cucumber part of the recipe, add some sambal oelek (an Indonesian/Malaysian chilli sauce) or other chilli condiment to the sauce. The sauce will keep for a few days but, like many sauces, it can get a bit flat in the fridge. Check the seasoning before using any leftovers.

This version of the recipe has cabbage as the lone vegetable in the mix. Of course, it will adapt to any vegetables you've got, but I think it's best to keep it down to one or two, three at a stretch, to avoid the dreaded 'mixed veg' syndrome, where individuals get lost in a crowd.

• Make the spiced cucumber: cut the cucumber in half lengthways and scoop out the seeds. Slice the remaining flesh into thin sticks about 4cm/1½in long and lay them out on a plate or tray. Sprinkle with the salt and leave for 20 minutes.

• Rinse off the salt, pat the cucumber slices dry with kitchen paper and put them in a bowl. Stir in the sambal oelek.

- Make the gingered honey almond sauce: put the almond butter, ginger, honey, soy sauce and lemon juice in a bowl and whisk in some hot water to make a thick paste. Continue whisking in more water, about 100ml/3½fl oz, until you get a light pouring consistency.

- Make the spring onion omelette: beat the eggs lightly with 2 tablespoons of cold water. Season with salt and pepper and stir in the spring onions and coriander.

- Brush a frying pan with vegetable oil and place it over high heat. Pour in the eggs and swirl to cover the base of the pan. While the omelette is cooking, lift the edge 2 or 3 times to allow the uncooked egg to flow underneath. After a minute or so, flip the omelette over and cook the other side for a further 30 seconds, then transfer the omelette to a chopping board. Cut it into slices about 6x1cm/2½x½in.

- Heat the 2 tablespoons of vegetable oil in a wide pan or wok over medium heat. Fry the onion for 5 minutes, stirring often, then add the cabbage. Continue to stir-fry for 5 minutes more, then cover the cabbage with baking parchment, lower the heat and leave to cook for 5–8 minutes more, until the cabbage is cooked to your liking.

- At the same time, bring a saucepan of water to the boil, drop in the rice noodles, stir until they have softened, then turn off the heat and leave for 7–10 minutes, until the noodles are done. Drain in a colander and return the noodles to the pan. Stir in the cabbage and half of the almond sauce.

- Serve the noodles in 4 warmed bowls. Drape some slices of omelette on top and drizzle over some more of the sauce. Finally, arrange some spiced cucumber on top.

Black kale & pumpkin with toasted millet in a tomato, almond & yoghurt sauce

Millet had been lost to me for so long I had forgotten it existed. My first cooking job was in Cranks on Tottenham Street in London, a site that was a furniture shop last time I checked. We used millet a lot; it seemed to be part of what you might call the 'vegetarian armoury' of the time and place, and so I assumed that millet was a widely available staple food. Not just any millet, mind you. I don't remember where the Cranks sourced theirs, but it was a highly refined white grain – and I mean that in a good way – that had a light, fluffy texture and nutty flavour.

Back in Ireland a couple of years later, the only millet I came across was wholegrain stuff, or partly hulled cracked grains with lots of gritty fibrous chewing material. Bird food, I think it was, but sold in wholefood shops to humans. That stuff gives vegetarians a bad name. So I let millet slip out of my mind and my repertoire.

Centuries later, or so it seemed, millet crept quietly back into my life, via a bulghur salad of all things. My girlfriend Maureen's sister Pati made one for a family gathering in Stratford and, while humbly absorbing the flying compliments, she mentioned that in British Columbia she usually made it from millet. Millet?! Millet exists!! While my mind screamed the words silently, complete with excited punctuation, my body stayed calm, save for a quizzical look across the table. 'That's a gritty little grain', I tentatively ventured. 'Not at all', came the reply, ever so slightly defensively, 'It has the texture of big fluffy couscous with better flavour, and so nutritious too!' 'And where, pray tell, might I find some of this fluffy and nutritious millet? Must I have it posted from some hippy homestead in the western hinterland?' (I speak very strangely when pretending not to be excited). 'Ah... no, not necessary... they sell it loose out of bins by the kilo out at that bulk sales place on the way out of town.'

How come nobody told me millet was widely available everywhere except Ireland? Someone's going to phone up next week and tell me where to get it in Ireland too. I bought a truckload – no I didn't, I bought a kilo. By the time I found the right aisle, I'd already spent my budget on salty, sugary, gram-flour-coated snacks that turned out to be stale. But the millet was as I remembered it. Like when a movie character goes back in time and still likes his childhood sweetheart.

Here's one thing to do with millet, after which you can make up your own dishes easily by adapting anything with rice, bulghur or couscous in it. It makes great porridge too. That was always a big hit in Cranks.

This is a rare recipe where I prefer to keep the stalk on the cavolo nero (black kale), chopping the whole leaf about 2cm/¾in thick crossways. The dish is cooked long enough to soften the stalk and keeping it gives structure to the dish. It's not compulsory, so feel free to cut all or some of it out.

- Preheat the oven to 150°C/300°F/gas mark 2.

- Toss the pumpkin in a little olive oil in an oven dish, then roast in the oven for 20 minutes, until the pumpkin is tender and beginning to caramelise.

- While the pumpkin is in the oven, make the almond and yoghurt sauce: put the almonds on an oven tray and toast them in the oven for 10 minutes, until lightly coloured. Blend in a food processor, adding a few tablespoons of water to get a smooth paste. Transfer to a bowl and stir in the yoghurt.

- Heat 2 tablespoons of olive oil in a heavy saucepan over medium heat. Fry the onion for 5 minutes, then add the garlic and spices, and cook for 2 minutes more. Add the kale and fry for 5 minutes, then add the tomatoes and soy sauce. Continue to cook for 5 minutes more, then add the pumpkin and the almond yoghurt sauce. Lower the heat and simmer for a further 5 minutes.

- At the same time, cook the millet: heat the olive oil in a heavy saucepan over low heat. Add the millet and toast for 7–8 minutes, stirring often. Add 600ml/1 pint boiling water and the salt. Lower the heat, cover the pan and simmer for 15 minutes, until the water has been absorbed.

- Stir the millet into the vegetables and serve in bowls. Or, if you prefer, serve the vegetables on top of the millet.

for 4

2 tbsp olive oil, plus extra for tossing and toasting
600g/1lb 6oz pumpkin or squash, peeled, deseeded and cut into 2cm/¾in dice
1 red onion, halved and thinly sliced
2 garlic cloves, sliced
2 tbsp grated fresh ginger
2 fresh green chillies, deseeded and thinly sliced
1 tbsp coarsely ground coriander seeds
2 tsp turmeric
200g/7oz black kale (cavolo nero), coarsely chopped
4 medium tomatoes, halved and thickly sliced
1 tbsp soy sauce

for the almond and yoghurt sauce
100g/3½ oz whole blanched almonds
6 tbsp natural yoghurt

for the toasted millet
1 tbsp olive oil
300g/11 oz millet
pinch of salt

Cauliflower, carrot & leek laksa with rice noodles and spinach-cashew dumplings

Laksa is a soup that's a meal in itself, made even more substantial here with the addition of deep-fried cashew dumplings. You can use any vegetables rather than this combination but, as always, try to limit it to no more than three types to avoid the dish becoming too confused. Beansprouts are very good in laksa too: uncooked and placed in the bowls after the vegetables and before the broth is poured over. If you don't want to go to the trouble of making and deep-frying dumplings, you might like to add some roasted cashews instead.

- Make the spinach cashew dumplings: cook the spinach briefly in boiling water, then cool it in cold water, drain and squeeze it as dry as possible. Put it in a food processor with the cashews and blend to a paste. Add the spices and the egg yolk, and pulse to mix. Transfer the paste to a bowl and stir in the gram flour. Season with salt and black pepper. Using lightly floured hands, form the paste into small, marble-sized balls, and store these in the fridge until needed.

- Make the laksa: put the tamarind pulp in a bowl, pour over 200ml/7fl oz hot water and leave to soak for 10 minutes. Strain the liquid through a fine sieve, pushing the pulp with the back of a spoon to squeeze all the liquid through the sieve.

- Break the cauliflower into florets, discarding the stalk. Peel away 1 or 2 outer leaves from the leeks and cut off some of the dark green ends. Cut the leeks in half lengthways down to just below where the leaves separate. Wash them under cold running water, then cut them at an angle into 2cm/¾in-thick slices. Peel the carrots and cut them at an angle into 1cm/½in-thick slices.

- Heat the vegetable oil in a wok or wide pan over medium heat. Add the garlic, chillies and ginger, and fry for 1 minute. Add the cauliflower, leeks, carrots and herbs, and continue to fry for 5 minutes, stirring often.

Continued on following page...

for 4

for the spinach-cashew dumplings
75g/3oz spinach
75g/3oz cashew nuts, lightly toasted
2½ tsp ground cumin
½ tsp turmeric
large pinch of freshly grated nutmeg
1 egg yolk
75g/3oz gram (chickpea) flour, sifted, plus extra for dusting
salt and pepper

for the laksa
2 tbsp tamarind pulp
1 medium cauliflower
2 leeks
2 carrots
2 tbsp vegetable oil
2 garlic cloves, sliced
2 fresh red chillies, deseeded and sliced
1 tbsp grated fresh ginger
2 tbsp chopped fresh coriander
1 tbsp chopped fresh mint leaves
2 tbsp chopped fresh Thai basil leaves
3 tomatoes, deseeded and diced
800ml/29fl oz coconut milk
400ml/14fl oz vegetable stock or water
2 tbsp light soy sauce

for the rice noodles
225g/8oz wide flat rice noodles
vegetable oil, for deep frying

Continued from previous page...

- Add the tomatoes, tamarind water, coconut milk, stock or water and soy sauce. Bring to the boil and simmer for 5–7 minutes, until the vegetables are tender.

- At the same time, cook the rice noodles: bring a saucepan of water to the boil, drop in the rice noodles and stir until they have softened. Turn off the heat and leave for 7–10 minutes, until the noodles are done. Drain in a colander.

- While the noodles are cooking, deep-fry the dumplings in hot (180°C/350°F) vegetable oil in a deep-fryer or saucepan for 2–3 minutes, until crisp and golden. Drain on kitchen paper.

- Put some noodles in deep bowls. Use a slotted spoon to take the vegetables from the broth, and divide them between the bowls. Pour some broth over each portion and place a few dumplings on top.

Wild rice, haloumi & ginger-braised leeks with sweet pepper, chilli & caper sauce

At first, this might not seem so much like a bowl dish as a carefully constructed plate arrangement. However, the crucial part of it is that the flavours of the separately cooked elements seep down through the dish to mingle with each other while also retaining their individuality. By the time you are scooping the last of the wild rice from the bottom of the bowl, there is a very exciting party going on. In the bowl, that is; I don't know what's going on over at your house. It's not at all as complicated as a first glance at the instructions might suggest. Basically, you cook some rice and some leeks, make a simple pepper sauce and, when everything is ready, fry some haloumi.

There are two ways to cook wild rice – either you measure exact quantities of rice and water and simmer slowly until the water has all been absorbed by the rice, or you boil the grain as you would pasta, in lots of water. I switch from one to the other, but here I recommend the pasta method, simply because it's easier to decide when the rice is done to your liking. I like wild rice just at the point at which it is opening up, when it becomes chewy rather than gritty. Not just because my teeth are aging, more that it seems to give up a little more of its nutty flavour then.

for 4

150g/5oz wild rice
30g/1¼oz butter
2 leeks
olive oil, for drizzling and cooking
2 tbsp grated fresh ginger
125ml/4fl oz dry white wine, plus extra for moistening (optional)
300g/11oz haloumi, cut into 8 slices about 5mm/¼in thick
1 lime, for squeezing
salt and pepper

for the sweet pepper, chilli and caper sauce
3 tbsp olive oil
1 red pepper, deseeded, quartered and thinly sliced
1 fresh red chilli, deseeded and thinly sliced
2 garlic cloves, sliced
115g/4oz cherry tomatoes, quartered
1 tbsp balsamic vinegar
1 tbsp small capers, rinsed

- Preheat the oven to 180°C/350°F/gas mark 4.

- In a large saucepan, bring about 2 litres/3½ pints of water to the boil, add the wild rice and a pinch of salt and simmer over medium heat for 30–40 minutes, until the rice is tender but not mushy. Drain in a sieve, return the rice to the pan and stir in half of the butter. Season with salt and pepper.

- While, the rice is cooking, discard the outer leaves from the leeks and cut them just below the point where they open up. Set aside the green tops to make soup. Cut the white parts at an angle into short slices about 1cm/½in-thick. Lay these slices in a single layer in an oven dish and drizzle generously with olive oil. Scatter the grated ginger on top and pour in the white wine.

Continued on following page...

Continued from previous page...

- Cover with baking parchment and place the dish in the oven. Bake for 20 minutes, until the leeks are tender. Check once or twice, and add a little water or more wine to keep them moist, if necessary.

- While the leeks cook, make the sweet pepper, chilli and caper sauce: heat 2 tablespoons of olive oil in a pan over medium heat. Add the red pepper, chilli and garlic, and sauté for 5 minutes, stirring often. Add the tomatoes, vinegar and capers. Lower the heat, cover the pan and simmer for 10–12 minutes.

- In a large frying pan, heat the remaining butter with a tablespoon of olive oil over medium-to-high heat. Cut the haloumi slices in half diagonally, place them in the pan and fry for 3–4 minutes on each side, until crisp and golden. Squeeze the lime juice over them at the end of cooking.

- Just before serving, stir the remaining tablespoon of olive oil and a tablespoon of water into the sweet pepper, chilli and caper sauce.

- To serve, spoon some wild rice into bowls, and top with the leeks, pouring the juices over. Place some haloumi slices on the leeks and spoon some sauce on top, allowing the juices to run down into the rice.

Black-eyed peas, aubergines, green beans & peppers in chilli, coconut & thyme

for 4

200g/7oz dried black-eyed
  peas, soaked in cold water
  overnight and drained
2 medium aubergines
2 tbsp olive oil, plus extra
  for tossing
200g/7oz flat green beans
4–6 small shallots, finely
  chopped
4 garlic cloves, finely
  chopped
2–4 fresh green chillies,
  thinly sliced
1 tbsp ground coriander
  seeds
1 tsp turmeric
2 green peppers
4–6 sprigs of fresh thyme
1 x 400g/14oz tin of
  tomatoes, drained and
  finely chopped
1 x 400ml/14fl oz tin of
  coconut milk
1 lime, for squeezing
nutmeg, for grating
salt

Black-eyed peas may have originated in India, but they have become synonymous with the Southern United States and the Caribbean, which is where this stew gets its interesting flavour combination of chilli and thyme. It's a proper bean stew, as distinct from a vegetable dish with a few polite beans added, as I tend to do more often than not. It's not that I don't like dried beans – my allegiance to the chickpea is well documented – but, with a few exceptions, like this particular recipe, I prefer them to play a supporting role most of the time.

Flat green beans will work better here than the more delicate pencil-shaped ones, because of their own stronger flavour and better ability to carry a sauce. And don't be tempted to replace the green peppers with sweet red or yellow ones. There are quite enough sweet flavours going on in the dish. If you really, really don't like green peppers, replace them with more green beans or a courgette sliced into thick batons.

If you make the stew in a casserole dish, you might like to simmer it in the oven instead of on the stovetop. In this case, turn the oven down to 150°C/300°F/gas mark 2 after roasting the aubergines. Serve it on its own, with flat bread or chunky bread, or with a little millet, rice or couscous.

- Bring a saucepan of water to the boil, add the black-eyed peas and simmer for 50–60 minutes, until just tender.

- Meanwhile, preheat the oven to 200°C/400°F/gas mark 6.

- Cut the aubergines in half lengthways, then cut them into slices 1cm/½in thick, discarding the ends. Toss the slices in olive oil to coat them evenly and lightly, then lay them in a single layer on baking parchment-lined oven trays. Roast in the oven for 10–15 minutes, turning once, until tender and browned.

- While these cook, slice the flat green beans at an angle into pieces about 4cm/1½in long. Bring a saucepan of water to the boil, add the beans and simmer for 2 minutes. Drain, and drop the beans into cold water to cool. Drain again and set aside.

- Heat the 2 tablespoons of vegetable oil in a heavy saucepan over medium heat. Add the shallots and sauté for 2 minutes, stirring. Add the garlic, chillies, coriander and turmeric, and sauté again for 2 minutes more, stirring.

- Cut the peppers in quarters lengthways, remove the seeds and pith and cut the flesh at an angle into slices about 1cm/½in thick. Add the peppers and thyme to the pan and continue to sauté for 5 minutes, stirring often.

- Add the chopped tomatoes, coconut milk and drained cooked black-eyed peas. Bring to the boil, cover the pan and reduce the heat to very low. Simmer for 30 minutes. Add the aubergine and green beans, and remove the thyme sprigs. Season with salt and check that the chilli heat is to your liking. Reheat briefly and gently, then serve.

- Squeeze some lime juice over each portion and finish with a dusting of lightly grated nutmeg.

Couscous pilaf of sprouting broccoli, aubergine & chickpeas with harissa sauce, chermoula & orange-marinated feta

I get asked for this recipe a lot by people who've lunched in Café Paradiso, and I always think – 'but you've already got this recipe somewhere'. 'If you've got the books, that is' – that's my next thought, eyeing a sale. 'Not this version', comes the response, and I vow to put it right one of these days. The elements are scattered through the earlier books, so maybe it is time to put down on paper an updated version of how we construct this simple but lengthy recipe.

The thing is that we often have a couscous pilaf on the lunch menu and, while it can seem like a complicated dish to describe in my lengthy menu-speak, to the restaurant kitchen it's mostly a simple task of putting things together. Chances are the chermoula and harissa sauce are on the dinner menu somewhere and roasted aubergine slices are being used for something too. The rest is easy.

The same applies to writing it out as a recipe here. There are loads of ingredients and it must look daunting. However, after you've made the back-up elements, it's like knocking up a stir-fry.

It would be hard to make smaller quantities of either the chermoula or harissa sauce, nor would I recommend it. Chermoula will keep for days in the fridge and can be frozen if you haven't found a use for it in that time. Essentially a pesto with a Moroccan twist, it adds a complex background flavour to any dish with Southern or Eastern Mediterranean leanings. Think roasted veg, aubergines, haloumi, sheep's cheese. The harissa sauce will be gone in a couple of days, I guarantee it. Its sweet, fiery hot and richly oily combination makes it a great sauce for rice as well as for couscous, not to mention pasta and noodles. If you find yourself drizzling a little on your morning eggs, fret not for you are not alone.

Having said all of that, there is of course no definitive version of the pilaf. But this one is close.

As well as the chermoula, harissa sauce and couscous being, in football-speak, the spine of the dish, you could say that the marinated feta and roasted aubergine are first-team regulars and the cherry tomatoes would be surprised to be left out of the big games.

Sprouting broccoli, to all appearances the star of the show, is a seasonal performer and through the year you might very well find green beans, rocket, kale, broad beans, a variety or roots and even asparagus doing a stint in the role.

Continued on following page...

for 4

2 medium aubergines
olive oil, for tossing,
 drizzling and cooking
12 cherry tomatoes, halved
325g/11½oz couscous
300ml/11fl oz vegetable
 stock or water, plus extra
 for cooking
2 red onions, halved and
 thinly sliced
2 tsp cumin seeds
300g/11oz sprouting
 broccoli
200g/7oz soaked and
 cooked dried chickpeas
salt

for the orange-marinated
feta
200g/7oz feta cheese, cut
 into 2cm/¾in dice
rind of 1 orange
100ml/3½fl oz olive oil

for the chermoula
1 tsp ground cumin seeds
1 tsp ground fennel seeds
50g/2oz fresh coriander
100g/3½oz fresh parsley
30g/1¼oz fresh mint
3 garlic cloves
3 tsp paprika
large pinch of cayenne
 pepper
finely grated zest of
 ½ lemon
finely grated zest of
 ½ orange
200–250ml/7–9fl oz olive oil

for the harissa sauce
1 large red pepper
225ml/8floz olive oil
4–6 tsp harissa paste

Continued from previous page...

- Well ahead, make the orange-marinated feta: put the feta in a shallow bowl. Cut the orange rind into 1cm/½in-wide strips and scatter these over the feta. Pour the olive oil over the cheese and leave for at least an hour.

- Preheat the oven to 200°C/400°F/gas mark 6.

- Cut the aubergines in half lengthways, then cut them into slices 1cm/½in thick, discarding the ends. Toss these slices in olive oil to coat them evenly and lightly, then lay them in a single layer on baking parchment-lined oven trays. Roast in the oven for 10–15 minutes, turning once, until tender and browned.

- When the aubergine goes in the oven, put the cherry tomatoes on an oven tray, and drizzle over a little olive oil and season with salt. Roast them for 7–8 minutes, until they are beginning to soften. Leave the oven on as you take them out.

- Put the couscous in a bowl and season it with salt. Warm the stock or water to hand temperature and quickly stir it into the couscous. Cover with a damp cloth and leave for 15 minutes.

- While the couscous is standing, make the chermoula: put all the ingredients, except 2 tablespoons each of the parsley and coriander and the olive oil, in a food processor and blend to a paste, then add enough oil to get a thick pesto-like consistency.

- Then make the harissa sauce: roast the pepper in the hot oven or under a hot grill, turning occasionally, until the skin is charred all over. Place the pepper in a bowl, seal with cling film and leave for 15 minutes. Peel and deseed the pepper, chop it coarsely and put it in a saucepan with the olive oil and 100ml/3½fl oz water. Boil for 1 minute. Blend with a hand-held blender until emulsified. Add the harissa paste and blend again. Leave to cool.

- Cook the vegetables for the pilaf: heat 2 tablespoons of olive oil in a wide pan or wok over medium heat. Add the onions and cumin seeds, and fry for 5 minutes, stirring often, until the onions are beginning to colour. Add the sprouting broccoli and chickpeas, and cook for a further 7–8 minutes, stirring often and occasionally adding a splash of stock or water, until the broccoli is tender. Stir in the roasted aubergine and cherry tomatoes, the reserved parsley and coriander and 4 tablespoons of the chermoula. Heat through again quickly.

- Sift the couscous with a fork, slotted spoon or, most efficiently, your fingers. Remove the pan of vegetables from the heat and stir in the couscous, then serve immediately.

- Serve the pilaf piled in the centre of shallow bowls. Pour some of the harissa sauce around each portion and place some of the marinated feta on top or on the side.

Oven

Oven

Every now and then, I get asked for a recipe or six for a media piece about things to cook for dinner in 20 minutes. My heart sinks. When did 20 minutes become the length of time allotted to cooking dinner? Will we starve to death if dinner isn't on the table at 20-past-getting-home-from-work? Or is it just part of our obsessive busyness? Did we skip lunch again and do we have no snacks in the house to stave off fainting? Apparently the answer is simply that we don't have any more time than that for cooking. At the end of a busy day, quality time has to be forcefully eked out of the short bit between the end of the commute and early bed-time. Relaxation is visual stimulation, cooking for more than 20 minutes is a chore.

(As an aside, the time allotted for eating isn't included in these briefs. That omission always reminds me of my first, unspoken, reaction to customers in Café Paradiso who wanted to know how long it took to have a main course and run to the theatre. I cook pretty fast when I need to. How fast can you eat? Would you like your food puréed?)

From years of knocking out 10-minute midnight solo suppers after 12-hour kitchen shifts, I know that it's possible to cook and eat well in a hurry. A bag of fresh greens in the fridge can be turned into a feast if the store cupboard is well stocked.

But, turning the prescribed thinking on its head, there is no better way to spend an evening than to make cooking dinner the focus of the evening's activity. All the better if it is a joint effort, helped along with a snack or simple starter to keep hunger at bay, and a shared bottle of wine to encourage kitchen improvisation. Operating somewhere between quick dinners and complicated recipes requiring constant attention are those that involve putting something together to bake, roast or braise in the oven. These give you time to fuss a little more over side dishes or desserts for fun, or to wander away to nibble at a starter, check out those compulsive screens or do something to sharpen your appetite for half an hour or more. You'll figure it out for yourselves, especially if you've opened that bottle.

Oven dishes are about mingling flavours and ingredients together in long slow cooking. In many of these recipes, the preparation time will come in under the 20 minutes that modern life has allotted, and the complex flavours that have developed usually mean that nothing more than a salad or some simple cooked greens is necessary to round out the meal. Your nose will usually tell you when it's time to eat and the pleasure to be had from dinner will be fuelled by the warm smells slowly developing in the kitchen. If you're not ready, turn the oven off and come back in your own time. Most oven dishes will wait for you to be ready to eat, and will make great leftovers too. Indeed, the fastest way to cook dinner in a hurry is to reheat last night's leftovers as a gratin or oven stew.

The recipes are infinitely adaptable in quantity, proportions, ingredients, spicing or richness. And they mostly involve ingredients that store well rather than being dependent on your having just picked fresh produce from the garden.

Cashew loaf with squash stuffing & chocolate-chilli gravy

for 6–8

200g/7oz squash or pumpkin, peeled, deseeded and diced
1 tbsp olive oil, plus extra for tossing
1 small leek, well washed and finely chopped
1 tbsp grated fresh ginger
finely grated zest and juice of ½ lemon
100g/3½oz parsnips, peeled and chopped
500g/1lb 2oz cashew nuts, lightly toasted and finely ground
1 tbsp sunflower oil
1 white onion, finely chopped
3 garlic cloves, crushed
2 celery sticks, finely chopped
1 tbsp finely chopped fresh sage
1 sprig of fresh thyme, leaves only
1 tsp ground cumin
¼ tsp cayenne pepper
100ml/3½fl oz dry white wine
100g/3½oz fine breadcrumbs
1 large egg, lightly beaten
salt and pepper

for the chocolate-chilli gravy
2 tbsp olive oil
1 red onion, finely chopped
½ red pepper, deseeded and finely chopped
1 celery stick, finely chopped
4 garlic cloves, chopped
1 fresh green chilli, deseeded and finely chopped
1 chipotle chilli, finely chopped
Continued...

I've been making variations on this recipe since I first started to learn the restaurant business back in the '80s in Cranks, a small London chain of vegetarian restaurants. The style of cooking may have, in the end, come to be seen as of its time, but in that time it was an innovative place to work that allowed a fair amount of creative freedom to the chefs so long as they could also turn out the classics. Among the small but eccentric kitchen team was a member of the Rajneesh quasi-religious group who wore orange clothes and spent the first fifteen minutes of every 6am shift sitting in total darkness in the tiny toilet smoking something sweetly pungent. What a brilliant cook used to emerge from that closet!

The Cranks festive loaf was certainly standing head and shoulders above anything else that included the words 'nut' and 'loaf' in the title. Still does. Nuts and loaves eventually became part of the clichéd portrayal of vegetarians – you know the one – sandals, beards, rabbit food... nut loaf. A lot of it was deserved, and good riddance to those dry, gritty concoctions of peanut, wholemeal bread and soy sauce. I carried on making the Cranks recipe once a year at Christmas for a while, but eventually fell victim to fashion, became embarrassed about it and put it away. Actually, that was helped by my now grown-up children telling me they, er... didn't care much for it. I thought for a while that they were just being silly children, but I gave in anyway.

The recipe has been stewing away in the back of my mind for a few years, as though it was quietly protesting – 'There was no call for throwing me out with all that other dull, brown stuff, and you know it. I'm class, I am... elegant and light, a tasteful blend of expensive and common ingredients, years of refinement packed into a style appropriate for the biggest feast days.' Ignored recipes sometimes make very dignified plea speeches.

When the voice got loud enough, it blocked out the mocking ones. So I took the recipe out for Canadian Thanksgiving.

I thought it might like the New World. I reverted, not to the Cranks classic, but to the last version I could remember in my head, a simplified one that was all about making a moist and very fine mixture from cashews, without too much padding. It was expensive, but worth it. Then, in honour of the continent I was on and the time of year, I replaced the chestnut stuffing with a squash one, and gave the red wine gravy a Mexican chocolate and chilli twist.

To make sure the loaf is soft, moist and pale, toast the cashews just a little and grind them as finely as possible; then add enough liquid at the end so that the uncooked mixture is just short of sloppy. If you can't find chipotle chillies for the sauce, use smoked paprika.

Without appearing to be singing a song of my own praise, I can't go on too long about how well this went down, and how appropriate to a celebration a seriously good cashew loaf can be. Now that so much time has passed, and with its new makeover, it's nice to have this one back.

1 tsp dried oregano
2 tsp ground cumin
2 tsp ground coriander
1 tsp ground allspice
1 x 400g/14oz tin of
  tomatoes, juice included
1 tbsp tomato purée
200ml/7fl oz red wine
500ml/18fl oz vegetable
  stock
25g/1oz dark chocolate,
  finely chopped
40g/1½oz butter, diced

- Preheat the oven to 220°C/425°F/gas mark 7.

- While the oven is heating up, start preparing the chocolate-chilli gravy: heat the olive oil in a pan and sauté the onion, red pepper, celery, garlic and chillies for 10 minutes, until soft. Add the spices and cook for 2 minutes more, then add the tomatoes and their juice, tomato purée, wine and stock. Simmer very slowly for 40–50 minutes.

- Toss the squash with a little olive oil in an oven dish and roast it in the oven for about 40 minutes, until tender and well coloured. When you take it out of the oven, reduce the temperature setting to 170°C/325°F/gas mark 3.

- In a wide pan, heat the tablespoon of olive oil and fry the leek over medium heat for 5 minutes. Add the ginger, lemon zest and juice and the roast squash. Cook for 2 minutes more, stirring to break up the squash into a coarse mash. Season with salt and pepper, and leave to cool.

- Steam or boil the parsnips then blend to a purée in a food processor. Put in a bowl with the ground cashews.

- Heat the sunflower oil in a small saucepan, add the onion and cook over medium heat until translucent. Add the garlic, celery,

Continued on following page...

Continued from previous page...

sage, thyme, cumin and cayenne. Cook for 2 minutes more, then add the wine and bring to the boil for 30 seconds.

- Add this mixture and 75g/3oz of the breadcrumbs to the parsnips and cashews and stir to get a firm but moist consistency. If necessary, add a little more white wine or water. Season well with salt, then stir in the egg. Add the remaining breadcrumbs to the squash.

- Line a 900g/2lb loaf tin with baking parchment. Press in half the cashew mixture, followed by the squash then finish with the remaining cashew mixture. Bake in the oven for 50–60 minutes, until firm and lightly coloured on top. Leave the loaf for 5–10 minutes in the tin before turning it out.

- Meanwhile, blend the chocolate-chilli gravy to a fine purée and pass it through a medium sieve. Return to the pan and whisk in the chocolate and butter. Season with salt.

- Turn the loaf out on a chopping board and cut it into 8 slices. Serve with the sauce.

Tian of aubergine, caramelised onion, spinach & polenta with feta crust and a fennel-chilli sauce

Much like the Moroccan tagine, tian is a French dish that's named after the container it's cooked in. Makes you think that if ratatouille were called 'big pot', it would never have been so world conquering. The tian vessel is essentially a rectangular gratin bowl and the dish cooked in it is classically a layered combination of vegetables with a crisp topping. This recipe might be more of a classic tian if it was baked in a gratin dish, and it certainly can be made that way. If you take that route, you might consider putting the fennel-chilli sauce inside the gratin too, spooning a layer on top of each layer of aubergine.

You will need four metal rings 7.5–8cm/3–3¼in in diameter and 3cm/1¼in high. The idea of using rings to shape the dish is to create individually baked tians that look very elegant on the plate, surrounded by the sauce. The flavour effect is different too, with each element of the dish retaining its separate character while forming part of the overall effect.

- Bring the stock to the boil in a saucepan and whisk in the polenta. Bring to the boil, reduce the heat and simmer for 20 minutes. Add the cheese and season well with salt and pepper. Spread the polenta about 1cm/½in thick on an oiled tray, cover with baking parchment and leave to cool.

- Heat the tablespoon of olive oil in a heavy frying pan. Add the onions and cook over medium heat for 10 minutes, stirring often. Add the vinegar and honey, cover loosely with baking parchment and reduce the heat. Simmer for 20–30 minutes until the onions are soft and caramelised. If the onions are soft but still wet, remove the lid and raise the heat for a little while.

- Preheat the oven to 200°C/400°F/gas mark 6.

- Brush the aubergine slices with olive oil and roast in the oven for about 15–20 minutes, until well done, turning once if necessary to brown both sides.

Continued on following page...

for 4

500ml/18fl oz vegetable stock
100g/3½oz coarse polenta
50g/2oz hard cheese, finely grated
vegetable oil, for oiling, plus extra for brushing
1 tbsp olive oil
4 red onions, quartered and thinly sliced
1 tbsp balsamic vinegar
1 tbsp honey
2 large aubergines, sliced into 2cm/¾in-thick rounds
200g/7oz spinach leaves, cooked, drained and chopped
salt and pepper

for the feta crust
200g/7oz feta cheese, crumbled
2 eggs
3 tbsp natural yoghurt
2 tbsp fine breadcrumbs

for the fennel-chilli sauce
4 tbsp olive oil
½ medium fennel bulb, cored and chopped into small dice
2 fresh green chillies, halved, deseeded and thinly sliced
2 garlic cloves, chopped
100ml/3½fl oz dry white wine
1 x 400g/14oz tin of tomatoes, juice included

Continued from previous page...

- Lower the oven setting to 190°C/375°F/gas mark 5.

- Prepare the feta crust: make a custard by beating the cheese, eggs and yoghurt together.

- Use 1 of the metal rings to cut the polenta into circles – you should have 8 in total.

- Line the rings with baking parchment with the paper rising 1cm/½in above the ring. Place a polenta circle in the bottom and top with an aubergine slice – or 2 if 1 is too small – some onion, then some of the cooked spinach and a spoonful of the custard. Repeat the aubergine, onion and spinach layers, and finish with a third layer of aubergine. Press down gently before adding a final layer of custard. Sprinkle some breadcrumbs on top.

- Place the tians on a baking parchment-lined oven sheet and bake in the oven for 15–20 minutes, until the custard is set.

- While they are in the oven, make the fennel-chilli sauce: heat a tablespoon of the olive oil in a pan and sauté the fennel, garlic and chillies for 5 minutes over medium heat. Add the wine and simmer for a minute, then add the tomatoes and their juice. Bring to the boil and simmer for 5 minutes. Purée the sauce with the remaining olive oil and season with salt. Serve at room temperature.

- Place a tian on each plate and carefully remove the ring and paper. Spoon some sauce around each tian.

Cardamom-roasted cauliflower with pistachio & green pepper salsa and leek, tomato & coconut pilaf

Having roasted cauliflower to star in a warm salad, as on page 76, I thought about pushing it a little further and making a main course of it. Cauliflower seems automatically to get posted with the big cheese flavours or subtle Indian spicing. As main courses go, it has enough support for the big cheesey ones, so I swung the other way. In terms of texture, I was thinking about the way I slice cauliflower for tempura, multiplying it by a big factor. Inside every floret of cauliflower is a beautiful cross-section slice, like a miniature of the trees you used to draw as a small child.

There's a lot of waste involved in this, the leafy bits that get trimmed away, as it were. I got in a spot of bother about that years ago when teaching a guest class in a cookery school where avoiding any waste was practically a requirement to pass. 'I suppose you make cauliflower soup with all those trimmings', came the loaded question from the boss at the back of the room. ''Course I do, cauliflower soup every day, that's my motto.' I don't make cauliflower soup every day, though I do like cauliflower soup. And, assuming you won't be doing this recipe every day, maybe you should indeed make soup the next day. In a restaurant setting, I just think it's worth the sacrifice to find the shape you see in a vegetable, without worrying what to do with the leftovers. You can't get beautiful cauliflower trees without making a bit of cauliflower by-product.

The roasting process is simple, but make sure you test the cauliflower often, as you want to serve it when it is crisp and browned, and carrying a good hit of spicing, but still with a nicely firm texture.

I've suggested a simple, slightly sweet rice pilaf as a foil for the cauliflower and salsa. Some even simpler buttered rice would be fine too.

• Cut a cauliflower on 2 sides of the central stem to get a flat single piece about 5cm/2in thick. Cut this in half again to get two thinner slices, then cut each in half across the middle to get 4 pieces. Repeat with the other cauliflower.

Continued on following page ...

for 4

2 medium cauliflowers
100g/3½oz butter, melted
2 tbsp olive oil
2 tbsp chopped fresh coriander
2 tsp turmeric
20 green cardamom pods, seeds only, crushed
1 tbsp coriander seeds, cracked
1 fresh green chilli, deseeded and finely chopped
juice of ½ lemon
salt

for the leek, tomato and coconut pilaf

2 tbsp olive oil
2 leeks, well washed and thinly sliced
2 garlic cloves, thinly sliced
1 tbsp grated fresh ginger
200g/7oz basmati rice
100ml/3½fl oz coconut milk
200g/7oz cherry tomatoes, halved

pistachio and green pepper salsa

60g/2½oz shelled pistachio nuts, roasted and coarsely chopped
½ green pepper, deseeded and finely diced
1 spring onion, thinly sliced
1 fresh green chilli, deseeded and finely diced
1 tbsp chopped fresh coriander
juice of ½ lemon
1 tbsp olive oil

Continued from previous page...

- Bring a large saucepan of water to the boil, then drop in the cauliflower pieces for 1 minute. Drain and place the cauliflower pieces in a single layer in an oven dish.

- Stir the butter and olive oil together and add the fresh coriander, turmeric, cardamom, cracked coriander and chilli. Add the lemon juice and a large pinch of salt.

- Brush this marinade on both sides of the warm cauliflower, then leave it to sit for 30 minutes.

- Preheat the oven to 200°C/400°F/gas mark 6.

- Put the marinated cauliflower in the oven and roast for 25-30 minutes, turning it halfway through cooking, until tender and browned.

- While the cauliflower is roasting, make the leek, tomato and coconut pilaf: heat a tablespoon of olive oil in a pan over medium heat. Add the leeks, garlic and ginger, and sauté for 5 minutes. Add the rice, coconut milk and 350ml/12fl oz of boiling water. Bring to the boil, then reduce the heat, cover the pan and simmer for 15 minutes.

- While that simmers, in another saucepan, heat the remaining tablespoon of olive oil over low heat. Add the tomatoes and a pinch of salt, and cook for 10 minutes, until the tomatoes have softened. Stir the tomatoes into the pilaf.

- Make the pistachio and green pepper salsa by combining all of the ingredients, and season with a little salt.

- Spoon some pilaf on to each plate, prop 2 slices of cauliflower on it and scatter some salsa across.

Saffron-braised squash with aubergine, pine nut & spinach stuffing and lentil-goat's cheese sauce

Small squash make great vessels for stuffing, but the dish only works if the squash itself is worth eating. Sure, the filling is highly flavoured, but put it in a doorstopper of a marrow and you might as well just eat it out of the pot. What you need here is a small winter squash that will make two portions when split in half. The skin must be edible and the flesh a nice deep orange colour with a dense texture and sweet flavour. Among the common varieties, the best for this are Acorn and Sweet Dumpling. Buttercup and the Japanese Hokaido, if you can get small ones, are good too.

The lentil-goat's cheese sauce could easily double up as a rich soup, which is worth keeping in mind as you serve. Be generous with it and, for best effect, use a wide, shallow bowl.

- Preheat the oven to 190°C/375°F/gas mark 5.

- Cut the squash in half across the middle and scoop out the seeds. Trim a little off the ends so that the squash can stand. Melt the butter with a tablespoon of the olive oil and the saffron. Brush this inside the squash, then place the squash halves, cut side down, in an oven dish. Brush the skins, then pour the wine and stock into the dish. Cover with foil and place the dish in the oven for 20 minutes.

- Meanwhile, in a wide pan, heat the remaining 2 tablespoons of olive oil over medium heat and sauté the onion for 5 minutes. Add the aubergine, garlic and spices, and cook for 10–12 minutes, stirring often, until the aubergine is tender and browned. Add the pine nuts and dates, cook for 2 minutes more, then stir in the spinach and season with salt and pepper.

- Turn the squash halves over and fill them with the aubergine stuffing. If the liquid has been absorbed, add a few tablespoons of water. Replace the foil cover and return the dish to the oven for 10 minutes.

- To make the sauce, bring the lentils and stock to the boil in a pan. Add the garlic, ginger, coriander, star anise and orange zest, and simmer for 20 minutes, until the lentils are tender. Remove the star anise. Blend the sauce to a purée and season with salt and pepper. Whisk in the goat's cheese. Adjust the consistency, if necessary, by adding a little more water or stock.

- Serve the squash sitting in a generous pool of the sauce.

for 4

2 small winter squash
15g/½oz butter
3 tbsp olive oil
1 pinch of saffron threads, crushed
100ml/3½fl oz dry white wine
100ml/3½fl oz vegetable stock
1 red onion, finely diced
400g/14oz aubergine, finely diced
4 garlic cloves, finely chopped
1 tbsp cumin seeds, ground
1 tbsp coriander seeds, ground
large pinch of ground cinnamon
3 tbsp pine nuts, coarsely chopped
4 dried dates, finely chopped
200g/7oz spinach leaves, blanched and finely chopped
salt and pepper

for the lentil-goat's cheese sauce
50g/2oz red lentils, washed
500ml/18fl oz vegetable stock, plus extra for thinning (optional)
2 garlic cloves, finely chopped
1 tbsp grated fresh ginger
2 tbsp chopped fresh coriander
2 star anise
finely grated zest of 1 orange
60g/2½oz fresh goat's cheese, crumbled

Asparagus & raspberry tartlets with strawberry champagne salsa

I made these for the wedding of a friend, the first wedding I ever got to cook for. Not that it was a huge ambition of mine to get into wedding catering, but it was one of those topics that cropped up over late-night beers after a tough kitchen service – preferences for one kind of service over another. Some chefs love big catering jobs and the challenges of one-off projects. I used to think I was the type who avoided such drama but, after putting a few toes in the water, it's something to which I seem to have developed a mild addiction. I'd rather not, thanks, but if you ask, there's a decent chance it will get a hold of the obsessive part of my brain.

This wedding was in a marquee, with a kitchen of hired equipment in a smaller tent tacked on to the side. A fair amount of care had been taken to ensure the dining room area was flat enough to avoid plates sliding from tables, or dancers sliding into the wrong hands, but the kitchen was on a 30-degree slope. We got this down to about 20 degrees with a few breeze blocks, and decided to put the ovens at the lower end. The chefs worked uphill and sideways for two days, developing good calf muscles but funny walks as a result.

The practical brief was to provide food that would be rich and pleasurable but still light and fruity. The conceptual brief was to create a menu that would tap into the love of the marrying couple, the food somehow playing its part in conjuring up an atmosphere that would leave everyone giddily reeling from the heavenly vibes in the air. Or something like that. No problem, I thought... this calls for some asparagus... and some bubbly... and raspberries and strawberries... The other courses had lots of artichokes, nuts and berries, and a little chocolate to finish, and we successfully avoided the only banished item – garlic. 'No bad breath' was in the brief, just below 'no heavy full bellies too bloated to dance'.

In proportion to the demanding and slightly obscure challenge, it was also incredibly successful and rewarding. When the kitchen team dragged its collective weary legs home, the dining room was in what turned out to be the still early stages of a mild delirium, fuelled mostly on an atmosphere of love deliberately conceived and created by the bride.

Continued on following page...

for 6

240g/8½oz plain flour
large pinch of salt
120g/4¼oz cold butter,
  diced
3 eggs, plus 3 extra egg
  yolks
6 tbsp crème fraîche or
  soured cream
18 thin asparagus spears
9 raspberries, halved
salt and coarsely ground
  black pepper

*for the strawberry
champagne salsa*
200g/7oz strawberries,
  hulled
2 tbsp champagne vinegar
1 tsp grated fresh ginger

Continued from previous page ...

I'm not saying the tart had a lot to do with it, but it fulfilled its role, and you can't ask more of a tart than that.

Practical issues? Yes, you can also make a large tart instead of individual ones. And hire a band that can switch from bluesy boogie to electro-pop-disco in mid-tune.

• Sift the flour and salt into a bowl then put them in a food processor with the butter. Pulse to get a fine crumb. Transfer back to the bowl, add 4 tablespoons of cold water and stir briefly to form a dough. Shape the dough into a ball with your hands, flatten it gently and chill for at least half an hour.

• Roll out the chilled pastry to a thickness of about 2mm/¹⁄₁₆in (a 10-pence coin) and cut out circles that will comfortably fit 6 tartlet cases with a diameter of 9cm/3½in. Press the circles into the cases and prick them all over with a fork. Chill again for 30 minutes.

• Preheat the oven to 180°C/350°F/gas mark 4.

• Blind-bake the pastry cases for 5–7 minutes.

• Whisk the eggs and extra yolks together, then stir into the crème fraîche. Season with salt and some coarsely ground black pepper.

• Slice the tops off the asparagus spears, just long enough to fit the tarts. Finely chop the remaining parts and put them into the pastry cases. Pour in some of the egg custard to almost fill the cases. Arrange 3 thin asparagus tops in a fan on top, and place a raspberry half in the gaps.

• Bake the tartlets for 10 minutes, until the custard has set.

• Meanwhile, make the strawberry champagne salsa: dice the strawberries and mix them with the champagne vinegar and ginger.

• Serve the tartlets with some salsa spooned over.

Sage & onion farinata with olive, caper & chilli peperonata

Farinata, a pizza-like pancake, is an Italian cousin of socca, which would suggest that recipes, like animals, birds and plants, don't have much time for borders. The recipe on page 173 is a cross between socca and crêpes, while this one here is a fairly traditional interpretation of farinata.

By its very nature, it is impossible to replicate street food, short of getting hold of the same ingredients and equipment and doing it on the street. The same street as you first ate it, that is. Which is by way of saying I am not hereby obliged to replicate authentic Ligurian farinata, only to make a decent stab at gram flour flat bread. Some recipes would suggest making two or three quickly cooked thin breads from this amount of batter; others would have even more batter and a longer cooking time for just one bread. As a snack, I like it thin; as an accompaniment to this spicy and oily peperonata, I like the farinata to be about 1cm/½in thick, like thin polenta.

The dough is left to stand so that it ferments a little to take on a slightly sour flavour. If you can leave it overnight all the better, but two hours will be of some use. A good, heavy ovenproof frying pan with decent non-stick qualities is important, though you could line the pan with baking parchment to help with that. You could also use a circular ceramic oven dish.

Because the farinata is slightly thick, it is best to finish it under a grill, to avoid the bottom burning while it waits for the top to catch up. If you've got a separate grill, that's hunky-dory. If not, just turn the oven to grill once the base of the farinata is browning.

The peperonata can be made early in the day or while you are working on the farinata. For this serving, I would also cook some wilted greens, such as spinach or kale, and sprinkle a little grated feta or other hard cheese over the plated dish.

for 4

100g/3½oz gram (chickpea) flour, sifted
1 tsp salt
4 tbsp olive oil
8 fresh sage leaves
2 red onions, halved and thinly sliced

for the olive, caper and chilli peperonata

2 tbsp olive oil
6 garlic cloves, halved
2–3 fresh green chillies, deseeded and thinly sliced
4 red peppers, quartered lengthways, deseeded and cut at an angle into 1cm/½in slices
12 black olives, stoned and halved
2 tbsp small capers, rinsed
salt

- Put the gram flour in a large bowl and whisk in 300ml/11fl oz water. Leave to stand for at least 2 hours. Skim any foam off the top of the batter, then stir in the salt and olive oil.

- While the batter is standing, make the caper and chilli peperonata: heat the olive oil in a deep pan over medium heat.

Continued on following page...

Continued from previous page...

- Add the garlic and chillies, and fry for 1 minute, then add the peppers, olives and capers. When the peppers are hot, turn the heat to low, cover the pan and simmer for 30 minutes. Season with salt and remove from the heat.

- Meanwhile, heat 2 tablespoons of the olive oil in a heavy iron frying pan over medium heat. Add the sage leaves, fry them for a minute and then remove them to drain on kitchen paper. When cool, crumble or chop them coarsely.

- Add the onions to the pan and sauté for 7–8 minutes, stirring often, until beginning to caramelise. Remove and set aside. Wipe the pan clean.

- Preheat the oven to 230°C/450°F/gas mark 8 and the grill to high.

- Put the remaining 2 tablespoons of olive oil in the pan and place it in the oven for a few minutes to heat up.

- Stir the batter and pour it into the pan. Put the pan on the top shelf of the oven for 2–3 minutes, to firm up the base, then quickly scatter the onion and sage over the farinata. Leave to bake in the oven for 8–10 minutes more, checking the base carefully once or twice with a spatula. When the base is browning, move the pan to the grill for a few minutes to finish the cooking and brown the top.

- Slide the farinata on to a chopping board, cut it into wedges and serve with the peperonata.

Braised artichokes with lemon hazelnut praline, cherry tomato sauce and a chard, potato & Puy lentil cake

for 4

1 lemon
6–8 medium globe
   artichokes
1 carrot, peeled and thinly
   sliced
2 celery sticks, thinly sliced
1 small onion, thinly sliced
4 garlic cloves, sliced
2 sprigs of fresh tarragon
2 sprigs of fresh thyme
100ml/3½fl oz olive oil,
   plus extra for oiling
150ml/5fl oz dry white
   wine
100ml/3½fl oz vegetable
   stock or water

*for the lemon hazelnut
praline*
100g/3½oz caster sugar
rind of 1 lemon, in long
   strips
50g/2oz hazelnuts

*for the chard, potato and
Puy lentil cake*
100g/3½oz Puy lentils
8 large chard leaves
3 tbsp olive oil, plus extra
   for brushing
1 onion, finely chopped
600g/1lb 6oz potatoes,
   boiled and peeled
2 tbsp chopped fresh
   parsley
50g/2oz hard sheep's
   cheese, grated
salt and pepper

for the cherry tomato sauce
250g/9oz cherry tomatoes,
   halved
3 garlic cloves, sliced
4 tbsp olive oil

In Café Paradiso, we tend to switch between pan-frying and braising artichokes. Sometimes it's just a matter of getting bored with one way and moving on to the next. More than that, though, braising seems to make sense, as the artichokes become more mature and have denser flesh and more of that annoying hairy choke at the centre. So, as the young ones grow up, we think about treating them differently. By the time they have huge chokes, we've moved on to stuffing recipes.

This recipe then, you might say, is for teenage artichokes, when you hope they don't have any choke but they usually do. The flavours are ones I've come to associate with artichokes – lemon, potato, lentils, chard, tomato, tarragon and thyme... and just a smidgeon of sheep's cheese, a high note not to offset the earthy tones.

Sprinkled over the dish is a dusting of lemon hazelnut praline. Sweet, yes, but in small crisp doses it's a fun way to add citrus and nutty flavours.

To make the chard potato cakes, which you are free to call timbales if the mood strikes, you will need four metal rings about 8–9cm/3¼–3½in in diameter and 2cm/¾in high.

- Make the lemon hazelnut praline: put the sugar in a small pan with the lemon rind and a tablespoon of water. Simmer over low heat until the sugar has melted and turned a light golden colour. Stir in the hazelnuts and immediately spread the mixture, including the rind, on baking parchment. Leave to cool.

- While they are cooling, prepare the chard, potato and Puy lentil cake: bring a saucepan of water to the boil, add the lentils and simmer for 15–20 minutes until tender but still firm. Drain in a colander and set aside.

- Meanwhile, cut the stalks from the centre of the chard leaves and dice the stalks finely.

- Bring a saucepan of water to the boil and cook the leaves for 4–5 minutes, until tender. Drain and cool in cold water, then drain again and dry on kitchen paper.

- Heat a tablespoon of the olive oil in a frying pan over medium heat. Fry the onion and diced chard stalks for 5 minutes, stirring. Turn the heat to high and add the remaining 2 tablespoons of olive oil.

- Break the cooked potatoes into a coarse mash with your hands and add them to the pan. Fry for 10 minutes, stirring constantly, until the potatoes are browned.

- Stir in the parsley and lentils, and season well with salt and pepper. Transfer to a bowl and leave to cool.

- While this cools, squeeze the juice of the lemon into a bowl of cold water and throw in the lemon too. Prepare the artichokes by pulling away the outer leaves and peeling the stem back to the edible core. Slice off the top of the remaining leaves, and cut the artichokes in half lengthways. If there is any hairy choke, scrape it out with a knife. Put the prepared artichokes in the water.

- Bring a saucepan of water to the boil, drop in the artichokes and simmer for 5 minutes, to part-cook them. Drain and place the artichokes, cut side up, in an oven dish.

- While these simmer, preheat the oven to 190°C/375°F/gas mark 5.

- When the potato lentil mixture is cool, stir in the cheese and brush the metal rings with olive oil. Use the cooked chard leaves to line them, with the edges overhanging the rims. Pack the lined rings with some of the potato lentil mix, fold over the overhanging leaves and press firmly to make a solid cake. Store on a baking parchment-lined oven tray in the fridge until needed.

- Put the carrot, onion, celery, garlic, herbs, olive oil and white wine in a small pan and bring to the boil. Pour this over the artichokes. Season with a little salt. Cover the dish loosely with baking parchment and place it in the oven for 30 minutes, until the artichokes are tender.

- While the artichokes are cooking, brush the chard cakes generously with some olive oil and sprinkle them with a little

Continued on following page...

Continued from previous page...

water. Put the tray in the oven for 12–15 minutes, until the cakes are warmed through.

- Make the cherry tomato sauce: put the cherry tomatoes, garlic and olive oil in a small saucepan over low heat. Cook for 10 minutes, until the tomatoes have softened. Add the balsamic vinegar, season to taste with salt and pepper, and then remove the pan from the heat.

- Just before serving, add a little of the artichoke braising liquid to make a wetter sauce.

- Break the praline into pieces and pulse these in a food processor to get a crisp crumb.

- To serve, flip the cakes over and place them on plates. Spoon the sauce around each one. Discarding the braising vegetables and herbs, arrange the artichokes on the cakes and sprinkle the praline over the dish.

Aubergine, spinach & potato gratin with fennel-braised Puy lentils

for 4

2 medium aubergines
1 tbsp olive oil, for tossing
  and oiling, plus extra for
  brushing
1 red onion, finely chopped
4 garlic cloves, thinly sliced
2 tsp cumin seeds, ground
2 tsp coriander seeds,
  ground
2 sprigs of fresh thyme,
  leaves only
1 x 400g/14oz tin of
  chopped tomatoes,
  drained
100ml/3½fl oz red wine
800g/1¾lb potatoes
400g/14oz spinach leaves
200g/7oz ricotta
100g/3½oz mozzarella
  cheese, grated
salt and pepper

*for the fennel-braised Puy
lentils*
100g/3½oz Puy lentils
45g/1¾oz butter
1 tbsp olive oil
½ red onion, finely diced
½ medium fennel bulb,
  cored and diced
1 fresh red chilli, deseeded
  and thinly sliced
finely grated zest of
  1 orange

The lentils were originally going into the gratin with everything else, but I put the brakes on the recipe, thought it through a bit more and decided to do a little deconstruction. This way, the earthy lentils get together with the fennel, chilli and butter to bring a new set of flavours to the plate – a cross between a sauce and a side dish.

- Preheat the oven to 200°C/400°F/gas mark 6.

- Cut the top and end off the aubergines, and remove a thin slice from 2 sides. Cut the remaining flesh into 1cm/½in slices. Brush these lightly with olive oil and place on a baking parchment-lined oven tray. Roast for 12–15 minutes, until coloured on both sides, turning once if necessary.

- Reduce the oven temperature to 180°C/350°F/gas mark 4.

- While the aubergine is roasting, heat the tablespoon of olive oil in a pan over medium heat and fry the onion for 5 minutes, then add the garlic, spices and thyme, and cook for 1 minute more. Add the tomatoes and red wine, bring to the boil and simmer over low heat for 15 minutes. Season with salt and pepper.

- At the same time, bring a saucepan of water to the boil. Peel the potatoes and cut into slices 5mm/¼in thick. Drop into the water and boil for 5 minutes to part-cook. Remove the potatoes from the water, drain them and toss in a little olive oil. Season well with salt and pepper.

- Drop the spinach into the boiling water for a few seconds, then remove and cool it in a colander under cold water. Squeeze the water from the spinach and chop coarsely. Stir it into the ricotta, and season.

- Brush a 20cm/8in square oven dish with a little olive oil. Place a layer of slightly overlapping potato slices in the dish and spoon over half of the tomato sauce. Top with a layer of aubergine slices, then all of the spinach-ricotta mixture. Follow this with another layer of potato, the remaining tomato sauce and another layer of aubergine. Press down firmly and cover with foil. Bake for 20 minutes, then sprinkle over the mozarella and return the dish to the oven, uncovered, for a few minutes until the cheese is melted and beginning to colour.

- Remove from the oven and leave to stand for a few minutes before slicing to serve.

- While the gratin is baking, make the lentils: bring 300ml/11fl oz of water to the boil in a saucepan, add the lentils and simmer for 12–15 minutes, until almost tender. Remove the pan from the heat.

- Meanwhile, in another saucepan, heat 15g/½oz of the butter with the olive oil over medium heat and fry the onion, fennel and chilli for 5 minutes until tender.

- Add the lentils and their remaining cooking liquid to the fennel mixture. Bring to the boil and cook over medium heat until the lentils are tender and the liquid has almost disappeared. Add the orange zest and the remaining butter. Season well and remove from the heat.

- Serve the gratin with some of the braised lentils spooned over and around each portion.

Portobello mushroom & aduki bean gratin with roast parsnip crust

for 6

250g/9oz aduki beans, soaked in cold water for 2 hours and drained
6 large Portobello mushrooms
2 tbsp olive oil, plus extra for drizzling
2 red onions, finely chopped
6 garlic cloves, chopped
2 carrots, peeled and diced
1 small celeriac, peeled and diced
2 sprigs of fresh thyme, leaves only
1 sprig of fresh rosemary, leaves only, chopped
150ml/5fl oz red wine
1 x 400g/14oz tin of tomatoes, diced
1 tbsp tomato purée
salt and pepper

for the roast parsnip crust
400g/14oz parsnips, peeled and diced
olive oil, for tossing
200ml/7fl oz milk
800g/1¾lb potatoes, peeled and halved
60g/2½oz butter
200g/7oz hard cheese, such as Cheddar or Gruyère, grated

With its dark, juicy portobellos and tiny dense aduki beans in a rich sauce underneath a pile of parsnip-flavoured mash, this winter gratin is clearly a distant relation to 'shepherd's pie'. I was wondering what to call it, so I took a stroll around the web wondering if anyone had a clever name for something similar that I might adapt or borrow. I came across a couple of feisty arguments about the 'proper' way to make the traditional English/Scottish dish, and about where it 'originated'. It seemed like the only fact that was pinned down was that the dish couldn't have been made at all until potatoes from the Americas were accepted into the common food culture of the British Isles.

We have similar arguments in Ireland about the correct recipe for things like colcannon. As though one morning a great leader came to the balcony and handed out strict instructions for mashing cabbage and potatoes together. The fun thing about peasant food is that recipes get handed down, not through authorities, but within families and communities. The variations and competition between one family, village or county and the next are part of what keeps it current and relevant.

It's one of the joys of being an untrained vegetarian cook that there are very few rules, little enough tradition and no hierarchy. When I put this recipe together, I wasn't trying to adhere to a proper way or imitate another dish, and I have made plenty of dishes that essentially consist of vegetables in a rich sauce under mash. When I stopped to wonder whether I should put cheese on top, I didn't have to consider whether it was correct or not, only whether it would make the dish nicer to eat. I voted yes; if you vote no, that's correct too.

In the end, I chose a rather prosaic title, a simple description of the dish. You can call yours anything you like. Serve it with a simple green – cabbage or kale lightly steamed or braised would be lovely.

- Boil the aduki beans in plenty of water for 50–60 minutes, until tender. Drain and set aside.

- Preheat the oven to 200°C/400°F/gas mark 6.

- Place the mushrooms on an oven tray, drizzle with olive oil and sprinkle with a little salt. Roast in the oven for 10 minutes, until tender. Chop the cooked mushrooms into medium dice.

- Lower the oven setting to 180°C/350°F/gas mark 5.

- Heat the 2 tablespoons of olive oil in a large, heavy saucepan over medium heat. Add the onion and sauté for 5 minutes. Add the garlic, carrots, celeriac and herbs, and cook for 8–10 minutes, until the vegetables are tender. Add the wine and the cooked aduki beans, and simmer for 5 minutes. Then add the tomatoes and tomato purée. Season with salt and pepper and simmer for 15 minutes. Stir in the roasted mushrooms.

- While these simmer, make the roast parsnip crust: toss the parsnips in a little olive oil in an oven dish, cover with baking parchment and roast in the oven for 20 minutes, until tender. Check occasionally and add a little water to keep the parsnips moist. Transfer to a food processor and blend to a purée, adding a little of the milk, if necessary.

- Steam or boil the potatoes until soft. Drain. Warm the milk and butter in a large saucepan, add the potatoes and mash. Season with salt and pepper, and stir in half of the cheese and the parsnip purée.

- Put the mushroom and aduki mixture in an oven dish and cover with the parsnip mash. Scatter over the remaining cheese. Bake in the oven for 30 minutes, until the top is golden, remove the dish from the oven and leave to stand for 5 minutes before serving.

Potato, squash & leek gratin

for 4

2 leeks, halved lengthways
  and well washed
15g/½oz butter
4 garlic cloves, thinly sliced
2 sprigs of fresh thyme,
  leaves only
8 fresh sage leaves, sliced
  into thin ribbons
2 tsp strong mustard
150ml/5fl oz double cream
300g/11oz squash or
  pumpkin, peeled and
  deseeded
olive oil, for tossing
800g/1¾lb medium floury
  potatoes, peeled
100g/3½oz strong melting
  cheese, grated
salt and pepper

On cold winter evenings, there isn't anything much more satisfying or nicer than a gratin of layered ingredients bubbling and mingling gently in the oven for an hour or so, filling the house with hunger-inducing smells and the sense of being safely tucked away from the mean weather. As usual, when the comfort levels of a dish get this mellow, I like to contrast them with something lively. I would suggest serving this gratin with some simple greens, such as broccoli, Brussels sprouts or kale quickly cooked with garlic and chillies or ginger. The cheese in the gratin should be a medium-hard one with good flavour and a melting texture, in the style of Gruyère, Emmental or Gouda. In Ireland, I would use Coolea or a young Gabriel.

- Preheat the oven to 180°C/350°F/gas mark 4.

- Cut the leeks at an angle into slices 1cm/½in thick.

- In a wide pan, melt the butter over medium heat, add the leeks and sauté for 5 minutes, stirring. Add the garlic and herbs, and continue to cook for 2 minutes more. Add half of the cream and half of the mustard, bring to the boil and then remove from the heat. Season well with salt and pepper.

- Quarter or halve the squash and cut into slices 3cm/1¼in thick and 5-8cm/2–3¼in long. Toss in a little olive oil. Slice the potatoes to the same thickness and toss separately in olive oil.

- Place a layer of potato slices, slightly overlapping, in an oven dish about 20cm/8in square. Top with a similar layer of squash slices. Scatter over half of the leeks. Repeat the layers and finish with a layer of potato.

- Press down firmly on the top layer and cover the dish with foil. Bake for 30–40 minutes, until the vegetables are tender – check by piercing with a knife.

- Pour in the remaining cream and sprinkle on the cheese. Return the gratin to the oven and bake for 10–15 minutes more, until the cheese is melted and beginning to colour.

- Remove the gratin from the oven and leave to stand for a few minutes before serving.

Baked pumpkin, leek & coconut curry with green bean salsa

I think of this curry as essentially Thai in its flavouring, though it's not in any way classic or traditional in its cooking method. Dishes from the region are more typically put together quickly on the stove over high heat, emphasising their fresh, lively flavours of herbs, coconut, spices and citrus.

In this case, the same flavours are treated to a slow simmer in the oven instead. This is partly because pumpkin likes to absorb flavours slowly, and partly for the simple pleasure of having time to do with what you will, while dinner fills the house with sweetly spiced aromas. Coming back downstairs, or from the basement office if you must keep working so late in the day, you quickly boil some rice and knock up the salsa, which miraculously puts all the lively zing back in the dish. You get the best of both worlds – slow cooking and a fresh herby finish.

- Preheat the oven to 200°C/400°F/gas mark 6.

- Chop the pumpkin into large pieces and toss them in a little vegetable oil in an oven dish. Bake for 10 minutes. Lower the oven setting to 170°C/325°F/gas mark 3.

- While the pumpkin is baking, cut the leeks just below the point where the leaves open. Slice the lower parts into 2cm/¾in-thick rounds. Trim away and discard the coarser part of the green tops. Slice the remaining green parts in half lengthways, wash them well and slice them to the same thickness.

- Heat the 2 tablespoons of oil in a large, wide pan over medium heat and cook the leeks for 3 minutes, stirring them often. Add the garlic, red chillies, ginger and basil, and cook for a further 1 minute.

- Press the lemon grass stalks to bruise them and add to the pan with the coconut milk, cream and soy sauce. Bring to the boil and pour it over the pumpkin.

- Stir and return the dish to the oven to bake for 30–40 minutes, until the vegetables are tender. The sauce should be still moist.

Continued on following page...

for 4

1.5kg/3¼lb pumpkin, peeled and deseeded
2 tbsp vegetable oil, plus extra for tossing
3 leeks
4 garlic cloves, sliced
3–4 fresh red chillies, deseeded and sliced
2 tbsp grated fresh ginger
1 small bunch of fresh Thai basil leaves, chopped
4 lemongrass stalks
1 x 400ml/14fl oz tin of coconut milk, plus extra for moistening (optional)
150ml/5fl oz double cream
1 tbsp soy sauce
salt

for the green bean salsa
200g/7oz fine green beans, halved lengthways
3 tbsp peanuts, roasted and skinned
1 fresh green chilli, deseeded and finely chopped
3 spring onions, finely chopped
3 tbsp chopped fresh coriander
juice of 2 limes

Continued from previous page...

If it has dried out too much, add more coconut milk or water and heat through for a few minutes more.

- While the curry is baking, make the green bean salsa: bring a small saucepan of water to the boil, add the green beans and simmer for 2 minutes. Drain and cool the beans in cold water. Drain again and place the beans in a bowl. Stir in the peanuts, green chilli, spring onion, coriander and lime juice. Season to taste with salt.

- Serve the curry with the salsa spooned over and some rice or bread on the side.

Artichoke, leek & brie tart in walnut pastry

While a tart or pie, or any such pastry, is often used as a way to use up or even hide ingredients, this one is best with some really good young artichokes – the kind with long edible stems and little hairy choke. In fact, rather than use tough old artichokes, my second choice here would be very good-quality pre-prepared ones from a jar.

Serve this as an elegant early summer dinner, with a simple leaf salad and new potatoes; or take it on a picnic – artichokes love to go on picnics, but I don't know why that is, they just do.

- Make the pastry: sift the walnuts with the flour and salt, then put these in a food processor with the butter. Pulse until you get a fine crumb.

- Transfer to a bowl, add 2 tablespoons and 2 teaspoons of cold water and stir briefly to form a dough. Shape the dough into a ball with your hands, flatten it gently and chill for at least 30 minutes.

- Roll the chilled pastry out to fit a 23cm/9in tart tin, leaving enough overhang to fold in and double up at the top. Use your fingers to make a fluted edge. Prick the pastry all over with a fork and chill again for 30 minutes.

- Meanwhile, prepare the filling: melt the butter in a pan over medium heat, add the leeks, garlic and thyme, and sauté for 7–8 minutes, stirring often, until the leeks are tender. Add the mustard and wine and simmer for 3–4 minutes more, until the liquid is gone. Season well with salt and pepper and leave to cool.

- Bring a saucepan of water to the boil. Squeeze the lemon juice into a bowl of cold water and throw in the lemon too. Prepare the artichokes by pulling off the outer leaves and peeling the stalk back to the edible cores. Cut the artichokes in half and remove any hairy choke and tough leaves at the centre.

- Cut each half into 3 slices lengthways. Drop the slices into the lemon water as you go. Transfer all the prepared artichoke slices and the lemon to the boiling water. Simmer for 2 minutes only, then cool the artichokes in another bowl of cold water.

Continued on following page...

Continued on following page...

for 4

for the walnut pastry
40g/1½oz walnuts, finely ground
150g/5oz plain flour
large pinch of salt
75g/3oz cold butter, diced

for the filling
30g/1¼oz butter
2 leeks, well washed and diced
2 garlic cloves
2 sprigs of fresh thyme, leaves only
1 tsp smooth mustard
100ml/3½fl oz dry white wine
1 lemon
4–6 small–medium artichokes
1 tbsp olive oil
6 slices of Brie, 5mm/¼in thick
salt and pepper

Continued from previous page...

- When cool, drain well and toss the artichokes in the olive oil, and season with salt and pepper.

- Preheat the oven to 180°C/350°F/gas mark 4.

- Weigh the pastry case down with dried beans in baking parchment and bake it for 8–10 minutes, until crisp.

- Remove the beans and paper, then spread the leek mixture into the pastry case. Arrange the artichoke slices on top.

- Bake the tart in the oven for 10 minutes, until the artichokes are beginning to colour. Arrange the Brie slices on top, from the edge to the centre, pressing them in gently. Bake the tart for a further 5 minutes until the Brie has melted.

- Remove the tart from the oven and leave to cool for a few minutes before slicing.

Broccoli, feta &
caramelised onion tart

Many, many years ago, in the early days of Café Paradiso, a couple of lunchtime diners, whom I thought of as somewhere between acquaintances and new friends, said the broccoli tart they had just eaten was, er, not very nice. I got a bit harrumphed for a short while, then thought about what it was they didn't like about it. Texture. We had blended cooked broccoli with eggs, cream and cheese, as you might do with spinach, to make a uniformly green tart filling. Except that the colour went a bit brown in the oven and the brassica flavour tipped over into boiled cabbage territory. It's actually not an uncommon way to go about making a tart with broccoli or other greens. I've eaten similar tarts in other restaurants, and it usually reminds me of that early Paradiso effort. Something about the process loses all the positive characteristics of the main ingredient.

Putting that one in the 'bad idea' box, I gave up on broccoli tart for a long time. Until one evening when I was thinking about making a tart for dinner and searching the fridge to decide what to put in it. You know that scenario – you decide to make something, your mind locks on it and only then do you check if you've got the ingredients to pull it off.

One thing I realised, with my head in the fridge, was that I don't think about broccoli very much but, like most people, I routinely buy it because it's so damn useful and looks so good for you. Kids eat it too, or at least you think they will when you buy it. Anyway, I decided to combine my leanings towards tart for dinner with an attempt to banish the bad broccoli tart memories.

If I've learnt anything in the intervening years, it is to take the time to adapt recipes to ingredients rather than force available ingredients into square-hole recipes designed for others.

This tart is a whole lot more respectful of broccoli's intrinsic qualities of texture, colour and lively flavour than the earlier one, helped by the fact that the green is in the good company of sweetly caramelised onions and the salty tang of feta.

Serve with some roast potatoes in winter or new ones in summer.

Continued on following page...

for 6–8

for the pastry
160g/5½oz plain flour
75g/3oz cold butter, diced

for the filling
olive oil, for cooking and
    tossing
250g/9oz red onions
2 tbsp soft brown sugar
2 tbsp balsamic vinegar
400g/14oz broccoli
3 eggs
150ml/5fl oz double cream
200g/7oz feta cheese
salt and pepper

Continued from previous page...

- Make the pastry: sift the flour and salt, then put them in a food processor with the butter. Pulse to get a fine crumb.

- Transfer to a bowl and stir in 2 tablespoons and 2 teaspoons of cold water with a few quick strokes to form a dough. Shape the dough into a ball with your hands, flatten it gently and chill it for at least 30 minutes.

- Roll the chilled pastry out to fit a 26cm/10½in pastry case and chill for about 30 minutes.

- Preheat the oven to 180°C/350°F/gas mark 4.

- Meanwhile, prepare the filling: slice the red onions in half, then into thin slices. Heat a little olive oil in a pan, add the onions and cook for 5 minutes over medium heat. Add the sugar and vinegar and cover loosely with baking parchment, then lower the heat and continue to simmer for 20–30 minutes, until the onions are soft and have taken on a slightly jammy texture.

- Break the broccoli into florets and slice these in half lengthways, or in quarters if they are very fat. Peel the lower part of the stalks and thinly slice them.

- Bring a saucepan of water to the boil, drop in the broccoli and simmer for 1 minute. Drain through a sieve and cool the broccoli under cold running water. Place it on a towel and pat it dry, then put it in a bowl and toss with a little olive oil, salt and pepper.

- Weigh the pastry case down with dried beans in baking parchment and bake it for about 10 minutes, until beginning to crisp. Leave the oven on when you take it out.

- Spread the caramelised onion on the base of the pastry and cover with the broccoli. Season with salt and pepper. Whisk together the eggs and cream, and pour over the tart. Crumble the feta on top and press down gently. Bake for 30 minutes, until the custard is set. Remove the tart from the oven and leave to sit for 10 minutes before serving.

Broad bean–stuffed braised artichoke on beetroot pastry with orange & caper aioli

Giving up on supplies of small or medium artichokes – those lovely things with long fleshy stems and little or no messy chokes to deal with – is always a drag. But there's no point in pouting: when they're gone, they're gone. You've seen it coming for weeks, and the remaining choice is whether to give up on artichokes entirely or switch to those affectionately known as green monsters. Affection might be an exaggeration. Best suited to being eaten slowly in the traditional leaf-by-leaf manner, it can be a tough physical chore to carve away their exterior to reveal the bases required for this recipe. The good part is that you only have to do one for each person. Ten minutes work, max, and well worth it, I promise you. Make sure you get the biggest, fattest artichokes you can find – and I don't say that too often about artichokes.

You can tell by looking at this dish that it's not a casual TV dinner. It is definitely designed to look pretty, bringing together in an appealing way ingredients that are always very comfortable with each other. It is certainly rich and satisfying, though not necessarily a huge feed. Rather than add to the plate, I would suggest serving this as part of a two- or three-course meal.

In the restaurant business, the issue of portion size is a constant balancing act. Ideally, when creating menus and their individual dishes, you expect people to eat two or three courses, and to feel pleasured and satisfied by those without feeling like foie gras geese. That can sometimes leave a big eater, or those who only order one course, with a nagging gap and an urge to go for chips on the way home. Weirdly, men with big appetites are often the ones to order only one dish, as though starters are for sissies and desserts for girls. In which case, you just have to put your hand up and recommend a good chippie.

From a word count, it has the look of a daunting recipe, but all the stages can be done ahead of time and lined up ready for a very simple finish. At a leisurely pace, caramelise the beetroot, bake the pastry, make the aioli and prepare and fill the artichokes. When your guests are ready to eat, it's a simple warming-up exercise.

- Preheat the oven to 180°C/350°F/gas mark 4.

- Make the beetroot pastry: grate the beetroot and put it in a pot with the balsamic vinegar, maple syrup and cayenne. Bring to the boil and simmer for 20 minutes, uncovered, stirring occasionally to prevent the beetroot from sticking. Season with a little salt and remove from the heat. When cooled, stir in the sheep's cheese.

- Cut four 8cm/3¼in squares from the puff pastry. Place these on a baking parchment-lined baking sheet and prick them all over with a fork. Bake for 12–15 minutes until golden. Leave the oven on when you remove them from it.

- While the beetroots are cooking and the pastry baking, prepare the artichokes: pull the outer green leaves from an artichoke, as close to the base as possible, until the leaves revealed are a pale yellow-green shade right up to the widest part of the artichoke. Now cut the top from each artichoke at this widest part, and peel the tough outer green skin from the base. Finally, use a spoon to scoop out the hairy choke from the centre. Halve the lemon, squeeze the juice into a bowl of water and drop in the squeezed lemon and the prepared artichoke bottom. Repeat with the other artichokes.

- Bring a saucepan of water to the boil and drop in the artichokes and the lemon. Simmer for 10–12 minutes, until the artichokes are tender but firm. Drain and cool in a bowl of cold water.

- Place the artichokes in a single layer in an oven dish. In a saucepan, bring the olive oil, wine, stock, thyme and garlic to the boil. Pour this over the artichokes, cover loosely with baking parchment and place the dish in the oven for 30–40 minutes.

- Meanwhile, make the broad bean stuffing: cook the broad beans in another saucepan of boiling water for 5 minutes, then cool them in cold water and peel off the outer grey skins. Mash the broad beans with a fork or by chopping briefly in a food processor. Stir in the ricotta and herbs, and season with salt and pepper.

Continued on following page...

for 4

4 large globe artichokes
1 lemon
3 tbsp olive oil
100ml/3½fl oz dry white wine
100ml/3½fl oz vegetable stock
2 sprigs of fresh thyme
4 garlic cloves, sliced
salt and pepper

for the beetroot pastry
2 medium beetroots, washed, cooked and peeled
1 tbsp balsamic vinegar
2 tbsp maple syrup
pinch of cayenne pepper
30g/1¼oz hard sheep's cheese, such as pecorino
½ sheet of frozen puff pastry, defrosted

for the broad bean stuffing
300g/11oz podded fresh broad beans
200g/7oz ricotta
1 tbsp chopped fresh basil leaves
1 tbsp chopped fresh chives

for the orange and caper aioli
1 garlic clove, chopped
finely grated zest of 1 orange
1 egg, plus 1 extra egg yolk
1 tsp smooth mustard
250ml/9fl oz olive oil
1 tbsp small capers, rinsed
juice of ½ orange

Continued from previous page...

- Drain the artichokes, discarding the liquid, and fill their cavities with the broad bean stuffing. Return the dish to the oven for 7–8 minutes, just to heat through.

- Make the orange and caper aioli: put the garlic, orange zest, egg and extra yolk and the mustard in a food processor. Blend for a minute, then slowly add the oil until you get a thick pouring consistency. Add the capers and orange juice, and pulse briefly to incorporate them. Season with salt and pepper.

- Carefully spoon some beetroot on each of the pastries, covering with a thin layer all but a 5mm/¼in border around the edge. Place the pastries back on the oven tray and return to the oven for 2 minutes to warm through.

- Decorate the plates with the aioli and place a beetroot pastry on top, with a stuffed artichoke on top of that again.

Swede & leek gratin in maple cream with sage & walnut crust

for 4–6

1 large swede
2 leeks, halved lengthways and well washed
30g/1¼oz butter, plus extra for greasing
3 garlic cloves, finely chopped
2 sprigs of fresh thyme
100ml/3½fl oz dry white wine
250ml/9fl oz double cream
4 tbsp maple syrup
salt and pepper

for the sage and walnut crust
8 fresh sage leaves
1 tbsp chopped fresh chives
50g/2oz white bread
50g/2oz walnuts
30g/1¼oz butter

When winter kicks in, I often find myself looking for ways to make main courses based on my favourite root, that giant of the underworld answering to the name of swede, rutabaga or neeps in various parts of the globe. In Ireland it is simply – and rather obstinately – known as turnip. Unlikely ever to become as fashionable as squash, burdened by associations with poverty and rude suggestions that it was developed for pigs, the swede soldiers on, loved dearly by those of us who pay it any attention. I think that most swede lovers have some degree of nostalgic or cultural reasons for their devotion. And for every one, there is another who dislikes them for the same reasons. One of my greatest pleasures as a cook is to see a smile of pleasure cross the face of one of the disbelievers as they say in the wonder of reconversion, 'that was a swede?'

In this dish, the swede's golden colour and the truly earthy sugars welcome the strong character and savoury sweetness of maple syrup. Long cooking seems to be the way to bring the best out of a swede, whether by boiling, braising or roasting.

Serve with some simple cooked greens, cabbage or broccoli maybe, for a hearty and belly-warming winter supper.

- Preheat the oven to 150°C/300°F/gas mark 2.

- Bring a large saucepan of water to the boil. Peel the swede, quarter it, then chop it into slices about 5mm/¼in thick. Simmer these in the water for 10 minutes, then remove and partly cool them in cold water. Drain and set aside.

- Chop the leeks into pieces about 2cm/¾in thick. In a large pot, melt the butter over high heat, add the leeks and garlic and cook, stirring, for 8–10 minutes. Add the thyme and white wine, and boil for 1 minute, then pour in the cream and maple syrup. Bring back to the boil and then remove from the heat. Season with salt and pepper.

- Grease an oven dish with butter and arrange a layer of swede slices on the bottom. Spoon one-third of the leeks on top and cover with another layer of swede. Repeat to get 3 layers of each, finishing with the leeks. Press firmly on the top and place the dish in the oven. Bake for 30 minutes.

- While the gratin is baking, make the sage and walnut crust: put the sage, chives and bread in a food processor and pulse to a fine crumb. Add the walnuts and butter, and pulse briefly to chop the walnuts coarsely.

- Increase the oven temperature to 180°C/350°F/gas mark 4.

- Scatter the sage and walnut topping over the gratin and return it to the oven for 5 minutes.

- Remove from the oven and leave to rest for 5 minutes before serving.

Sweetness

Sweetness

I've been developing something of a sweet tooth as I get older. And not just when it comes to dessert-time either. Scattered throughout the savoury recipes of this book, you will find dishes that create one of my favourite flavour combinations (and, indeed, that of many people) – rich, spicy-hot and sweet. The sugar content comes from straight-up sweeteners like honey and maple syrup, from citrus, berries and stone fruit or from cooking methods that coax out the natural sugars of vegetables like peppers, tomatoes and fennel.

My interest in desserts has also shifted from a starting position of rarely even looking at the last part of a menu out of anything more than professional curiosity. Not that I was ever as disinterested as an old friend who used to say that he would prefer to have another plate of spuds thanks. My sister never touched a piece of chocolate or ordered a dessert until she turned 40; now she's got sweet treats stashed around the house for times when her surprising new cravings kick in. Meanwhile, I find myself getting (just a little) excited at the thought of a dish of ice cream or a scattering of strawberries across a meltingly soft pavlova.

Perhaps it is just part of an aging (or maturing, as I like to see it) palate. A reverse of how other people seem to go, gradually losing their childish taste for sugar and drifting towards the rhubarb as the years go by.

I tell myself that it also has to do with a better (maturing again?) understanding of the role of dessert in a multi-course meal. If dinner has been low-key, dessert might be an exciting showstopper; or it might be the rich follow-up to a light main course; or a calm, soothingly pleasurable landing after a dramatic dinner.

In the construction of savoury dishes, both texturally and in flavour combinations, I like to play with contrasts, using richness to balance light, and spiking comfort zones with spice and crunch. The 'afters' – as dessert was so literally named when I was a child – of such a meal should be a sublime experience. There's only so much excitement one meal can stand. Dessert should make you go 'Mmmmm...' when dinner has elicited the occasional 'Wow!',

'Cripes!', or the ultimate compliment of 'Holysweetjesusdivine-tonight, that's bloody good'. Rhubarb dishes excepted, of course. Rhubarb will always demand attention.

A scan through the recipes of this chapter shows that they almost all have one thing in common – a combination of seasonal fruit with something rich and sweet. Fruits are a perfect, naturally sweet way to end a meal, though on their own they can seem too frugal and you'll rarely convince a child that an apple constitutes dessert. That reminds me of another friend – note how comprehensive my research is in this field – a regular at Café Paradiso who, confronted by a chocolate and clementine dessert we used to serve, would flick the oranges to the edge of her plate, saying that when she orders chocolate she wants chocolate and anyway oranges are for breakfast. Such a forcefully made point has to be taken on board, so now our chocolate desserts have little or no fruit embellishment to dilute the sinful pleasure. Ultimately, that's it – dessert is pure pleasure, a frippery of delightful taste with no purpose other than to soothe your soul and put a grin on your face.

While the recipes follow my taste preferences, they also reflect my basic skill levels. Never having spent much time in the pastry section, where the work tends to be precise, exact and sticky-fingered, I am more at home with the flexible and intuitive type of cooking required to make the savoury parts of a meal. So I can promise you that the recipes here can be made by anyone with a little bit of patience, weighing scales and a measuring jug.

Olive oil chocolate mousse with salt & chilli sesame praline and cherry salsa

It started – as many restaurant dishes do – with a chatty post-service kitchen conversation about the nature of menu language, a topic that has long fascinated me. Although ordering something to eat – about as physical as things can get – restaurant diners have to make their choices based not on taste or even appearance but on the pitch of a sentence. Some menus are familiar; others almost deliberately obtuse, and the rest of us are making an honest effort to help you choose between unusual dishes, using only typed words. You read the menu over and over, trying to find combinations of words that excite your palate, while your mind tries to visualise the dish and your stomach tries to influence the decision based on which dishes sound most filling. (Never listen to your stomach in a good restaurant; you're there for the pleasure of eating, not to get full.)

So, without being misleading, there was an element of playfulness in constructing the sentence describing this dessert. The idea was to write the sentence in a way that would largely suggest a savoury dish, beginning with 'olive oil' and ending in 'salsa'. In between, there is salt, chilli and sesame on one side of the fence and chocolate, praline and cherries on the other.

Semantics is fun, but if it was only for a laugh we would have left this on paper. The fun thing is that the flavours work really well together. Another menu writer might well put it this way – chocolate, olive oil, chilli, salt, sesame, cherries. I'd order that. Be generous with the praline on the plate – it's an integral part of the balance, not a garnish.

for 6

200g/7oz dark chocolate
175ml/6fl oz light, fruity
   olive oil
5 eggs, separated
160g/5½oz caster sugar
pinch of salt

*for the salt and chilli
sesame praline*
200g/7oz caster sugar
125g/4½oz sesame seeds,
   lightly toasted
2½ tsp salt flakes,
   crumbled
8 dried bird's eye chillies,
   deseeded and ground

for the cherry salsa
100g/3½oz caster sugar
3 tbsp kirsch
200g/7oz cherries, stoned
4 fresh mint leaves, finely
   chopped

- In a heatproof bowl set over a saucepan of simmering water (but not touching the water), melt the chocolate and slowly stir in the olive oil.

- Beat the egg yolks with half the sugar until pale and fluffy. Stir in the chocolate and oil mix.

- Whisk the egg whites with the salt until stiff, then continue whisking while adding the remaining sugar gradually in small batches. Fold the egg white mix into the chocolate.

Continued on following page...

Continued from previous page...

- Line 6 dessert rings with baking parchment, rising above the rings a little to give a higher structure. Spoon some mousse mix into each and smooth the tops. Chill for 4 hours or overnight.

- Make the salt and chilli sesame praline: put the sugar in a small saucepan over low heat and leave until the sugar has melted and turned golden brown. Stir in the sesame seeds and immediately spread out on a sheet of baking parchment. When cool and hard, break up the praline and chop it to a coarse ground in a food processor. Stir in the salt and chilli.

- Make the cherry salsa: place the sugar, 3 tablespoons of water and the kirsch in a small saucepan and simmer for 5 minutes. Leave this syrup to cool to room temperature. It should be slightly thickened, just enough to coat the back of a spoon.

- Just before serving, chop the cherries into small dice and add syrup according to your own taste. Stir in the mint.

- To serve, place a mousse on a plate. Lift off the ring and carefully peel away the baking parchment. Beside it, arrange the cherry salsa in a line and the praline in another.

Honey-roasted figs on a yoghurt, cardamom & pistachio tart

That sentence up there wrote itself when I put pencil to notebook and started with the words 'honey' and 'figs'. No, that's not quite right, this is the second version. The first was a very simple 'honey roasted figs with cardamom yoghurt'. The easy version is a very delicious and quick dessert in its own right, but I decided to pre-empt the editor's likely request to, er, tart it up a little. If you close your eyes and murmur the title quietly to yourself repeatedly for five minutes, you'll find yourself under the warm Mediterranean sun somewhere between Greece and Lebanon. If you do this after eating the dish, you might find it hard to return. This is wonderful therapy on a chilly autumn evening, especially with the central heating cranked up.

The tart, made with a foolproof, no-rolling pastry, can be served at room temperature or chilled, and so can be made well in advance on the day.

- Put the ground pistachio nuts, the 50g/2oz sugar, flour and butter in a bowl and stir to get a firm dough. Place this in a 23cm/9in tart tin or pie dish, and press with your fingers to make a tart case. Chill the case for 30 minutes.

- Preheat the oven to 180°C/350°F/gas mark 4.

- Bake the chilled tart case for 5–7 minutes, until crisp. Remove from the oven and allow to cool. Keep the oven on.

- Combine the yoghurt, the 2 tablespoons of sugar and the citrus zests in a bowl, and stir in the eggs. Remove the seeds from the cardamom pods, coarsely grind them and add to the bowl.

- Fill the pastry case with the yoghurt custard, and place the tart in the oven to bake for 20–25 minutes, until the custard has set. Remove from the oven and leave to cool.

- While it cools, prepare the honey-roasted figs: put the honey and butter in a small saucepan and heat gently to melt. Put the quartered figs in an oven dish and pour over the honeyed butter. Roast in the oven for 5–7 minutes.

- To serve, place a slice of tart on each plate and spoon some of the figs over each portion.

for 6

100g/3½oz shelled
  pistachio nuts,
  finely ground
50g/2oz caster sugar, plus
  2 tbsp more for the filling
100g/3½oz plain flour
75g/3oz butter, softened
300ml/11fl oz natural
  yoghurt
finely grated zest of
  1 lemon
finely grated zest of
  1 orange
3 eggs, lightly beaten
15 green cardamom pods

for the honey-roasted figs
3 tbsp honey
30g/1¼oz butter
9–12 black figs, quartered

Rhubarb & strawberry trifle with prosecco, orange mascarpone & pistachio-lemon praline

for 4

1 bunch (600g/1lb 6oz) of
  rhubarb
200g/3½oz sugar
200g/7oz strawberries
100ml/3½fl oz prosecco
4 sponge finger biscuits

*for the pistachio-lemon
praline*
100g/3½oz caster sugar
rind of 1 lemon, in long
  strips
50g/2oz shelled pistachio
  nuts

for the orange mascarpone
200g/7oz mascarpone
  cheese
finely grated zest of 1
  orange
1 tbsp icing sugar
200ml/7fl oz double cream

The crossover period of rhubarb and strawberries as spring turns into summer is one of the loveliest accidents in food. They don't even seem a very likely pair, and yet they get on so well.

I first made this for my mother's 80th birthday party, 40 of them in rented martini glasses. I liked making it, eating it and just looking at it so much I put it on the Café Paradiso menu a few weeks later... with maternal permission, of course.

It's a very simple layered construction, and the parts that require any effort can be done in advance. You can even make up most the individual trifles, leaving the mascarpone and praline to be put on top just before serving. Of course, you can also make it in a single dish and scoop it out like classic trifle, but a lot of the fun in this is its very appealing appearance in large martini glasses.

- First make the pistachio-lemon praline: put the sugar in a small saucepan with the lemon rind and a tablespoon of water. Simmer over low heat until the sugar has melted and turned a light golden colour. Stir in the pistachios and immediately spread the mixture on a large sheet of baking parchment. Leave to cool. Break the praline into pieces and pulse in a food processor to get a fine crisp crumb.

- Chop the rhubarb into pieces about 2cm/¾in long and put these in a saucepan with 160g/5½oz of the sugar. Simmer for 8–10 minutes, until the rhubarb is soft. Check the sweetness and adjust with a little more sugar if necessary.

- Slice the strawberries thinly into a bowl and add the prosecco and the remaining sugar.

- Make the orange mascarpone: soften the mascarpone with a spoon and stir in the orange zest and juice and the icing sugar. Whisk the cream to soft peaks, then fold it into the mascarpone.

- Place a spoon of rhubarb in each martini glass. Break the biscuits in half and place a layer in the glass. Top this with some strawberries. Pipe the orange mascarpone over the strawberries and sprinkle some praline on top. Serve at room temperature.

Roast pears with ginger steamed pudding & mascarpone ice cream

for 4

4 medium pears, halved
    and cored
60g/2½oz butter, melted

*for the mascarpone ice
cream*
2 egg yolks
80g/3¼oz icing sugar
225g/8oz mascarpone
2 drops of vanilla extract

*for the gingered spiced
syrup*
250g/9oz caster sugar
1 cinnamon stick
3 cloves
1 star anise
50g/2oz stem ginger in
    syrup, syrup included,
    coarsely chopped

*for the ginger steamed
puddings*
40g/1½oz butter, softened,
    plus extra for the
    greasing
75g/3oz light muscovado
    sugar
1 egg, lightly beaten
½ tsp grated fresh ginger
large pinch of ground
    ginger
5 cloves, ground
80g/3¼oz plain flour
½ tsp baking powder
½ tsp bicarbonate
    of soda
50g/2oz stem ginger in
    syrup, syrup included,
    coarsely chopped
¼ sweet apple, finely
    grated

Put aside your delicate poaching of pears, and try this simple way of cooking them instead. It's much more up my street anyway. The pears are roasted in butter only, but the cooking process really draws out and concentrates their flavour. Besides, there is plenty of sweetness going on in the other parts of the dish, particularly the syrup and puddings, which are flavoured with three different gingers – mostly stem ginger in syrup, plus a little dried and fresh too.

There are a few stages in the recipe, but they can mostly be done ahead of time, and the individual puddings will cook while you eat dinner. The idea of serving individual puddings is purely for aesthetic reasons. We use narrow ones, 6cm/2½in tall with a capacity of 150ml/5fl oz, filled just a little over halfway to allow for rising.

- Make the ice cream: beat the egg yolks and icing sugar until creamy, then stir in the mascarpone and vanilla. Churn this mixture in an ice-cream machine, or simply freeze it in a covered container.

- To make the gingered spiced syrup: put the sugar, cinnamon, cloves, star anise and 3 tablespoons of water in a small saucepan, and simmer gently to get a lightly coloured syrup. Remove from the heat. Blend the stem ginger with its syrup to a purée and add it to the spiced syrup. Leave to cool, then pass through a sieve.

- Preheat the oven to 200°C/400°F/gas mark 6.

- Toss the pears in the melted butter and place them in a baking parchment-lined oven dish. Roast in the oven for 20 minutes, until they are tender and lightly coloured. Remove from the oven and set aside. Lower the oven setting to 180°C/350°F/gas mark 4.

- Make the ginger steamed puddings: bring a saucepan of water to the boil. Brush the ramekins with softened butter and place a small piece of baking parchment in the bottom of each one.

- Cream the butter and sugar, then stir in the egg. Mix the ginger, cloves, flour, baking powder and bicarbonate of soda together, then stir into the egg mix, together with the stem ginger and apple.

- Fill the ramekins just over half-full with this mixture and place them in a deep baking dish. Pour in enough boiling water to come just over halfway up the sides of the ramekins, and place the dish in the oven.

- Cook for 40 minutes, until the puddings have risen and set softly. Remove from the oven and leave to cool a little in the ramekins.

- Put the pears back in the oven to warm through. At the same time, remove the puddings from the ramekins by sliding a knife around the edges and turning the ramekins upside down.

- Serve 2 pear halves per portion, with a pudding, a scoop of mascarpone ice cream and a drizzle of the spiced ginger syrup.

Lavender set custard with honey & berries

for 6

for the lavender set custard
5 heads of lavender flowers
450ml/16fl oz single cream
4 egg yolks
75g/3oz caster sugar

to serve
4 tbsp honey
18–24 raspberries,
  blackberries, blueberries
  or figs

Despite the sequence of words in the title, this one's all about the honey, in my mind at least. When we harvested our first batch of Paradiso honey, I wanted to put it on the menu in at least one way that didn't hide it in complex or cooked flavours; a way that would say simply that we made this and isn't it good? Or even just plain 'we made this'. At the heart of the philosophy of using local or self-made ingredients is not so much the idea that it is the best that is available, but simply that it is your own. Restaurants don't make their own bread because they are the best bakers in town, they do it because it validates their sense of the unique nature of what they are offering. And the same is true of local vegetables or cheeses. Café Paradiso is lucky to have one of the best growers working anywhere right on its doorstep, but if he was merely ordinary, we would still buy from him first because of the deeper needs of belonging to a food culture and supporting the lifeblood of it – those who grow or make primary ingredients.

The combination of delicately flavoured classic set custard and fresh berries leaves room for the warm honey to state its case as the strongest flavour on the plate. Without it, the dish hums nicely, but the honey makes it sing. You can make this with any honey, you can make it even better with good honey and you can make it special with local honey. If you know the bees or the beekeeper, you will stop after every bite to think about that, and therein lies a pleasure beyond recipe making. Get some bees!

If you get in touch with that part of the dish, it matters little whether you use raspberries, blackberries, blueberries or figs. Use the best available at the time.

- To make the lavender set custard: preheat the oven to 150°C/ 300°F/gas mark 2.

- Put the lavender flowers and cream in a saucepan and heat gently to just below boiling point. Remove the flowers.

- Stir the egg yolks and sugar together. Pour into the hot cream and stir with a spatula. Leave this custard to settle for a minute, then remove the foam that remains on top.

- Place six 150ml/5fl oz ramekins or steel rings lined with cling film in a baking dish. Fill with the custard. Pour boiling water into the baking dish to come halfway up the sides of the ramekins and place the dish in the oven. Check after 20 minutes and again every 10 minutes until the custards are firm on top but still slightly wobbly when moved gently.

- Remove from the oven and leave in the water dish for 30 minutes, then lift the ramekins out of the water and chill for 4 hours. They can also be kept overnight or up to 2 days in the fridge.

- To serve, carefully remove the custards and place 1 on each plate. Drizzle with the honey and serve with fresh berries or figs.

Liquorice ice cream with blood orange juice & pistachio-anise biscotti

As a teenager, I wasn't a fan of liquorice. Which is no big deal, you might think, except that liquorice, in the form of long tubular straps, was cool, and cool kids liked liquorice. Liking liquorice isn't something you can fake, and it's still quite the divider between those who get excited by the mere reading of the word and those who wouldn't touch it. I crossed the border somewhere in my adult life. I don't remember it happening, I just ended up on the liquorice side of the fence, though too late to impress anyone.

We first tried to make liquorice ice cream using a recipe we came across that involved infusing the custard with actual pieces of dried liquorice root. The result was a very faint flavour and no discernable hint of colour, which was all very disappointing. So the pastry chef, a man so innately cool he was born sucking liquorice, went to the sweet shop to get some black straps. It took a bit of trial and testing to get the balance right, part of the problem being that liquorice lovers will tend to make the ice cream too strong for normal folk. Those who profess to have a revulsion for liquorice won't go for this, but I've seen plenty of fence-sitters converted by its rich, creamy texture and strong, yet somehow subtle, flavour.

I looked at different ways to serve the blood orange with the ice cream, from salad to sorbet and back again. But what I really wanted was the full complex sweet/sour flavour of really good blood oranges, and a straight shot of juice on the side seemed the best way to do it. You can sip the juice to follow a spoonful of ice cream, or you might prefer to repeatedly pour some of the juice over the ice cream as you eat.

The biscotti are a little bit of trouble to make but well worth it, and they will keep for weeks in a sealed jar or tin.

- First make the pistachio-anise biscotti: preheat the oven to 170°C/ 325°F/gas mark 3.

- Grind the fennel seeds with a mortar and pestle briefly so that they are cracked and opened, but not ground.

- Mix the flour, sugar and baking powder together in a food mixer.

for 4

375ml/13fl oz milk
100g/3½oz liquorice, chopped
5 egg yolks
125g/4½oz caster sugar
125ml/4½fl oz double cream
juice of 4 blood oranges

for the pistachio-anise biscotti
2 tsp fennel seeds
200g/7oz plain flour
200g/7oz caster sugar
2 tsp baking powder
2 eggs, lightly beaten
finely grated zest of 1 lemon
40g/1½oz sultanas
75g/3oz dried apricots, sliced
100g/3½oz shelled pistachio nuts, coarsley chopped

Continued on following page...

Continued from previous page...

• Add 1 egg and mix well, then add the second egg and beat well to get a soft, slightly sticky dough. Stir in the lemon zest, dried fruit, pistachios and fennel seeds.

• Divide the dough into 3 pieces. Roll each piece into a long tubular shape of about 3–4cm/1¼–1½in in diameter. Place these well apart on baking parchment-lined oven trays, and bake for 30–40 minutes until pale golden. Remove from the oven and leave to cool for 15 minutes. Turn the oven setting down to 130°C/250°F/gas mark ½.

• Slice the cooled biscotti dough across at an angle into slices of about 1cm/½in thick. Lay the slices on the oevn trays and bake them again in the cooler oven for 10 minutes, then turn the slices over and bake for 10 minutes more. The biscotti will still be slightly soft, but will become crisp very quickly as they cool.

• Put the milk and liquorice in a saucepan, and bring slowly to the boil. Blend with a stick blender, then remove the pan from the heat and leave to infuse for 30 minutes.

• Whisk together the egg yolks and sugar until pale and creamy. Strain the cooled licorice milk through a sieve into the egg mix. Heat this custard gently for 10 minutes or so, stirring all the time, until it has thickened slightly, then cool it completely. Stir in the cream, and freeze the custard using an ice-cream machine.

• Serve the ice cream in deep glass bowls with a shot glass of orange juice and some biscotti on the side.

Citrus, sultana & maple rice pudding with raspberries

Poor old rice pudding… Despite occasional hints at a comeback, it remains solidly unfashionable, unable to shake off associations with British school meals and Victorian cooking. Those of us who have been spared both still suffer the associations through childhood addictions to literary classics like *The Beano* comic and the 'Secret Seven' novels. As if that wasn't enough to be going on with, there is a hard-to-shake-off sense that rice pudding is too heavy to be a modern dessert.

Well, it doesn't have to be that way. I'm not out single-handedly to make rice pudding fashionable – more enthusiastic pudding-makers than me have gone down that road and come back crying – but I'd like to say a few words in its favour.

If the core criteria of a dessert are sweetness and a rich but light and pleasurable texture, then it only takes a little care and attention for a rice pudding to go there instead of turning out dry and heavy. As with all cooking, having a good idea of how you want the result to be is very important; as you work, you keep that goal in mind and make adjustments to recipes or techniques to end up there.

This recipe won't get you there all by itself, but it is a useful blueprint. The most important part is your focus on the goal – sweet, light, rich and pleasurable. Once you've got the ingredients to hand – and you should always have extra in case you need to make adjustments – the most important part of the process is long slow cooking of the rice so that it becomes soft and richly infused with cream and maple syrup. Another critical requirement is a willingness to make adjustments as needed at the end to get it right. No two ovens are the same, so don't just ignore the baking rice. Check it occasionally towards the end of the cooking time, and add more milk or cream if you think the dish is drying out too quickly.

The target you're aiming for is a pudding of meltingly, almost disappearingly, soft rice with the texture of creamy risotto – as one delightful spoonful slips down your throat, your mind is thinking it wants just a little more.

Just because the recipe says that this quantity feeds six doesn't mean you have to divide it into six portions!

Continued on following page…

Continued from previous page...

for 6

100g/3½oz caster sugar
750ml/1¼ pints milk
600ml/1 pint single cream
15g/½oz butter, for
  greasing
150g/5oz pudding rice
50g/2oz sultanas
finely grated zest and juice
  of 2 lemons
finely grated zest and juice
  of 1 orange
3 tbsp maple syrup, plus
  extra for drizzling
30 raspberries

If you gave your guests no more than a few salad leaves, three hungry people could eat this. If they've been feasting on rich food, flip the focus of the dessert around by serving it as a dish of maple-dressed fresh raspberries with just a smidgeon of rice pudding on the side.

• Preheat the oven to 170°C/325°F/gas mark 3.

• Set aside 25g/1oz of the sugar for later. Put the rest in a saucepan with the milk and cream, and stir over a gentle heat until the sugar has dissolved, then bring to the boil and remove from the heat.

• Grease an ovenproof dish with butter and scatter the rice and sultanas in the bottom. Stir the citrus zests and juices into the milk, add the maple syrup and pour over the rice. Mix well, cover with foil, then bake for 1 hour, until almost all the liquid has been absorbed and the rice is tender.

• Preheat a hot grill. Dust the top of the pudding with the remaining sugar and place under the grill to brown the top.

• Serve in shallow bowls with raspberries scattered on top. To finish, drizzle a little more maple syrup over.

Pear & maple tart tatin
with rosemary ice cream

I made puff pastry once. That's not just a confession of mine, it's something I hear a lot of people say. Usually followed by 'and that once was enough'. It isn't that it's a very difficult technique, more the time and labour involved, only to find yours is almost as good as top-quality frozen stuff. That's my excuse anyway; others have their own.

Without the pastry-making, tart tatin is a very simple and quick dessert to knock up. And that comes from someone who finds dessert-making a bit intimidating, especially those from what might be called the classic canon. There's something a bit daunting about the mystique that builds up around classics. Nothing real to fear here, though, I promise. Use a heavy iron pan that can go in the oven. Or... and this is ever so slightly controversial... have an oven dish prepared, warmed and buttered when the fruit is ready to be covered with pastry. Make the transfer quickly, pop the pastry on top and carry on. It will work fine, believe me.

Rosemary ice cream brings a savoury touch to the dish, something pear and maple are very comfortable with.

- Well ahead, make the ice cream: slowly bring the milk and rosemary sprigs to the boil in a saucepan, then remove the pan from the heat and leave to infuse for 30 minutes.

- Whisk together the egg yolks and sugar until pale and creamy. Discard the rosemary sprigs and strain the milk through a sieve into the egg mix. Heat this custard gently for 10 minutes or so, stirring all the time, until it has thickened slightly, then let it cool completely.

- When it is cool, stir in the cream and freeze the custard using an ice-cream machine.

- About an hour before you want to serve: preheat the oven to 200°C/400°F/gas mark 6.

- Place an ovenproof frying pan over medium heat and melt the butter in it. Add the sugar and maple syrup, and stir gently until beginning to caramelise.

for 6–8

50g/2oz butter
30g/1¼oz caster sugar
3 tbsp maple syrup
6 medium firm pears,
  peeled, quartered and
  cored
½ tsp ground cinnamon
¼ tsp freshly grated
  nutmeg
1 packet of frozen puff
  pastry, defrosted

for the rosemary ice cream
375ml/13fl oz milk
3 sprigs of fresh rosemary
5 egg yolks
125g/4½oz caster sugar
125ml/4½fl oz single
  cream

Continued on following page...

Continued from previous page...

- Add the pears and spices, and stir to coat. Continue cooking the pears, stirring occasionally, for 10 minutes, until the syrup has thickened. Push the pears with a spatula to make sure they are packed towards the centre of the pan.

- Roll the pastry out to a round big enough to cover the pears and leave an overhang, and place it over the pears. Cut off any excess, leaving 2–3cm/¾–1¼in all round. Use a spatula to push this excess into the pan and around the pears. Prick the pastry with a fork. Place the pan on an oven tray and put this in the oven. Bake for 20–30 minutes, until the pastry is browned and crisp.

- Remove the dish from the oven and leave to stand for 10 minutes. Place a plate on top and carefully flip the pan over to invert the tart on to the plate. If any pears get stuck, free them with a spatula and press them back on to the tart.

- Cut the tart into 6 or 8 slices and serve warm or at room temperature with the rosemary ice cream.

Lavender & summer berry pavlova with passion fruit syrup

Lavender is a weird thing to eat, being more commonly recognised as a seductive scent for perfumes, soaps and body oils. But, hey, if people are going to rub strawberries, chocolate and peaches on each other's bodies, cooks can raid the flower garden for ingredients. Used subtly – usually as an infusion – lavender has a wonderful affinity with summer fruit. In this sunshine pavlova, the flower buds are ground with sugar and added to the dish. Be careful with the quantities, as subtlety is the key here and too much lavender will taste like soap. The variety commonly known as French Lavender is the best for culinary use.

Use a combination of the common summer fruits in season – strawberries, which should be sliced, raspberries and currants. Peaches, nectarines and apricots are lovely too, though not combined with the berries.

Pavlova can be made as much as a couple of days ahead, as can the passion fruit syrup. After that, you're only a few minutes cream-whisking and fruit-slicing away from a real sensual pleasure on a warm summer's evening. Assuming you're eating it, of course.

for 6

4 lavender flower buds
450g/1lb caster sugar
whites of 8 eggs
½ tsp lemon juice
1 tbsp cornflour
1 tbsp white wine vinegar
200ml/7fl oz double cream
200g/7oz berries

for the passion fruit syrup
50g/2oz caster sugar
4 passion fruit, halved

• Preheat the oven to 140°C/275°F/gas mark 1.

• Grind the lavender buds with 2 tablespoons of the sugar with a mortar and pestle.

• Whisk the egg whites to stiff peaks, adding the lemon juice in drops as the whites thicken. Slowly add 350g/12oz of the sugar, still whisking, until fully incorporated. Then add the remaining sugar with the cornflour, and finally the vinegar.

• Spread the mixture on a large baking parchment-lined oven tray, shaped into a wide disc about 6cm/2½in high.

• Bake in the oven for 50 minutes. Lower the oven setting to 110°C/225°F/gas mark ¼ and bake for another 30 minutes. Remove from the oven and leave to cool for an hour.

Continued on following page...

Continued from previous page...

- Make the passion fruit syrup: heat the sugar and 100ml/3½fl oz water in a small saucepan over low heat for 4–5 minutes, until it forms a thin syrup.

- Scoop the passion fruit flesh and seeds into the pan of syrup, simmer for 1 minute more, then transfer the syrup to a jug and leave it to cool.

- Whisk the cream to soft peaks and spread it evenly on the pavlova, then cover this generously with the berries.

- Serve slices of the pavlova with some of the passion fruit syrup poured over each portion.

Beamish stout ice cream with a whiskey maple chaser

Classically, a whiskey chaser is a shot to toss back after a pint, but the combination of stout and whiskey is too good to be pinned down into a traditionalist corner. Some prefer to down a whiskey before spending a contemplative hour sipping a pint. As a child, I remember my grandfather and his peers perched on bar stools, each contemplating a half pint and shot side by side, though I have no memory of which went down first. I have no memory of them drinking at all, just sitting there savouring the potential.

The half pint has come to be seen as an unmanly measure, but the classic Irish half-pint glass is a thing of beauty, an elegant tall flute that makes for easy drinking. The volume proportions of half pint of stout and an (Irish) measure of whiskey are in perfect balance.

I can't promise you'll get the same result from this dessert but, following a good meal, you never know where it will lead. Just don't be tempted to drink the chaser – it's a sweet concoction intended for the ice cream. The hard core among you might be tempted to replace it with a straight shot, with my blessing. It doesn't matter whether you use bottled or canned stout. If you can't find Beamish, the other brands will work too, with just a little less magic.

for 4

175ml/6fl oz Beamish stout
375ml/13fl oz double cream
5 egg yolks
125g/4½oz caster sugar

for the whiskey maple chaser
150ml/5fl oz Irish whiskey
200ml/7fl oz maple syrup

- Put the stout in a saucepan, bring to the boil and simmer for a few minutes, until reduced to 150ml/5fl oz.

- In another saucepan, bring the cream slowly to the boil, then remove the pan from the heat.

- Whisk together the egg yolks and sugar until pale and creamy. Add some of the cream to the mixture, whisking to blend it in smoothly.

- Whisk this mixture into the cream pan, bring it back to the boil and simmer slowly, stirring all the time, until a slightly thickened custard has formed. Transfer to a bowl and let it cool completely, then churn it in an ice-cream machine.

- Make the maple whiskey chaser: put the whiskey and maple syrup in a saucepan and bring to the boil. Transfer to a jug and leave to cool to room temperature.

- To serve, scoop the ice cream into short sundae glasses and serve the chaser in a shot glass on the side. (To eat, pour the chaser over the ice cream!)

Ouzo-poached greengage plums with pine nut tart & honey-citrus mascarpone cream

for 8–10

1 sheet of frozen puff
   pastry, defrosted
130g/4½oz ground
   almonds
finely grated zest of
   1 orange
225g/8oz caster sugar
1 tbsp orange flower water
25g/1oz honey
2 eggs, lightly beaten
2 tbsp light olive oil
115g/4oz pine nuts

*for the ouzo-poached
greengage plums*
3 tbsp ouzo
1 cinnamon stick
100g/3½oz caster sugar
16 greengage plums,
   halved and stoned

*for the honey-citrus
mascarpone cream*
150g/5oz mascarpone
finely grated zest of
   1 orange
finely grated zest of
   1 lemon
1 tbsp honey
150ml/5fl oz double cream

This is such a rich tart that it is best served as an accompaniment to a fruit-based dessert. Think in terms of a sliver of sinfully sweet baklava rather than slab of granny's apple pie. One tart will easily serve 8–10 people, which is why I've given large quantities below for the greengage plums. The plums will keep for a couple of days, and they make a lovely breakfast served over yoghurt. Greengages are small, intensely flavoured plums, with a beautiful dusty shade of green skin. If you can't find any, other plums will work fine here, as will apricots or peaches.

• Preheat the oven to 180°C/350°F/gas mark 4.

• Roll the pastry out and use to line a 23cm/9in tart tin, prick it all over with a fork and bake the pastry for 7–8 minutes, until lightly browned and crisp.

• Beat together the ground almonds, orange zest, sugar, orange flower water, honey, eggs and olive oil. Stir in the pine nuts and pour the mixture into the pastry case. Bake in the oven for 20–25 minutes until slightly puffed and just set. Leave to cool.

• Prepare the ouzo-poached greengage plums: bring the ouzo, cinnamon, sugar and 150ml/5fl oz water to the boil in a saucepan. Drop in the plums and simmer for 3–4 minutes. Remove the plums and allow them to cool to room temperature. Simmer the syrup for a few minutes more over low heat, stirring occasionally, until it has thickened a little. Transfer it to a jug and leave to cool.

• Make the honey-citrus mascarpone cream: soften the mascarpone with a spoon and stir in the citrus zest and honey. Whisk the cream to soft peaks and fold it into the mascarpone.

• Serve a thin slice with the plums and mascarpone cream on the side, and drizzle some of the ouzo syrup over the plums.

Index

pasta with aubergines, honey, dates, pistachio & feta 196–7

roast squash flowers, with feta, currants & capers in a tomato, thyme & orange sauce 179–81

tian of aubergine, caramelised onion, spinach & polenta with feta crust and a fennel-chilli sauce 241–3

figs, honey-roasted on a yoghurt, cardamom & pistachio tart 285

fingerling potato, watercress & walnut salad 62–3

g

garlic:

roast garlic & fennel mash with lemon-braised chickpeas & aubergine 134–5

wild garlic & roast cherry tomato risotto with lemon-braised artichokes 98–9

wild garlic mash with grilled asparagus & citrus tarragon-dressed Puy lentils 136–7

goat's cheese:

beetroot risotto with lemon-fennel oil, goat's cheese and broad beans 88–91

celeriac soup with walnut & green pepper salsa and goat's cheese cream 110

saffron-braised squash with aubergine, pinenut & spinach

stuffing and lentil–goat's cheese sauce 247

salad of rosé-poached rhubarb, baby carrots, rocket and fresh goat's cheese with hazelnut citrus praline 60–1

gratin:

aubergine, spinach & potato gratin with fennel-braised Puy lentils 258–9

Portobello mushroom & aduki bean gratin with roast parsnip crust 260–1

potato, squash & leek gratin 262–3

Swede & leek gratin in maple cream with sage & walnut crust 276–7

h

haloumi:

braised chard timbale of haloumi, roast tomato & Puy lentils with citrus fennel butter 164–5

spiced haloumi on a warm Puy lentil, spinach & beetroot salad 46

wild rice, haloumi & ginger-braised leeks with sweet pepper, chilli & caper sauce 225–7

i

ice cream:

Beamish stout ice cream with a whiskey maple chaser 304–5

liquorice ice cream with blood orange juice & pistachio-anise biscotti 292–4

pear & maple tart tatin with rosemary ice cream 298–300

k

kai-lan:

& shiitake, braised with crisped vermicelli and a peanut, ginger & chilli dressing 48

maple-glazed tofu with rice noodles & kai-lan in a miso broth 199–201

kale:

black kale & pumpkin with toasted millet in a tomato, almond & yoghurt sauce 220–1

chestnut & sheep's cheese ravioli with kale in pumpkin broth 210–11

lentil, potato & kale soup 123

Socca crêpe of roast squash, caramelised red onion, kale & pine nuts, with tomato coriander salsa & goat's cheese cream 172–4

l

laska, cauliflower, carrot & leek with rice noodles and spinach-cashew dumplings 222–4

lavender:

& summer berry pavlova with passion fruit syrup 301–3

set custard with honey & berries 290–1

leek:

& cauliflower risotto with chilli walnut crumbs & fried capers 86

& potato soup with watercress pesto 114–15

& wasabi mash with oyster mushrooms and choi in coconut tamarind sauce 130–1

artichoke, leek & brie tart in walnut pastry 267–8

aubergine, leek & tofu parcel on sesame cabbage with gingered pumpkin sauce 166–9

orecchiette with broad beans & baby courgettes 190–1
ouzo-poached greengage plums with pine nut tart & honey-citrus mascarpone cream 306–7
oven 234–77

p

pancakes:
buttermilk with honey & berries 28
corn pancakes of courgettes, pine nuts & roasted onion with warm Sungold tomato & caper salsa 152–3
egg roll pancakes of roasted Brussels sprouts & sweet potato with green onion, tamarind & coconut sauce 162–3
pumpkin maple pancakes with orange cream & walnuts, spiced 34–5
sweet potato pancake with avocado, pumpkin seed, pomegranate & feta salad and herbed yoghurt, spiced 44–5
pappardelle with Brussels sprouts, leeks & truffle cream 195
parsnip mash with sage-grilled Portobello & caramelised red onion 138
pasta:
fresh pasta ribbons in walnut & sheep's cheese sauce with maple-braised endive 188–9
with aubergines, honey, dates, pistachio & feta 196–7
see also under individual pasta name
pavlova, lavender & summer berry with passion fruit syrup 301–3
pear:
& maple tart tatin with rosemary ice cream 298–300
roast pears with ginger steamed pudding & mascarpone ice cream 288–9
peperonata:
basil mash with olive & caper peperonata 132–3
sage & onion farinata with olive, caper & chilli peperonata 251–3
pepper:
black-eyed peas, aubergines, green beans & peppers in chilli, coconut & thyme 228–9
roasted aubergine & pepper soup with honeyed cabbage and leeks & chilli oil 109
shallot & thyme eggy bread with rocket and spiced pepper compote 32–3
summer squash, borlotti beans & roasted pepper soup with basil chilli oil 120–1

wild rice, haloumi & ginger-braised leeks with sweet pepper, chilli & caper sauce 225–7
pilaf:
caradamom-roasted cauliflower with pistachio & green pepper salsa and leek, tomato & coconut pilaf 244–6
couscous pilaf of sprouting broccoli, aubergine & chickpeas with harissa sauce, chermoula & orange-marinated feta 230–3
polenta:
almond cake with blood orange & pink grapefruit salad, spiced 29
tian of aubergine, caramelised onion, spinach & polenta with feta crust and a fennel-chilli sauce 241–3
Portobello:
& roast tomato Florentine 22–4
mushroom & aduki bean gratin with roast parsnip crust 260–1
roast parsnip mash with sage-grilled Portobello & caramelised red onion 138
potato:
aubergine, spinach & potato gratin with fennel-braised Puy lentils 258–9
egg roll pancakes of roasted Brussels sprouts & sweet potato with green onion, tamarind & coconut sauce 162–3
leek & potato soup with watercress pesto 114–15
lentil, potato & kale soup 123
Mussaman curry of new potatoes, cauliflower, chickpeas & green beans with cucumber coriander salsa 216–17
new potato crush with courgettes, broad beans & cherry tomatoes 140–1
potato crêpes of asparagus & brie with tarragon butter and warm beetroot & Puy lentil salsa 150–1
potato, squash & leek gratin 262–3
Savoy cabbage terrine of potatoes, leeks, apple & smoked cheese with balsamic beetroot syrup 176–8
sweet potato pancake with avocado, pumpkin seed, pomegranate & feta salad and herbed yoghurt, spiced 44–5
see also mash
pumpkin:
baked pumpkin, leek & coconut curry with green bean salsa 264–6
black kale & pumpkin with toasted millet in a tomato, almond & yoghurt sauce 220–1
chestnut & sheep's cheese ravioli with kale in pumpkin broth 210–11

About the author

Denis Cotter is the owner and chef of the celebrated Café Paradiso in Cork, Ireland, where his unique take on vegetarian cooking is heavily influenced by local vegetable and cheese producers. He is the author of three previous books, *The Café Paradiso Cookbook* (1999), *Paradiso Seasons* (2003), which was the winner of the 'Best Vegetarian Cookbook in the World' at The Gourmand World Cookbook Awards, and most recently, *Wild Garlic, Gooseberries... and Me* (2007). He divides his time between his native Ireland and Canada.

To find out more about Denis and Café Paradiso visit www.cafeparadiso.ie

Acknowledgements

Thanks to Jenny Heller at HarperCollins for her faith in me, and her patience and guidance when I kept changing horses in midstream; to everyone else at HarperCollins, led by Lizzy Gray, for turning a pile of recipes into such a lovely production; to Lewis Esson for his careful editing, William Lingwood for his photography and Fergal Connolly for cooking the food with such a love of his work; to Brendan Tangney for the loan of his hideaway house when I needed somewhere to concentrate the mind; to Geraldine and her team at Café Paradiso for just plain being the best; and most of all to Maureen...for the love.